REGIONAL VARIATIONS IN BRITAIN

Regional Variations
in Britain

Studies in Economic and Social Geography

B. E. Coates

SENIOR LECTURER IN GEOGRAPHY, UNIVERSITY OF SHEFFIELD

and

E. M. Rawstron

READER IN GEOGRAPHY,
QUEEN MARY COLLEGE, UNIVERSITY OF LONDON

B. T. BATSFORD LTD LONDON

First published 1971
© B. E. Coates and E. M. Rawstron, 1971

Made and printed in Great Britain
by T. & A. Constable Ltd, Edinburgh
for the publishers B. T. Batsford Ltd
4 Fitzhardinge Street, London W1

7134   2103 7

Contents

Acknowledgments

Our grateful thanks are due to Professor M. J. Wise for realizing the extent of our common interests and effecting an introduction; to Professors Alice Garnett, S. Gregory, A. E. Smailes and R. S. Waters for encouraging and facilitating our research and writing, and to Miss Margaret Wilkes for much assistance in tracking down and analysing data.

We are indebted to the draughtsmen and photographic technicians of the Departments of Geography in the University of Sheffield and Queen Mary College for kindly making our rough efforts fit for reproduction: Messrs Gary Brannon, John Hall, Christopher Jones, Peter Morley, Don Shewin and Harold Walkland, and Misses Pauline Evans and Sheila Ottewell will be able to judge the extent of our indebtedness to them by the extensive use we have made of their time and skills. We are very grateful to Miss Linda Bull, Miss Heather Sangar Davies, Miss Carol Dean, Mrs Mary Putney, and Mrs Penny Shamma for typing the manuscript.

Numerous civil servants in government departments in London, Cardiff, Edinburgh and Belfast, including members of the Departments of Health and Social Security, Education and Science, the former Board of Trade, the Inland Revenue and the General Register Office, were most generous in giving their time to answering our queries and providing us with unpublished data.

Finally, to our respective wives Shirley and Marjorie and our children Andrew, David and Anna, Philip and Catherine, we apologize for being preoccupied with preparing these studies for publication, and for neglecting more important matters.

B. E. C.
E. M. R.

List of Figures

List of Tables

I

Scope and Aims

Britain is much more varied than many far larger areas of the earth's surface. Yet, while some of the variations have been surveyed and mapped with great accuracy, others have not. On geology maps, for example, a host of well-defined regions result from survey, and are accepted without major dissent as true statements about this aspect of spatial reality. Cretaceous regions are distinguished from Jurassic; Permian from Carboniferous. The Upper Greensand regions are shown separately from the Chalk, and the Elland Flagstones can be distinguished from other strata in the Coal Measures of the West Riding to form minor regions therein. Geological information about the earth's surface is accurately portrayed and available to those who are interested and wish to pursue its meaning.

For the relief map, the Ordnance Survey has measured the variation from place to place in height above mean sea-level and has provided a detailed summary of its findings by using contours. No one doubts that the height of any point in Britain can be read within seconds from a contoured map of the Ordnance Survey to an accuracy of a few feet, or that far greater accuracy can be quickly obtained when needed. This variation has been well and truly measured, and from its measurement many supplementary findings can be derived.

The contour interval, which varies with the scale of the map, sets the limit to the definition of relief shown on the map. Within this limit many degrees of generalization can be obtained, from the still useful twofold division of the country into Highland and Lowland Britain down to small geomorphological features. In other words, the use of a contour system can lead to the discernment of major spatial trends and large regions or of minor trends and small regions. But it should be clearly recognized that the discernment of a trend does not automatically indicate the existence, and likely discovery, of a clearly delimited region.

Climatic variations over the country are also well served by measurement and mapping, while the meteorological synoptic chart, familiar now in its summary form to most people, results from the careful measurement of weather phenomena. At frequent intervals throughout each day meteorological data from a multitude of stations are assembled and mapped for analysis, often using adaptations of the contour method. Not only can spatial

trends at a particular time be discerned from any one chart but also, by
using the data from a chronological sequence of synoptic charts, changes in
trend and thus in weather can be predicted with considerable short-term
accuracy.

The task of the meteorologist differs, therefore, from that of either the
geologist or the land surveyor-cum-geomorphologist. The latter two study
phenomena that change only very slowly in most areas. Their major tasks are
first, to survey accurately variations from place to place and, secondly, to
show how these variations came about. The meteorologist likewise needs his
accurate survey and an understanding of meteorological processes, but his
major aim is to predict future changes in the spatial distribution of weather
conditions. He is concerned with a sequence of maps extending from the
past through the present and, as far as his techniques and knowledge will
allow, into the future. In contrast, the geologist and the geomorphologist
must, for the most part, begin and end with the map of the present, for much
of their intervening work is concerned with reconstructing the past so that
in the end they may better understand the present.[1]

These and other variations in the physical geography of Britain are not
the topics to be dealt with here, although there is clearly much in the methods
of survey, portrayal and analysis used in physical geography that could be
helpfully applied to the topics we shall examine. Our purpose is to measure
and portray, albeit far less precisely, some of the economic and social variations from area to area in Great Britain and, when conveniently possible,
within the United Kingdom as a whole. As yet there can be no portrayal by
the equivalent of a close contour interval to give clear definition to our maps
for, unlike temperature or altitude, social and economic phenomena are not
continuities over the earth's surface and thus there can be no effective sampling
of the economic weather by taking point readings at economic weather
stations, nor can the visual and photogrammetric skills of the land surveyor
be applied. All we offer at this stage in the evolution of spatial measurement
in human geography is a series of more or less blurred portrayals which may
be helpful to those who seek some improvement upon subjective impression,
or to those who may wish to set their more detailed local knowledge into a
wider perspective. It is hoped also that our collection of studies may add some
momentum to the process of establishing the *national survey* that alone could
develop our reconnaissance into a comprehensive survey.

This book is not, therefore, concerned with data either for the country as a
whole or for small areas such as individual towns or rural parishes. For the
most part it contains studies undertaken at intermediate levels between these
extremes, hence the use of the term 'regional variations' in the title. In the
present context this equivocal term is used simply to mean a level of analysis
that is less than national but more than local. It is intended here to signify

[1] This theme is taken up again in chapter 11, p. 291

neither an analysis by the large Economic Planning Regions established in 1964 nor an attempt to discover the existence of valid and clearly delimited economic and social regions by applying the concept of the spatially continuous break of slope or trend to effect their discernment.

The analytical framework most used in this book is that provided by the pattern of counties in the United Kingdom, and many of the maps presented herein employ that framework. It is coarse, uneven and scientifically frustrating; something far more detailed and regular is needed as a 'scanning' device so that the economic and social geography of the United Kingdom may be portrayed almost as clearly as a picture on television. The county framework does not attain even the same low quality of picture as did John Logie Baird's early experiments in television using a perforated, rotating disc. If counties were all the same size and shape, the portrayal would be improved. Since they are not, the portrayal is quixotically distorted, but not to so great an extent that the resultant maps are either grossly misrepresentative or uninteresting. Like early maps of agricultural land-use and crop distributions, the maps presented in subsequent chapters whet one's appetite for a less crude recipe and for the feast to follow.

Of course, it would be possible to examine some of the topics in this book by employing a more intricate framework. The areas of local authorities and employment exchanges are two such frameworks. But at a local level, areas applied to one set of data seldom coincide with areas applied to another. Furthermore, some data are not available below county level. The great virtues of the county framework are that most data are available in this form or can fairly readily be converted to it, and the framework has existed with little change for a long time. Thus comparability through time can be maintained.

A very large range of topics is open for study in economic and social geography. We have chosen only six, namely: personal income; employment; overseas born; health services; mortality; and education. We have been guided in our choice, first, by the availability of data amenable to spatial analysis and, secondly, by our own particular interests.

Our choice of personal incomes for the first study fits both of these principles, but there is another reason which may be more fundamental. If a single yardstick is to be found that will give coherence to the spatial analysis of the multitude of phenomena that comprise the field of study of economic geography, it is the income derived from the occupation and use of a given area of land. The sum and component structure of this income-yield provide a basis for comparative spatial analysis and interpretation; and the yield can be measured as monetary quantities of either consumption or production, of expenditure or value-added. Analysis of personal incomes goes part of the way towards attaining this twofold aim of economic geography to study spatial patterns of both production and consumption. For various reasons,

B

explained in chapter 2, the analysis of personal incomes is an imperfect tool, but it is the best available at the moment.

Chapters 3, 4 and 5 are concerned with various aspects of employment. In the volumes of the decennial censuses of population a great deal of demographic data is available for geographical study, but most attention has been given in the past to changes in population as such, and relatively few studies have been devoted to the industry tables of the censuses wherein data on employment are presented. These and other tables in the censuses of 1951 and 1961 form the basis for chapters 3, 4 and 5. Unfortunately the equivalent tables for the sample census of 1966 were not published early enough to be used fully in this book and analyses undertaken to incorporate these later data in chapter 5 showed up defects which compelled us ultimately to forgo reference entirely to the results of the sample census. Certain inadequacies and technical problems inherent in the use of data collected by the Department of Employment and Productivity have likewise prevented their use. Thus the study of employment ends at 1961, whereas the other chapters incorporate later data.

Employment relates to both economic and social geography. People provide the work-force – the labour factor of production – and the consuming-force, being not only the major earners but also the major spenders of money. What they have to spend and what they do for a living often set the tone to the social geography of a locality. The chapters on employment thus link the predominantly economic geography of personal income to the social geography of subsequent chapters.

Immigrant population is currently an important social and political issue which has its geographical perspective. This we have attempted to portray in chapter 5 by analysing statistics of place of birth overseas. Race, colour and creed cannot be effectively mapped using these or any other data, but a quite detailed series of portrayals of place of origin is presented. Some of the resultant maps tally fairly closely with some of those for income and employment.

Chapters 7, 8 and 9 deal with the health services and mortality. If the efficiency of the former is found to vary from place to place it is reasonable to assume that the incidence of the latter may vary in somewhat similar fashion. Moreover, variations in both may relate to patterns of income and employment. Clearly the analyses presented cannot be either comprehensive or precise, but they can stimulate further thought, research and remedial action.

The penultimate chapter contains an examination of selected aspects of the geography of education in England and Wales. Like immigration, education is currently an important issue, and strong spatial components are clearly apparent among the problems it presents to society for solution. Perhaps the goal of equal opportunity in education is crucial among the issues now facing British society. Certainly income, employment, place of birth and upbringing, and health have a bearing upon education locally received, and it in turn has a bearing upon them.

To enhance the future well-being of Britain increasing attention must be given to the spatial patterns of the topics we have chosen. Special attention to any one of them alone will not serve as a panacea, but among them the geography of education may prove ultimately to be the most important. Apart, therefore, from the conclusions presented in the final chapter, education comes last but we believe it to be far from the least important.

The aim of this book is to undertake a reconnaissance of a number of spatial variations in the human geography of Britain, each of which merits further research in depth. Most of the topics have hitherto been discussed only subjectively. We have attempted to add a measure of objectivity and to demonstrate the relevance of the spatial factor and geographical research to the solution of socio-economic problems in the future. Too often in the past decision-makers have used information at only two levels. They have based their decisions either on statistics for the country as a whole, thus neglecting its parts, or on local data helpful, when available, in solving pressing local problems. Recently a corrupt version of the regional idea has become widely accepted, as illustrated by the setting-up in 1964 of the Regional Economic Planning Councils and Boards.

An additional aim in this book is to show, mainly by implication, how the regional idea can be and needs to be defined and developed. The importance of trends over area and changes in them through time are emphasized. The analogy with weather forecasting is drawn, but with the following essential difference. When rain is forecast, one carries an umbrella, for nothing yet discovered will stop the rain from falling if nature intends that it shall fall. The only sensible action is to take protective action. In contrast, when social or economic rain is forecast locally, or when an economic cold-front is observed moving across the country, action can be taken to stop it and to make the front withdraw. Rain is still natural. An economy, such as exists today in Britain, is man-made. The plea therefore, implicit throughout this book and explicit in the concluding chapter, is for the establishment of a 'meteorological office' for the socio-economic geography of Britain. Once in effective operation, this new kind of measuring and forecasting office would provide decision-makers with a firm foundation for good judgment and efficient action in national, and ultimately international, economic and social management.

Analysis by the rudimentary county framework (shown for reference on fig. 1.1 and used in much of this book) yields informative indications of desirable lines of action. A scientific framework, if adopted by a national office for economic and social survey, would provide a scientific basis not only for regional decisions and socio-economic geographical management, but also for research and teaching in human geography equal in scientific quality to

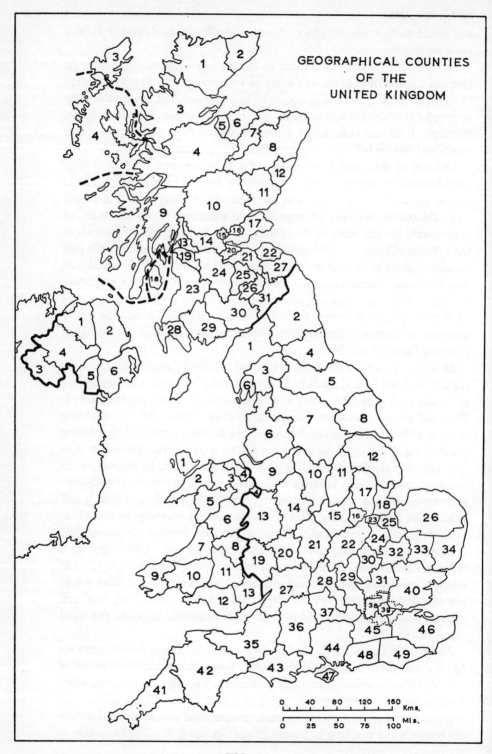

GEOGRAPHICAL COUNTIES
OF THE
UNITED KINGDOM

FIG. 1.1

KEY TO FIG. 1.1

ENGLAND
1 Cumberland
2 Northumberland
3 Westmorland
4 Durham
5 North Riding, Yorks
6 Lancashire
7 West Riding, Yorks
8 East Riding, Yorks
9 Cheshire
10 Derbyshire
11 Nottinghamshire
12 Lindsey, Lincs
13 Shropshire
14 Staffordshire
15 Leicestershire
16 Rutland
17 Kesteven, Lincs
18 Holland, Lincs
19 Herefordshire
20 Worcestershire
21 Warwickshire
22 Northamptonshire
23 Soke of Peterborough[1]
24 Huntingdonshire
25 Isle of Ely[2]
26 Norfolk
27 Gloucestershire
28 Oxfordshire
29 Buckinghamshire
30 Bedfordshire
31 Hertfordshire
32 Cambridgeshire
33 West Suffolk
34 East Suffolk
35 Somerset
36 Wiltshire

37 Berkshire
38 Middlesex
39 London[3]
40 Essex
41 Cornwall
42 Devon
43 Dorset
44 Hampshire
45 Surrey
46 Kent
47 Isle of Wight
48 West Sussex
49 East Sussex

WALES
1 Anglesey
2 Caernarvonshire
3 Denbighshire
4 Flintshire
5 Merionethshire
6 Montgomeryshire
7 Cardiganshire
8 Radnorshire
9 Pembrokeshire
10 Carmarthenshire
11 Brecknockshire
12 Glamorgan
13 Monmouthshire

SCOTLAND[4]
1 Sutherland
2 Caithness
3 Ross and Cromarty
4 Inverness-shire

5 Nairnshire
6 Morayshire
7 Banffshire
8 Aberdeenshire
9 Argyllshire
10 Perthshire
11 Angus
12 Kincardineshire
13 Dunbartonshire
14 Stirlingshire
15 Clackmannanshire
16 Kinross-shire
17 Fifeshire
18 Buteshire
19 Renfrewshire
20 West Lothian
21 Midlothian
22 East Lothian
23 Ayrshire
24 Lanarkshire
25 Peeblesshire
26 Selkirkshire
27 Berwickshire
28 Wigtownshire
29 Kirkcudbrightshire
30 Dumfriesshire
31 Roxburghshire

NORTHERN IRELAND
1 Londonderry
2 Antrim
3 Fermanagh
4 Tyrone
5 Armagh
6 Down

[1] Now joined with Huntingdonshire
[2] Now joined with Cambridgeshire
[3] The area of the Greater London Council is shown by the dotted boundary
[4] Less Orkney and Zetland

that of geomorphology and meteorology. Human geography would then cease to be so much an art and would become the science that it is now striving to become through the use of statistical methods, the so-called quantitative techniques, and model building.[1]

A model is only as good as its materials and its design. We are conscious of many of the defects in ours in both respects, but we are anxious also lest those who design better models should for ever lack the materials with which to construct and test their models effectively and to useful purpose.

[1] (i) Chorley, R. J., and Haggett, P. (eds.), *Models in Geography*, 1967
      (ii) Cole, J. P., and King, C. A. M., *Quantitative Geography*, 1968
      (iii) Gregory, S., *Statistical Methods and the Geographer*, 1968

2

Personal Incomes

The foundation to the science of economic geography should be measurement of the variation in intensity from place to place of the creation of wealth and its disposal. The one is often called income, the other expenditure. Both can be measured in terms of money, and both should be mapped by contours or isopleths in much the same way as relief, barometric pressure, rainfall or temperature.

One would then know in objective cartographic terms, whence the national income is derived within Britain and where it is spent; and the spatial morphologies of both income and expenditure would be displayed for analysis. The land-forms of the economy would appear clearly for the first time, for unlike those of true relief they cannot so readily be detected by the mapless observer because there is no economic force of gravity to tell him when he is going uphill or down, and there are no vantage points or economic belvederes to guide his visual judgment. Moreover, unlike true relief, but more like weather, the spatial expression of the economy changes quite quickly through time. The amplitude of such change is probably less in a year than that of weather in a day, except very locally as when a coal-mine closes down or a factory changes from one use to another. Nevertheless economic-geographical change is important.

As yet this ideal foundation to the science is well beyond reach, though the gap is narrowing more and more rapidly. Before 1939 little more had been attempted than to quantify international comparisons. By the early fifties variation from country to country for much of the world was being statistically presented by the United Nations. So, to a framework at that time of less than 100 divisions,[1] spatial analysis of income on a world scale had officially begun. An interest in regional economics slowly developed during the fifties to quicken during the sixties.[2] Thus in Britain a provincial frame-

[1] Each division represented a member of the United Nations Organisation
[2] (i) McCrone, G., *Scotland's Economic Progress 1951–60*, 1965
   (ii) McCrone, G., 'The application of regional accounting in the United Kingdom', *Regional Studies*, 1, 1, 39–45, 1967
  (iii) Ministère de l'Economie et des Finances, République Française, *Comptes économiques régionaux, Etudes et conjonctures*, numéro special, 1966
  (iv) Central Statistical Office, *Abstract of Regional Statistics*, 1965, annually
   (v) Hammond, E., *An Analysis of Regional Economic and Social Statistics*, 1968
  (vi) Needleman, L. (ed.), *Regional Analysis*, 1968

work, comprising the so-called Economic Planning Regions, was set up in 1964. It cannot be said yet that a major task for this framework is to measure how the gross domestic product varies from region to region, but problems and statistics relating to regional income and expenditure are being explored. Investigation of income (the production side of the economy) is making more progress than investigation of expenditure (the consumption side). This is so partly, one assumes, because both applied economics and economic geography have placed more emphasis in the past upon study of the production of goods and services than upon their consumption; partly also because since 1951 the Inland Revenue has published[1] quinquennial returns[2] of personal incomes on regional and county frameworks. In addition, from 1965-6 it was decided, in keeping with the newly created Economic Planning Regions, to publish annual returns for these areas in the 'Regional Abstract of Statistics'.

We cannot, therefore, attempt to explain, analyse or even discuss official maps either of income or expenditure for none exist, notwithstanding that they are as essential a foundation to economic planning as the maps of the Ordnance and Geological Surveys are to physical planning. Nor can we attempt ourselves, usefully, to produce contoured maps either of the economy or even of the Inland Revenue's data on personal incomes. Maps of this ideal kind should result for some aspects of the economy, but not for income, from the Censuses of Population for 1971.[3] So a major advance may be expected in published form by about 1975, or sooner if increased funds are allocated for the purpose. There should then be only a small gap to close to lay the ideal foundation to economic geography, spatial economics and in due course econo-geographical management and planning.[4]

These prospects for the future are no help to the present. Action taken now can be based only upon attempts to interpret current data of which the best now available are those prepared quinquennially for personal incomes by the Inland Revenue. Although they do not represent the national income as a whole they form a large part of it (about 80 per cent), and are therefore likely to reflect the spatial morphology *per capita* of the national income.

Four important points must be borne in mind from the outset. First, the data for personal incomes are not divided below county level anywhere in Britain, except that separate figures for the City of London are given until 1959/60, and the major conurbations are separately quoted annually from 1964/5.[5] Secondly, the data of both the Inland Revenue and the Industry Tables of the Censuses (used to map employment in chapters 3, 4 and 5)

---

[1] Annual Reports of the Commissioners of H.M. Inland Revenue
[2] For tax years 1949/50, 1954/5, 1959/60 and 1964/5
[3] Chapter 11, p. 291
[4] Chapter 11, pp. 291-4
[5] In parts of Scotland counties are aggregated in the statistical tables of the Inland Revenue (see footnote 4, p. 11). Thus it is not possible to obtain data for individual counties in these areas

refer basically to place of work[1] rather than place of residence. Thirdly, personal incomes below the tax-base, which rose with inflation during the period studied, are excluded from the data.[2] Fourthly, certain items of expenditure, such as payments of interest on mortgages, are deducted from *gross* personal incomes before tax is calculated. Thus differences among counties are greater than they appear to be from the data used here, if only because mortgages on property are higher in some parts of the country, notably the south-east, than in others. The taxable residue is referred to as *net* income. Where this term is encountered in the pages that follow it does not, therefore, refer to the income available for spending after tax.

Mean Net Income before Tax[3]

Figs. 2.1a, b and c for 1949–50, 1959–60 and 1964–5 respectively show clear differences in mean net income before tax among the counties of the United Kingdom for each of these years, and how the pattern of difference changed during the period. The county means[4] are mapped according to an evenly graded scheme of shading which in turn is related proportionally to the national mean for each date. Thus on all three maps the two top grades are used for counties with means above that for the United Kingdom, the remaining four grades being below that level. County boundaries are inserted only where necessary to indicate shading changes.

All three maps show that the range around the national mean is not enormous. Certainly it is far less than the range between countries on a world scale or, for example, between northern and southern Italy. In 1959–60 (fig. 2.1b) Armagh £524, Argyll and Bute £645, Anglesey £579 and Cornwall £642 were the counties with the lowest mean incomes in Northern Ireland, Scotland, Wales and England respectively. The highest mean was that of the County of London (£874), but within it the City of London had £1,158. Although small in area, there were 353,000 incomes above the tax-base in the City in 1959–60, a figure greater than that for Midlothian, about equal to that for Sussex, and not far short of that for the whole of Northern Ireland.

[1] Place of work is at its most accurate for personal incomes when Schedule E incomes are being discussed
[2] This point is taken up later, pp. 35–41, fig. 2.8a and b
[3] (i) Rawstron, E. M., and Coates, B. E., 'Opportunity and Affluence', *Guardian*, 26 July 1965, and *Geography*, **51**, *1*, 1–15
(ii) Coates, B. E., and Rawstron, E. M., 'Regional Incomes and Planning', *Guardian*, 11 and 17 April 1967, and *Geography*, **52**, *4*, 393–402
[4] Lincolnshire, Suffolk and Sussex are not divided into administrative counties in the primary data, whereas Yorkshire's three Ridings are listed separately. The Isle of Wight is included in Hampshire. In Scotland the primary source makes the following groupings: Aberdeenshire, Banffshire, Moray and Nairn; Angus and Kincardineshire; Argyll and Bute; Berwickshire, East Lothian, Peebles, Roxburgh and Selkirk; Caithness, Inverness, Orkney, Ross and Cromarty, Sutherland and Zetland

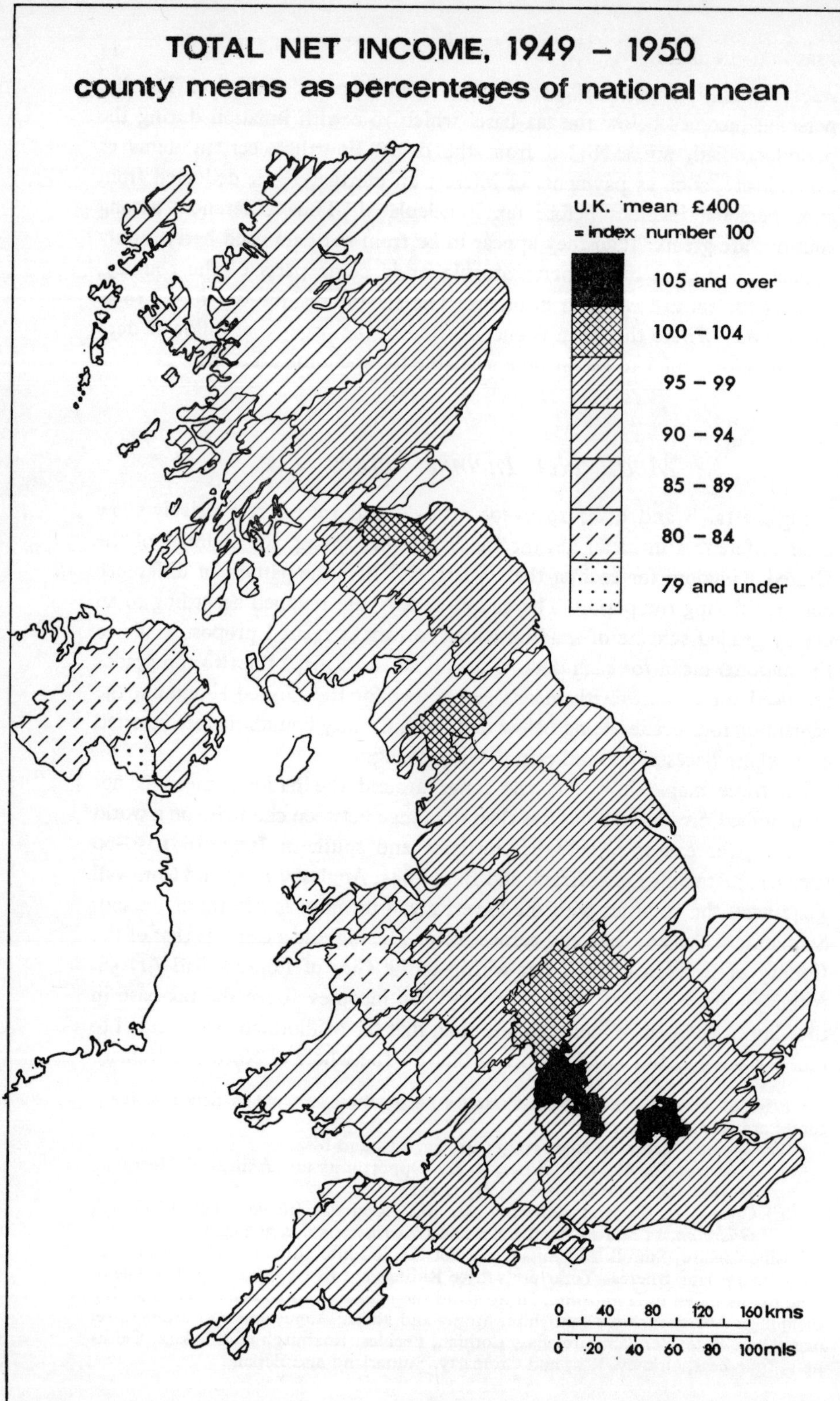

TOTAL NET INCOME, 1949 – 1950
county means as percentages of national mean

U.K. mean £400
= index number 100

■	105 and over
▨	100 – 104
	95 – 99
	90 – 94
	85 – 89
	80 – 84
⋰	79 and under

0 40 80 120 160 kms
0 20 40 60 80 100 mls

FIG. 2.1a

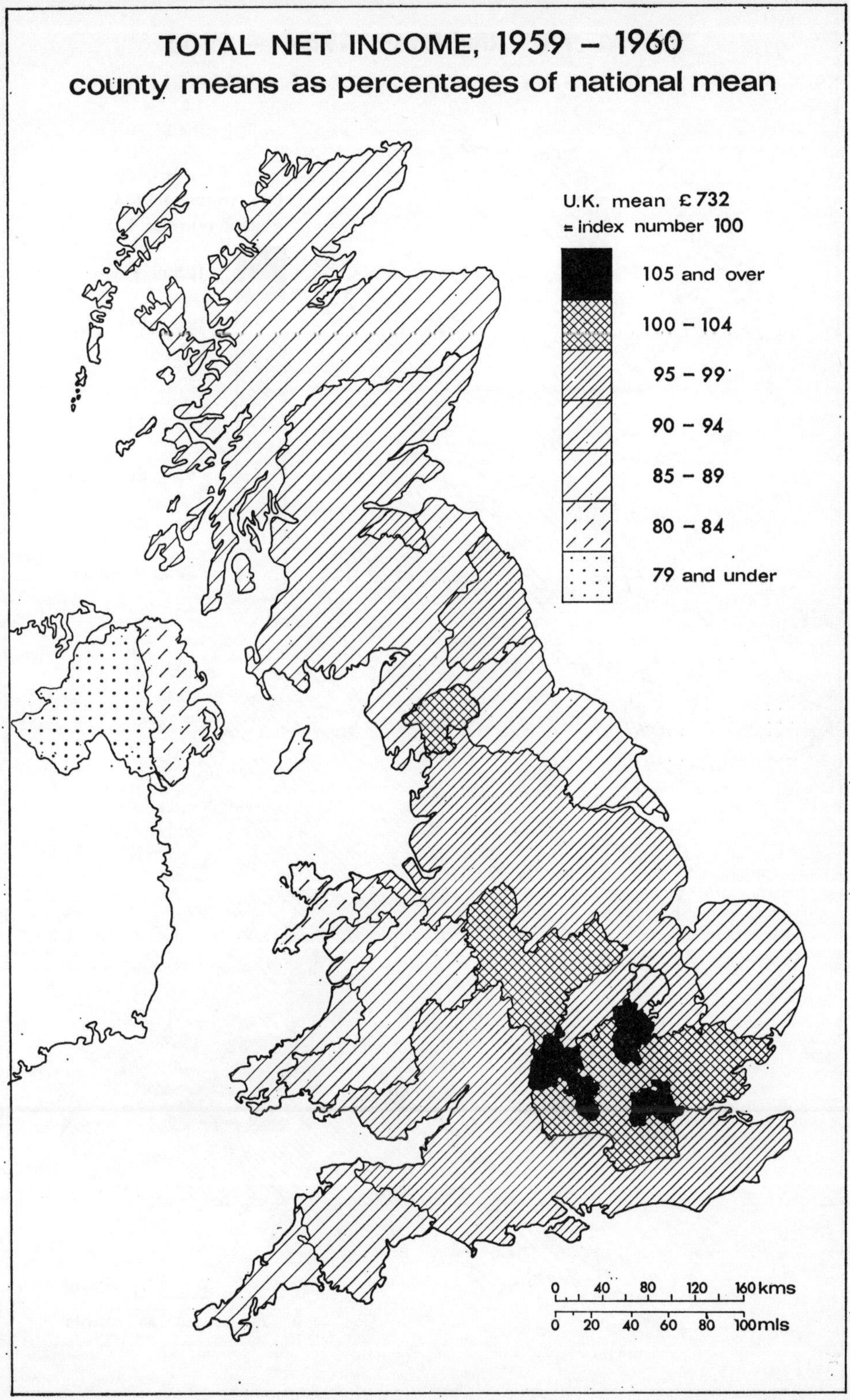

TOTAL NET INCOME, 1959 – 1960
county means as percentages of national mean

U.K. mean £732
= index number 100

105 and over
100 – 104
95 – 99
90 – 94
85 – 89
80 – 84
79 and under

0   40   80   120   160 kms
0   20   40   60   80   100 mls

FIG. 2.1b

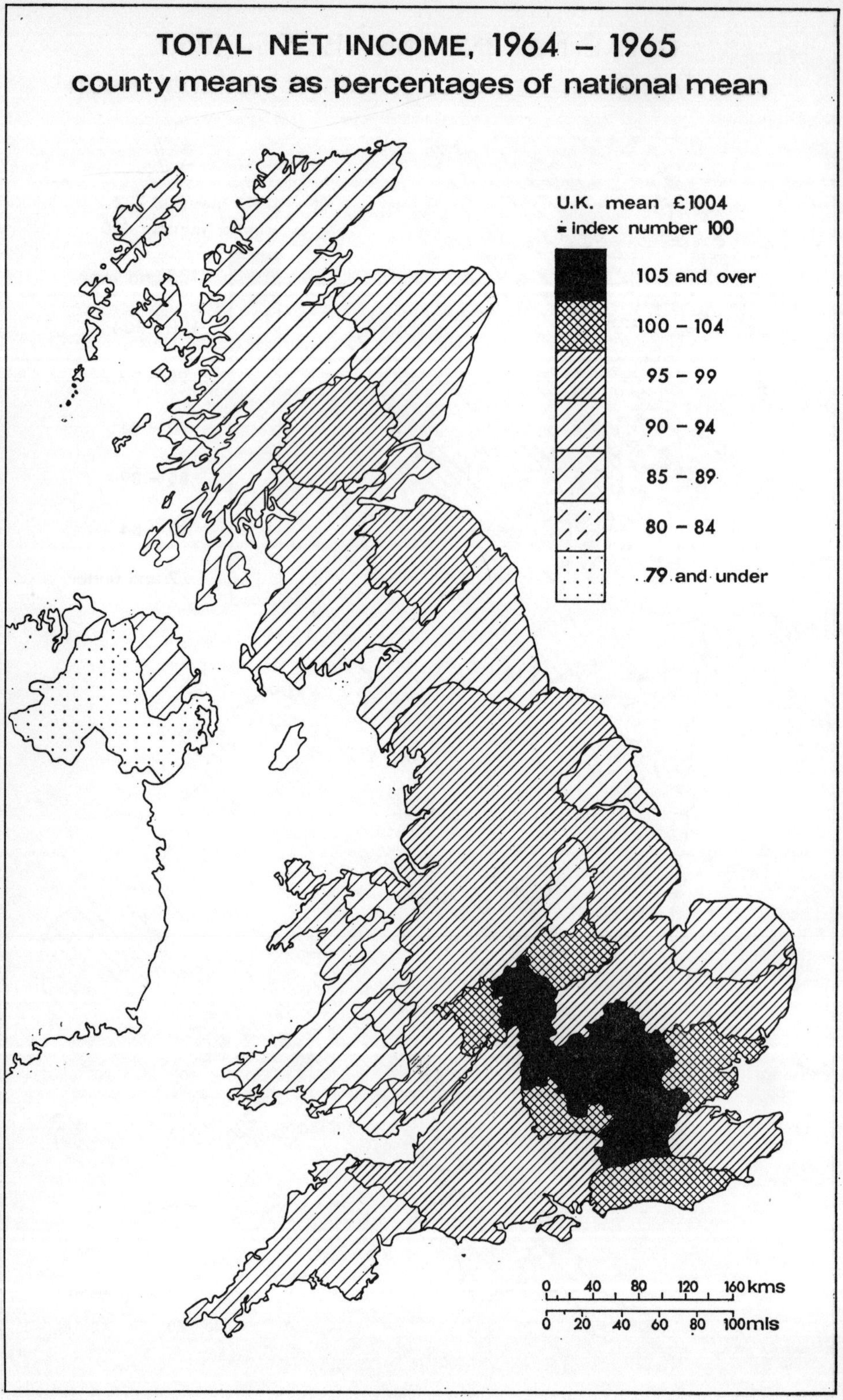

TOTAL NET INCOME, 1964 – 1965
county means as percentages of national mean

U.K. mean £1004
≈ index number 100

■	105 and over
▨	100 – 104
▥	95 – 99
▦	90 – 94
▧	85 – 89
▨	80 – 84
⋮	79 and under

0   40   80   120   160 kms
0   20   40   60   80   100 mls

FIG. 2.1c

While not enormous over much of the country, the range at all three dates is large enough in itself and in its consequences to warrant measurement and portrayal. Since the percentage intervals are both equal and identical on all three maps, the technique of representation is akin to that of the standard vertical interval used for contouring by the Ordnance Survey. Thus the maps should give some indication of the broadly trending surface of incomes over the country. In 1949–50 (fig. 2.1a) the surface was both less smooth and less favourably inclined upwards towards the south than in either 1959–60 (fig. 2.1b) or 1964–5 (fig. 2.1c). The phrase 'up to London' is as true for incomes on all three maps as it is on the railways or in common parlance. The same could be said of Oxford but not, be it noted, of Cambridge. But in 1949–50 London (including Middlesex) and Oxfordshire with Warwickshire and Leicestershire were separate islands in a sea of moderate incomes. By 1959–60 the two islands had coalesced and lay in a continuous area, as it were of newly emergent land, with incomes above the national mean. This area stretched from Essex and Surrey in the south to Staffordshire and Leicestershire towards the north. Meanwhile, Midlothian and West Lothian had sunk 'beneath the waters' of the national mean. By 1964–5 (fig. 2.1c) the island of the south had extended slightly in area and had increased in height, such that a high income ridge had appeared from Surrey to Warwickshire.[1] Thus we see emerging in these three maps a great island of prosperity stretching from Essex to Worcestershire and from Sussex to Leicestershire. Whether Staffordshire was eroded away during the process of emergence we shall never know.[2]

In sequence with these changes, the area graded as having 95 to 99 per cent of the national mean diminished in size during the 15 years after 1950, though there appeared to be some recovery in Scotland between 1960 and 1965. There was improvement on Severnside, but in south-west England and in Northern Ireland there seems to have been deterioration throughout the period covered by the three maps.

Net income before tax is, however, an intricate compound of income from different sources, namely, profits and professional earnings, investment, and employment. By far the largest of these is employment (Schedule E), which in 1964–5 comprised 76·5 per cent of total personal net income in the United Kingdom. As the largest and internally most consistent source, income from employment merits closer attention and greater credence in spatial analysis than either the other major sources or average net income as a whole.

[1] The disappearance of Westmorland from a high grade in 1964–5 results from an apparently rapid diminution there of Schedule D earnings (profits and professional earnings). Whether this fall really happened or was an error made in sampling a small Schedule D population is not known

[2] By a computing error in the primary data, Staffordshire cannot be separated statistically from Warwickshire in 1959–60. The inclusion of Staffordshire in the high income area for that date may not, therefore, be correct

Mean Income from Employment (Schedule E)

Income classified under Schedule E consists mainly of wages and salaries from which tax is deducted by the employer before payment to the employee. There is little scope for avoidance by the taxpayer and even less scope for ignorance at the Inland Revenue of the size of the employee's income before tax. The reliability of the data upon which this section is based cannot, therefore, be in doubt except in so far as techniques for producing the data have improved through time, and provided that clerical collection and sampling were properly carried out. In other words, fig. 2.2c (1964–5) may well be more accurate than fig. 2.2a (1949–50).

The range of incomes from employment is proportionately about the same as that for total net income, and is mapped for the three dates by a similar method. The chief difference is that a 10 per cent interval is used for employment income, not one of 5 per cent as on figs. 2.1a, b and c. At the bottom of the range of incomes from employment in 1964–5 were Armagh £620, Argyll and Bute £699, Montgomery and Radnor £720, and Cornwall £724, the same counties in Northern Ireland, Scotland and England, but not Wales, as for total net income in 1959–60. At the top were Greater London with £986 (there are no data for the City in 1964–5), and Bedfordshire with £963. The highest in Wales, Scotland and Northern Ireland respectively were Flint £903, Midlothian £830, and Antrim £764.

Between 1950 and 1965 the pattern of incomes earned as wages and salaries changed considerably. High incomes were more widespread in 1949–50 (the presence of the West Riding and Derbyshire in this category on fig. 2.2a should be noted) than in 1964–5 especially. If figs. 2.2a, b and c are considered by analogy to represent three successive synoptic situations of Schedule E income, what they may be deemed to show is a coalescent, southerly shift of high income systems and a smoothing of the income surface into a downward slope outwards from a Thames–Severnside–Midlands ridge (1964–5), with very high recordings for Greater London and Bedfordshire. These very high areas were apparent also in 1959–60 (fig. 2.2b). Changes occurred too in the pattern of moderate and low incomes, but they do not seem to merit detailed discussion. Suffice it that the three synoptic situations record significant movement in the pattern and thus plead the case for (a) the reduction of uncertainty regarding the detailed quality of the data,[1] and (b) the removal of the distortions inherent in the obligatory use, however elaborate the techniques, of the county framework as a statistical foundation for spatial analysis. Truly convincing and useful morphological surfaces will never be clearly discernible and therefore applicable to the solution of locational problems until this distorting framework, with its minute and even fragmented,

[1] Good as the statistics may seem to be in general, one is bound occasionally to doubt their accuracy in detail

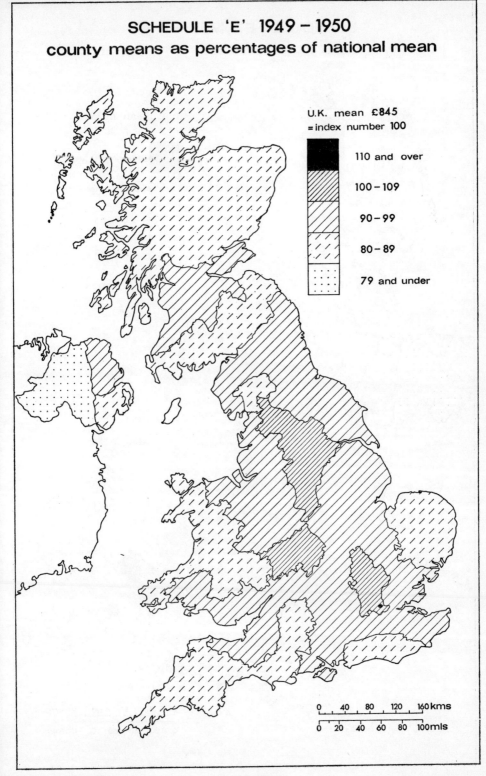

SCHEDULE 'E' 1949 – 1950
county means as percentages of national mean

U.K. mean £845
= index number 100

110 and over

100 – 109

90 – 99

80 – 89

79 and under

0   40   80   120   160 kms

0   20   40   60   80   100 mls

FIG. 2.2a

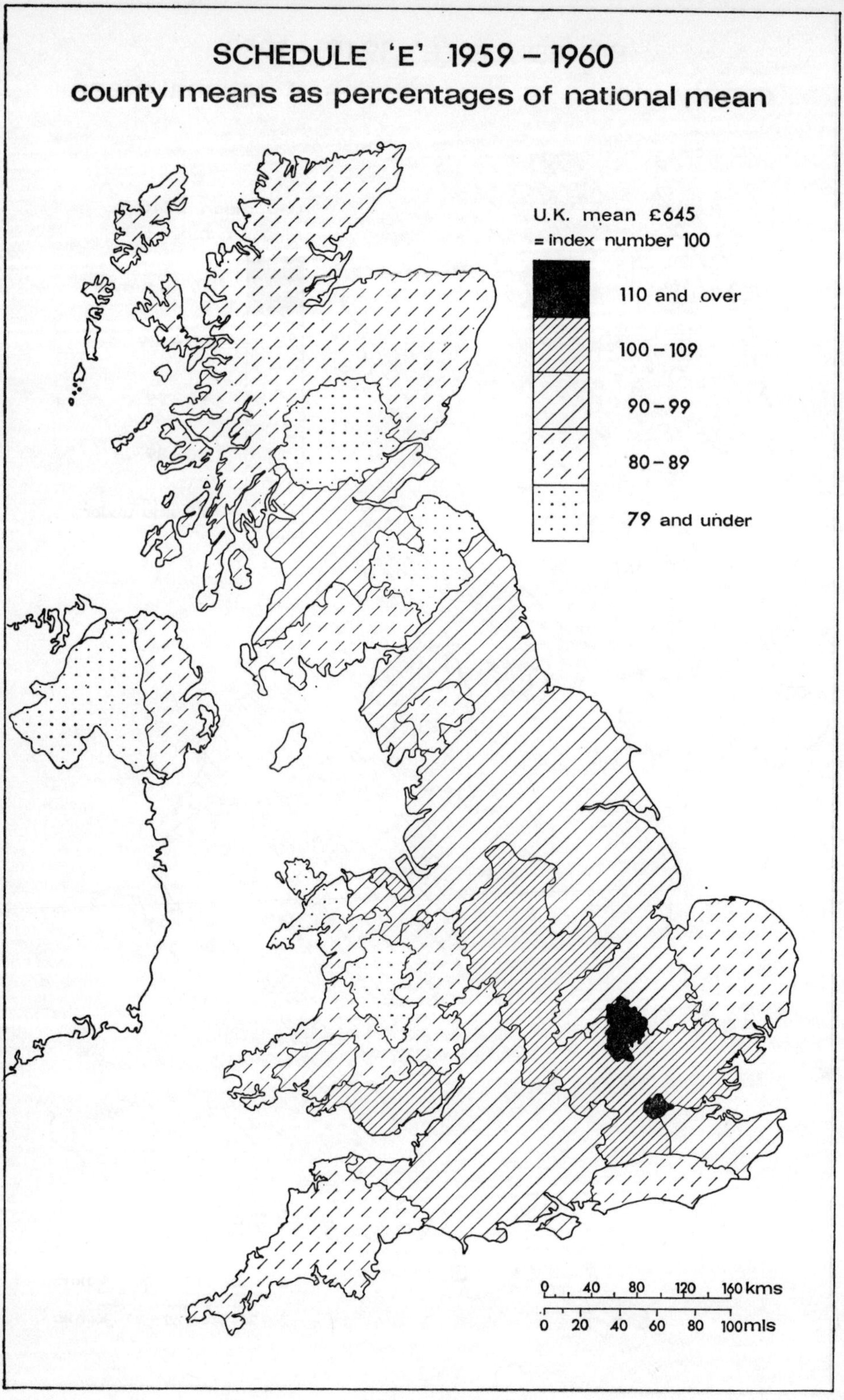

SCHEDULE 'E' 1959 – 1960
county means as percentages of national mean

U.K. mean £645
= index number 100

110 and over

100 – 109

90 – 99

80 – 89

79 and under

0   40   80   120   160 kms
0   20   40   60   80   100 mls

FIG. 2.2b

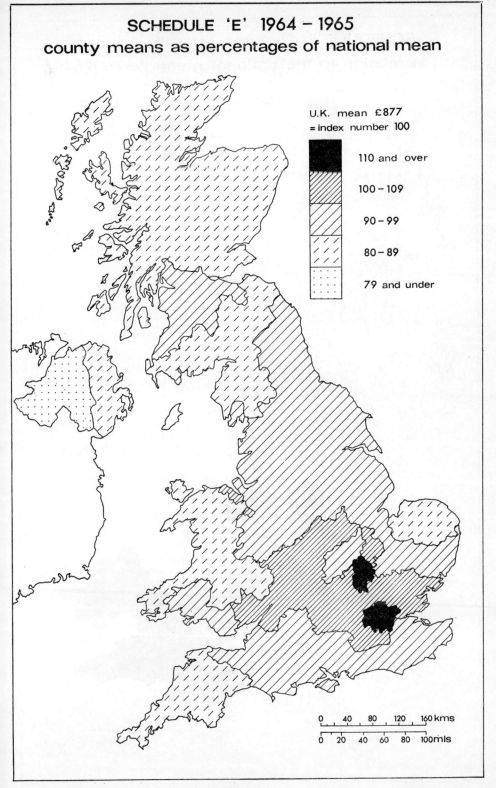

SCHEDULE 'E' 1964 – 1965
county means as percentages of national mean

U.K. mean £877
= index number 100

110 and over

100 – 109

90 – 99

80 – 89

79 and under

0   40   80   120   160 kms

0   20   40   60   80   100 mls

FIG. 2.2c

C

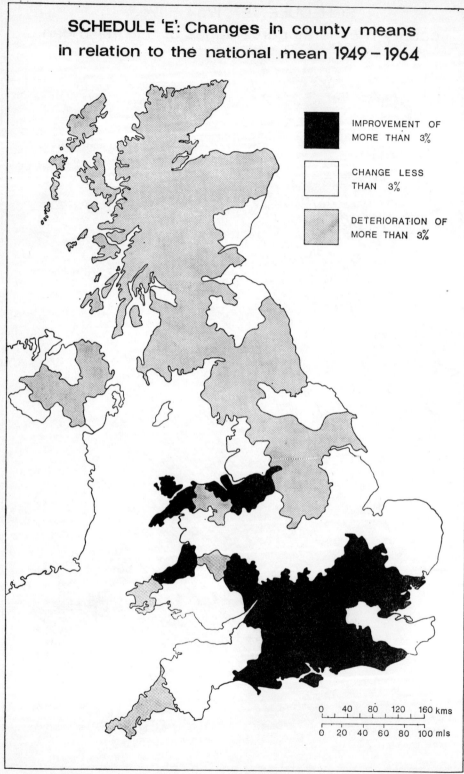

SCHEDULE 'E': Changes in county means
in relation to the national mean 1949 – 1964

IMPROVEMENT OF
MORE THAN 3%

CHANGE LESS
THAN 3%

DETERIORATION OF
MORE THAN 3%

| 0 | 40 | 80 | 120 | 160 kms |

| 0 | 20 | 40 | 60 | 80 | 100 mls |

FIG. 2.3a   (see table 2.1)   Data are not available for the Greater London Council area

Flintshires and its large Lincolnshires, Devons and Norfolks, is replaced by a standard grid for statistical purposes.

Even using the county framework, however, and without elaborate techniques, the statistics can be further explored to show relative change over the period studied. Fig. 2.3a examines the data of each county in relation to a national index of 100 for the extreme dates, 1949–50 and 1964–5. A change of more than 3 per cent between these dates for a given county is taken, arbitrarily, to be significant.

Thus, for example, while the West Riding deteriorates from 100 in 1949–50 to 95 in 1964–5, Durham from 99 to 93, Derbyshire from 104 to 99 and Antrim from 92 to 87, Lancashire remains fairly steady (97 to 95), as do Angus (88 to 87), Kent (94 to 96) and Shropshire (96 to 96). But marked increases are recorded by Berkshire (93 to 104), Buckinghamshire (100 to 109), Hertfordshire (102 to 108), Bedfordshire (103 to 110), Flintshire (96 to 103) and even Cardiganshire (82 to 87). The County of London, Middlesex and the area of the Greater London Council cannot be assessed on fig. 2.3a because of the boundary changes affecting them. These areas are thus left blank on the map. In short, fig. 2.3a shows a tilting of the morphological surface of changing Schedule E incomes in favour of much of southern England, just as figs. 2.2a, b and c showed a shift of incomes to form a Thames–Severnside ridge in 1964–5.

This broad tilting was not consistently maintained throughout the 15-year period, however, for table 2.1 shows that individual counties often changed more in one quinquennium than in the others, and that the quinquennium of greatest change was not everywhere the same. Hertfordshire, for example, improved most between 1949 and 1954. Northumberland deteriorated most between 1959 and 1964, while Buckinghamshire had two spurts of improvement, 1949 to 1954 and 1959 to 1964.

To illustrate these differences and to see whether the southerly trend was maintained towards the end of the period under review, fig. 2.3b was drawn for the last quinquennium, 1959 to 1964. It shows that improvement was not wholly restricted to the southern half of Britain, since several counties to the north, east and south of London that increased by more than 3 per cent over the 15-year period as a whole are excluded. Nor did deterioration affect most of the northern half of Britain or the whole of Northern Ireland. It was restricted to a compact area of northern England, comprising Cumberland, Northumberland, Durham, Westmorland and the West Riding. Further to the north, most of Scotland appeared to be 'holding its own', or improving, in some of the less populous areas. Perhaps, therefore, the early regional policies were beginning to have enough influence in some areas to register their positive effects on this simple map. Possibly their failures register too. One cannot safely draw a definite conclusion without a more elaborate analysis and an enhanced confidence in the accuracy of the data. But it does appear

TABLE 2.1   Index of Schedule E incomes for the four quinquennial surveys
(*The order of presentation is that used by the Commissioners of Inland Revenue*)

	1949–50	1954–55	1959–60	1964–65
United Kingdom	100	100	100	100
Cumberland	92	92	93	89
Durham	99	102	97	93
Northumberland	99	100	98	95
Westmorland	89	85	88	84
North Riding	96	96	95	96
East Riding	98	97	94	94
West Riding	100	100	98	95
Derbyshire	104	107	100	99
Leicestershire and Rutland	99	102	101	100
Lincolnshire	97	96	95	95
Northamptonshire	96	95	97	95
Nottinghamshire	100	103	98	96
Bedfordshire	103	107	112	110
Cambridge	90	92	93	95
Essex	98	102	104	104
Hertfordshire	102	106	107	108
Huntingdonshire	90	93	93	101
Norfolk	88	84	85	87
Suffolk	90	89	88	90
City of London	124	144	148	—
London County	—	—	116	—
Greater London	—	—	—	112
Kent	94	96	96	96
Surrey	99	101	101	103
Sussex	88	87	88	91
Berkshire	93	96	100	104
Buckinghamshire	100	104	105	109
Dorset	87	90	—	91
Hampshire	93	94	93	96
Oxford	99	100	106	106
Cornwall	86	84	82	82
Devon	86	85	85	88
Gloucester	95	99	—	100
Somerset	91	93	—	92
Wiltshire	90	91	93	95
Hereford	85	84	86	89
Shropshire	92	91	89	91
Staffordshire	100	103	106	99
Warwickshire	107	110	106	107
Worcestershire	101	100	98	100
Cheshire	95	98	98	98
Lancashire	97	98	96	95

	1949–50	1954–55	1959–60	1964–65
Anglesey	84	84	79	87
Brecknock	85	84	87	85
Caernarvon	85	82	79	88
Cardigan	82	82	84	87
Carmarthen	93	97	93	92
Denbigh	92	94	88	88
Flint	96	98	101	103
Glamorgan	99	100	100	97
Merioneth	83	80	87	84
Monmouth	99	108	100	101
Pembroke	88	85	87	85
Radnor	86	89	78	82
Aberdeen, Banff, Moray and Nairn	89	86	83	84
Angus and Kincardineshire	88	85	85	87
Argyll and Bute	87	77	80	80
Ayr	95	—	92	91
Berwick, E. Lothian, Peebles, Roxburgh and Selkirk	85	82	79	83
Caithness, Inverness, Orkney, Ross and Cromarty, Sutherland and Shetland	85	84	76	82
Clackmannan and Kinross	94	98	90	87
Dumfries, Kirkcudbright and Wigtown	84	84	82	81
Dunbarton	96	97	91	91
Fife	95	96	91	89
Lanark	98	97	93	94
Midlothian	98	96	94	95
Perth	84	81	79	80
Renfrew	96	95	96	94
Stirling	96	94	91	92
West Lothian	99	100	93	94
Antrim	92	91	—	87
Armagh	75	73	69	71
Down	81	77	—	80
Fermanagh	73	76	69	74
Londonderry	76	72	73	72
Tyrone	75	77	69	72

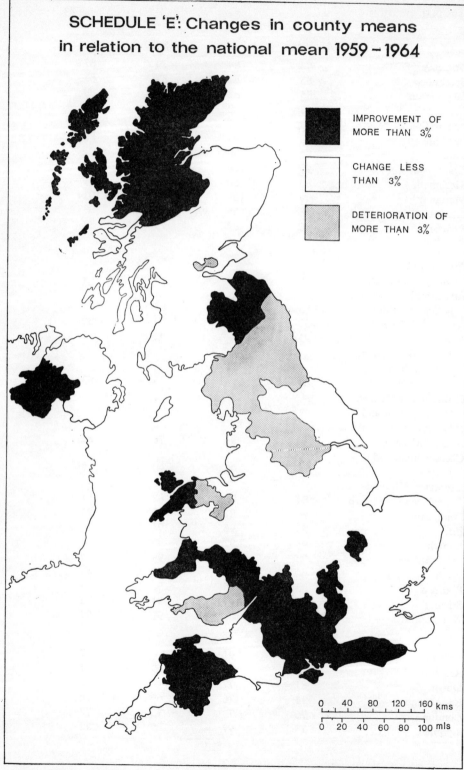

SCHEDULE 'E': Changes in county means
in relation to the national mean 1959–1964

IMPROVEMENT OF
MORE THAN 3%

CHANGE LESS
THAN 3%

DETERIORATION OF
MORE THAN 3%

0   40   80   120   160 kms

0   20   40   60   80 100 mls

FIG. 2.3b   (see table 2.1)   Data are not available for the Greater London Council area

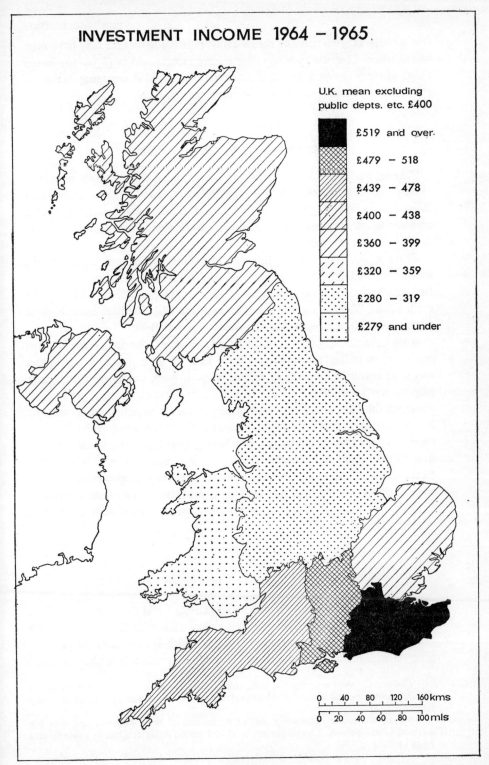

INVESTMENT INCOME 1964 – 1965.

U.K. mean excluding
public depts. etc. £400

£519 and over.

£479 – 518

£439 – 478

£400 – 438

£360 – 399

£320 – 359

£280 – 319

£279 and under

0 40 80 120 160 kms

0 20 40 60 .80 100 mls

FIG. 2.4

that a check in some areas to the so-called regional imbalance may have been taking place. The results of the next county income-survey (1969-70) should show whether or not a new and more complex trend is emerging to replace the relatively simple morphology apparent on fig. 2.3a.

Income from Investment

Detailed analysis of sources of income other than employment (Schedule E) must await further research. Fig. 2.4 indicates, however, that investment income especially might well merit investigation, notwithstanding that it amounts to only 7·5 per cent of total net income shared among almost 19 per cent of taxable incomes.[1]

There is a cultural tone to fig. 2.4. The south of England, especially the south-east, leads the country in investment. Scotland, Northern Ireland and East Anglia follow some way behind. The Midlands and North of England are low, and Wales is right at the bottom of the table. Perhaps there is some truth after all in the reputation the Scots have for thrift.

What influence this very unbalanced pattern may be having on the national economy, including the southerly trend that we have just been discussing and shall encounter repeatedly in this book, is quite unknown. But savings help create the capital necessary to sustain and increase future production. Although the influence of local savings upon local development is undoubtedly less today than it was before the modern banking system had evolved, nevertheless savings may still be expected to have greater impact upon the economy near by than upon the economy of more distant areas. Perhaps this proximity factor may work more strongly among private and small companies than among large corporations. Perhaps it is relevant also to the successful functioning of London as a seed-bed and nursery for the growth of small-scale enterprises of many different kinds.

Income Structure

The discussion thus far has depended entirely upon the simple expedient of calculating the mean income of a county or region by dividing its taxable fund by the number of its incomes.[2] No incomes below the minimum level of taxation were included. The sizes of the resultant means will not have escaped

[1] The regions shown on fig. 2.4 were used transitionally by the Inland Revenue in the changeover period from the old Standard Regions to the new Economic Planning Regions

[2] An income is not necessarily that of an individual since husband and wife are counted as one person. The minimum level of taxation stood at £180 in 1959–60 and £275 in 1964–5

notice, and some readers may consider them surprisingly small. Even the mean for Greater London is quite likely to be deemed a rung to be climbed on the ladder of income rather than a height to be reached and held before vertigo sets in. Whether or not these inferences are valid, it is certain that the mean alone can give little indication of the slope of the ladder, and that analysis of the structure of incomes is therefore desirable. Such analysis is indeed possible both for counties and for regions, and the structural distribution on the national ladder provides a yardstick for comparative assessment.

In 1964–5 there were just over 21 million net incomes above £275 before tax. These were distributed among 17 brackets of income. The brackets vary in the range of incomes they represent. Apart from the lowest, £275 – 299, they rise by steps of £100 from £300 to £999. Thereafter the intervals are £1,000 – 1,199, £1,200 – 1,499, £1,500 – 1,749, £1,750 – 1,999, thence by steps of £1,000 up to £4,999, and finally £5,000 – 9,999 and over £10,000. The monetary distance between each rung on the ladder increases therefore towards the higher end of the scale, and there is a statistically unsatisfactory interval of £300 (£1,200 – 1,499) interposed between steps of £200 and £250 respectively below and above it.

Two histograms showing the percentages in each of these brackets (without aggregation) for the United Kingdom and Northern Ireland, respectively, in 1964–5 are drawn on fig. 2.5. The intervals are statistically ill-chosen but the diagrams make a very striking visual contrast. The median income for the United Kingdom was between £800 and £899, probably about £840. That for Northern Ireland was about £630, while in Greater London it was £900.[1]

By aggregation of brackets we have tried to give some indication on fig. 2.6a to 6e of the weighting on the rungs of the ladder of incomes in each county in relation to the national weighting. The aggregates used are: £275 – 399; £400 – 699; £700 – 999; £1,000 – 1,499; £1,500 – 1,999; and over £2,000. The national percentage for 1964–5 in each of these aggregates respectively was: 10·55; 26·09; 25·68; 26·18; 6·70; and 4·79. A more evenly populated set of aggregates could be derived if only four were chosen. We have, however, used an unbalanced set of six in an attempt to reveal a little more information about the top and bottom of the ladder than four rungs would allow, on the grounds that an excess of incomes at the bottom is a guide to the distribution of poverty and distress, while an excess towards the top is a guide to the distribution of wealth, influence and decision-making. In so far as this justification is accepted, the fact that those with influence tend to be concentrated in one part of the country is a point worth implying on the maps.

These are very simple maps since they are based solely upon the criterion that for an area to be shaded it must have more than the United Kingdom percentage of incomes in both adjacent aggregates of rungs on the ladder.

[1] The amount for Greater London excludes the incomes of civil servants

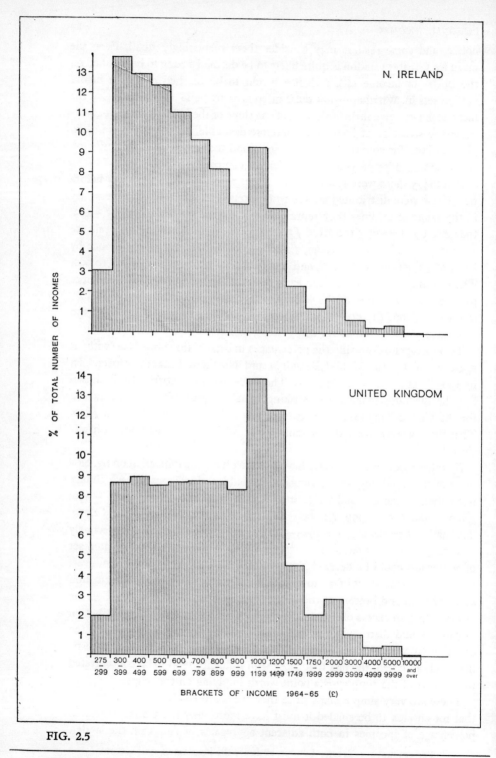

FIG. 2.5

FIG. 2.6 Shaded areas on each map have a higher proportion of income than
national means in *both* of the brackets indicated

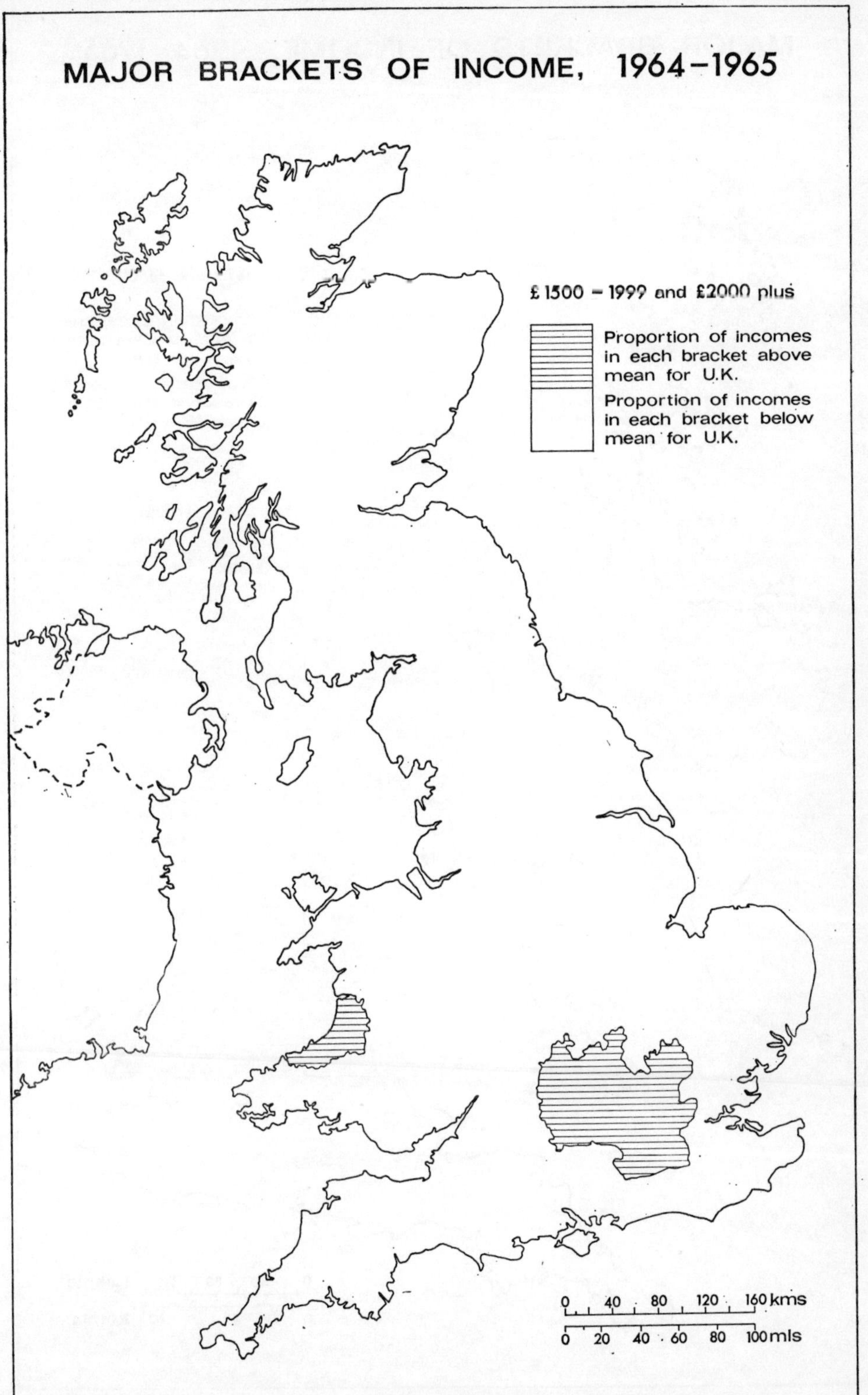

MAJOR BRACKETS OF INCOME, 1964-1965

£ 1500 – 1999 and £2000 plus

Proportion of incomes in each bracket above mean for U.K.

Proportion of incomes in each bracket below mean for U.K.

0 40 80 120 160 kms

0 20 40 60 80 100 mls

FIG. 2.6a

MAJOR BRACKETS OF INCOME, 1964-1965

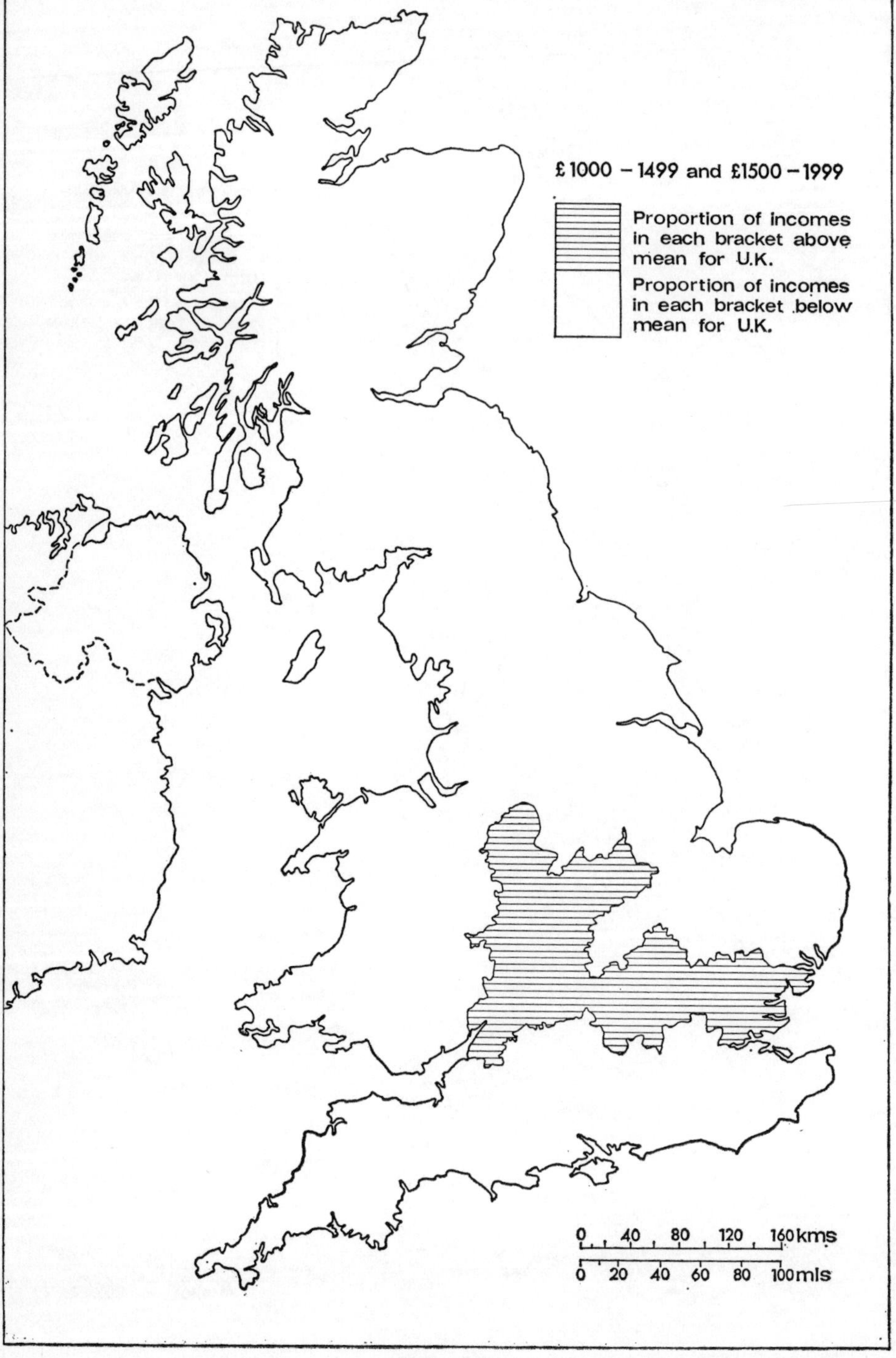

£1000 – 1499 and £1500 – 1999

Proportion of incomes in each bracket above mean for U.K.

Proportion of incomes in each bracket below mean for U.K.

```
0    40   80   120   160 kms
0   20   40   60   80   100 mls
```

FIG. 2.6b

MAJOR BRACKETS OF INCOME, 1964-1965

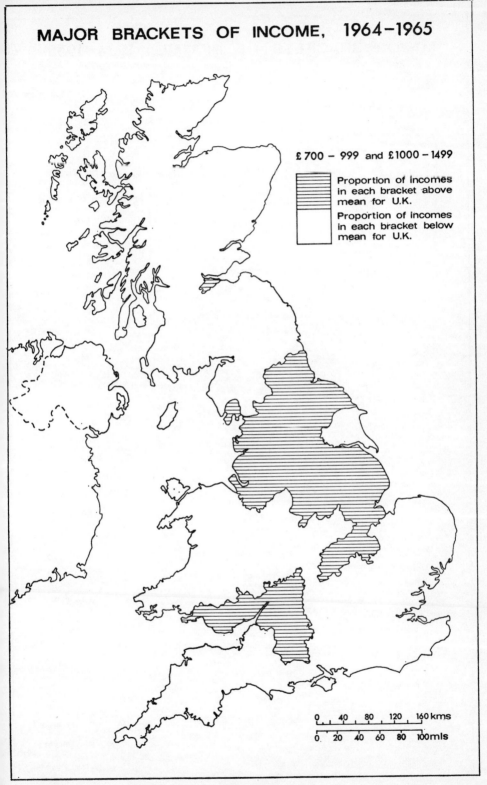

£ 700 – 999 and £1000 – 1499

Proportion of incomes in each bracket above mean for U.K.

Proportion of incomes in each bracket below mean for U.K.

0   40   80   120   160 kms

0   20   40   60   80   100 mls

FIG. 2.6c

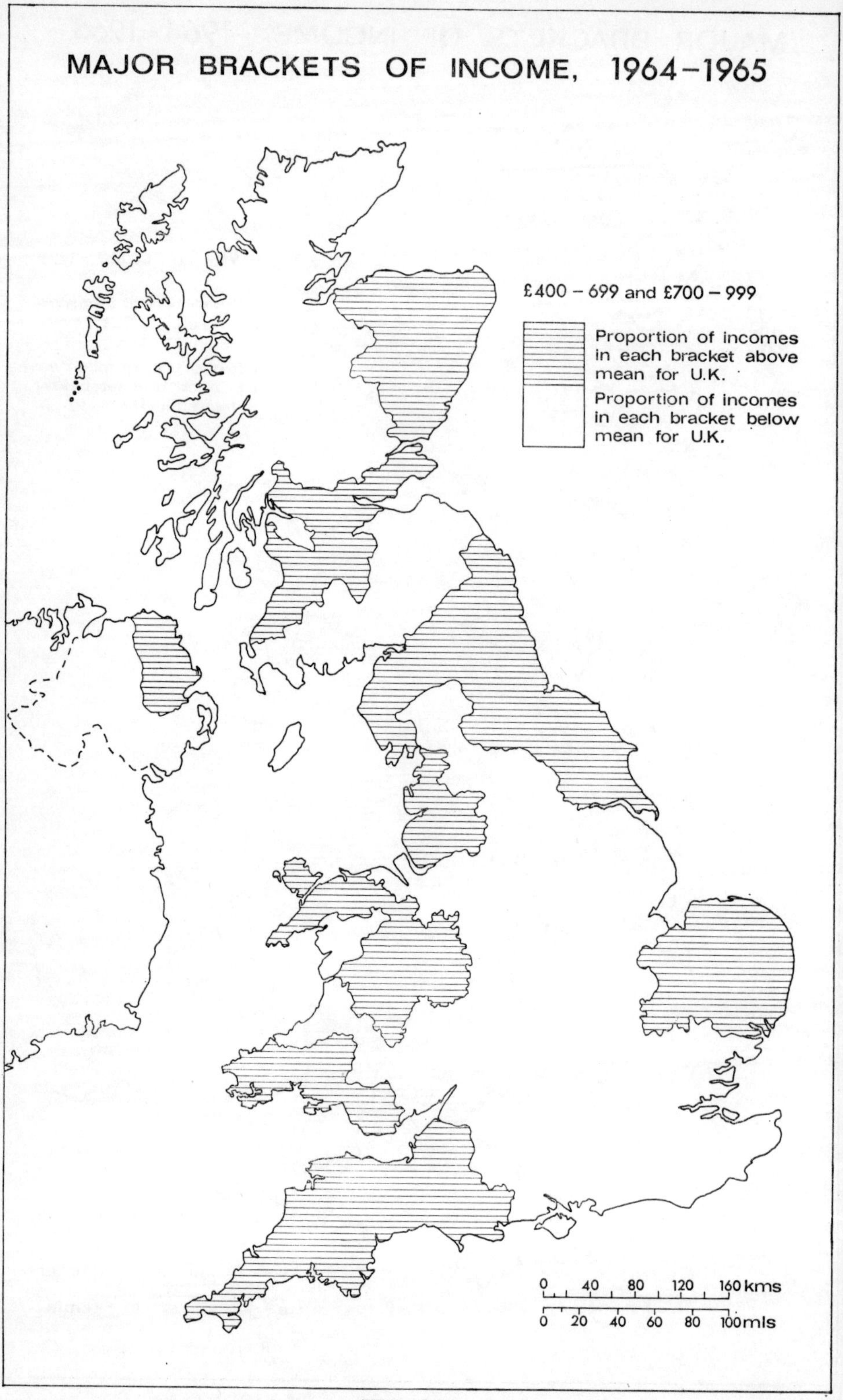

MAJOR BRACKETS OF INCOME, 1964–1965

£400 – 699 and £700 – 999

Proportion of incomes
in each bracket above
mean for U.K.

Proportion of incomes
in each bracket below
mean for U.K.

0   40   80   120   160 kms
0   20   40   60   80   100 mls

FIG. 2·6d

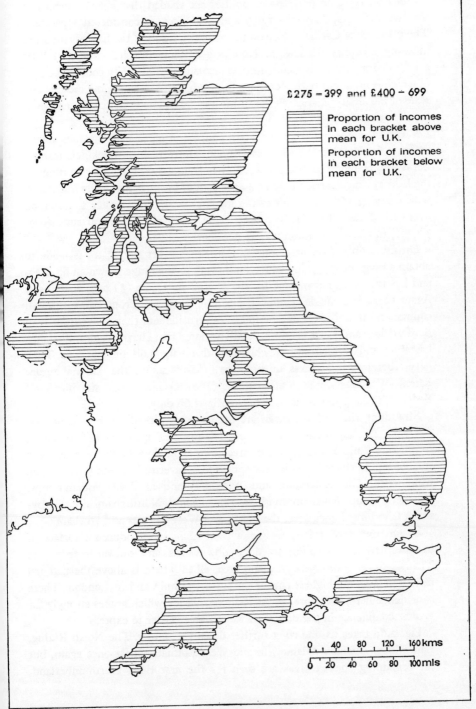

MAJOR BRACKETS OF INCOME, 1964–1965

£275 – 399 and £400 – 699

Proportion of incomes
in each bracket above
mean for U.K.

Proportion of incomes
in each bracket below
mean for U.K.

0   40   80   120   160 kms

0   20   40   60   80 100 mls

FIG. 2.6e

Over-weighting for one of these aggregates does not, therefore, compensate for under-weighting on the next.

Thus on fig. 2.6a only those counties are shaded that have a surplus in the two brackets, £1,500 – 1,999 and over £2,000, considered separately. The presence of Cardiganshire on this map is a result of the hazards involved in using a county framework. Here is a sparsely peopled county of little economic importance but containing an expanding university college the staff of which is no doubt both increasing in number and climbing the incremental scale of university salaries. Perhaps this one enterprise is sufficient to account for the anomaly.

Clearly there is only one important concentration of high incomes shown on fig. 2.6a. It comprises Greater London, Hertfordshire, Buckinghamshire, Berkshire, Oxfordshire and Surrey. In this compact area the top two rungs of the ladder, which carried only 11·49 per cent of incomes nationally in 1964-5, were carrying 16·19 per cent of the incomes arising in Greater London, an overload of two-fifths (41 per cent). The overload on the top rung (over £2,000) in Greater London was 52 per cent.

On fig. 2.6b a descent of one step in the bracket aggregates is made to obtain a range of weighting which both overlaps the range shown on fig. 2.6a, and has the mean net income for the United Kingdom (£1,000) at its base. Again there is a single, compact area but it extends from Essex through counties north and west of London to Severnside and thence northwards to Staffordshire and Leicestershire. It will be noted that Hertfordshire, Buckinghamshire and Oxfordshire are shaded both on fig. 2.6b and fig. 2.6a. They have, therefore, an excess in all three brackets above the national mean. Essex, Worcestershire, Staffordshire, Warwickshire, Leicestershire and Bedfordshire register their presence on fig. 2.6b only.

Straddling the national mean are the counties picked out by shading on fig. 2.6c. Among them, only Gloucestershire has appeared before. Apart from West Lothian which may be treated as anomalous by virtue of its very small size, the shaded area is now split into a Severnside group (Glamorgan, Monmouth, Gloucestershire and Wiltshire) and an East Midland-cum-Northern group (Northamptonshire, Lincolnshire, Nottinghamshire, Derbyshire, Cheshire, Lancashire, the North and West Ridings and Durham).

So far, therefore, this sequence of three maps has produced a surface of income structure seeming to slope downwards and outwards from the Thames–Severnside–West Midland area, all of which is above the national mean but with the highest part of the surface around and in London. There is evidence here, therefore, of internal consistency which argues strongly for greater confidence in the data than we felt able earlier to express.

Fig. 2.6d takes us one rung further down the ladder. The North Riding, Lancashire, Durham, Glamorgan and West Lothian appear once again, but the remaining shaded areas are seen for the first time. Northumberland,

Cumberland and most counties in central Scotland are among them, and Antrim is the first to appear in Northern Ireland. Within England and Wales. however, the outward trending surface is maintained.

The series is completed by fig. 2.6e which portrays surplus in the bottom pair of brackets. There is considerable repetition of shaded areas on figs. 2.6d and e, and Lancashire and the North Riding appear on all three maps dealing with brackets below the national mean. Cardiganshire returns to claim a place at the bottom of the league as well as at the top. The morphology of income structure is not, therefore, quite so simple a surface as we implied after discussing fig. 2.6c. It cannot clearly be explained in terms of distance from London, for distance seems to have different values and effects in different directions. The surface slopes most steeply towards East Anglia and Sussex, and least steeply towards Cheshire, the West Riding and Severnside. Finally it should be noted that three counties, Flintshire, Hampshire and Kent, remain unshaded on all five maps because their income structures do not contain surpluses in any two adjacent aggregates.

It is impossible to show how income structures have changed over time. Data are available, but by virtue of inflation, changes in bracket intervals and obstacles preventing satisfactory comparative aggregation of brackets, it is not deemed worthwhile to pursue the task. The bracket analysis has however been undertaken for 1959-60, and part of it appears elsewhere.[1] The resultant findings are similar to those portrayed on the sequence of maps that have just been examined.

Clearly there is more to income structure than it has been possible to present here or to analyse. Further research into structure is likely also to be more helpful to effective decision making than the study of averages, and it is probable that the application of more elaborate statistical and geographical techniques to existing and future structural data could provide very refined indicators of how the spatial pattern, the local and regional parts of the national economy, change in the course of time and respond to policy measures. To justify this opinion and to glimpse the variety of structures that exist, diagrams have been prepared for a selection of counties (fig. 2.7). Little comment is needed, save to pose the questions: why do these differences exist; is it efficient or necessary that they should exist; can and should policies be aimed to change them?

Poverty

The foregoing analysis of statistics produced by the Inland Revenue shows where the lowest taxable incomes form the largest proportion of the taxable population. But the primary data exclude the very low incomes that

[1] Coates, B. E., and Rawstron, E. M., 'Regional variations in income', *Westminster Bank Review*, February 1966, 28-46, figs. 3 and 4

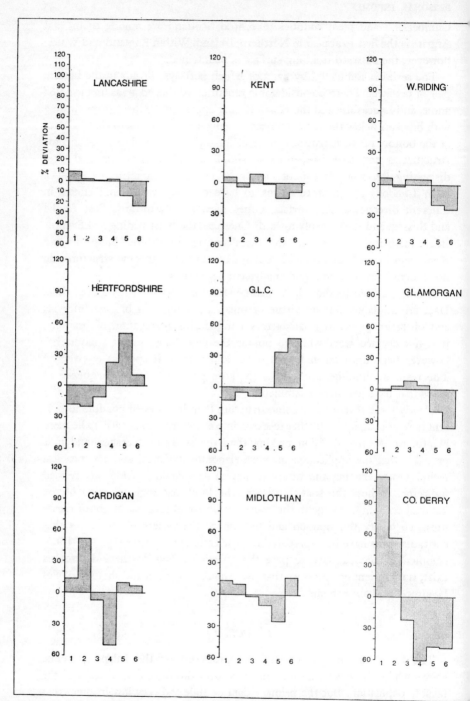

FIG. 2.7 Percentage bracket-deviations for selected counties, 1964-5

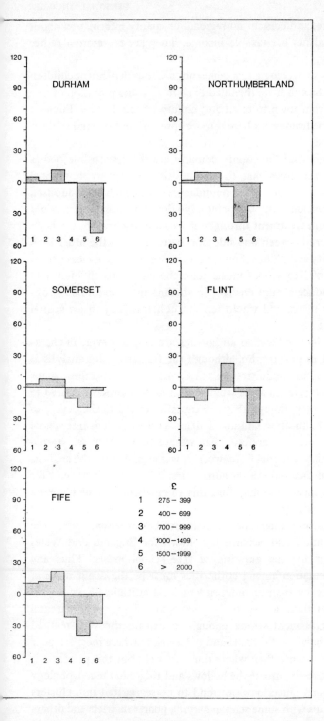

fall below the tax-base, and contain no regional or county information about the number of dependants per taxable income. They are therefore a rather poor index of poverty.

In an attempt partly to overcome this deficiency so far as dependent children are concerned, figs. 2.8a and b are included to show how the provision of free school meals varied from town to town and county to county over England and Wales in 1966. The framework here is more appropriate to spatial analysis than it was for incomes.

The county boroughs and the county councils are the responsible bodies for education. Thus the areas that these authorities serve are functional regions each with a clearly demarcated boundary within which one education committee alone has the authority to operate. No doubt a committee may not give completely uniform treatment throughout its statutory area, but policies are likely to differ more between one side of a boundary and the other than within a single statutory area. Thus if one authority were markedly less generous in its provision of free school meals than the next, this difference in behaviour should produce abrupt changes in shading in a random and confused manner on our maps, and would tend to obliterate any major spatial trend in poverty itself.

The boundaries of local education authorities are not, however, in themselves directly related to poverty. So, although the framework for analysis is functionally relevant in an administrative sense, one still sees on these maps a series of averages that refer to areas which are in no way causally related to the distribution of poverty, though they are causally related to the degree to which the provision of education and its ancillary services such as free school meals is effective. It seems, therefore, that we are back where we started with just as inappropriate a spatial framework as was available for the analysis of incomes. Indeed, if local education authorities differ in their policies for providing free school meals one may find this roundabout way of mapping poverty totally unsatisfactory.

Fortunately two factors intervene to redeem the situation. First, the Department of Education and Science lays down for England and Wales mandatory regulations for the granting of free school meals. Thus any difference in implementation among authorities must be the result more of administrative inefficiency than of independent local attitudes. Secondly, it is highly unlikely that there are spatially graduated differences in parental pride or child embarrassment strong enough to explain the very marked graded distributions shown on figs. 2.8a and b. Certainly where most are poor it is easier to accept assistance than where most are rich, but this principle is likely to do no more than accentuate the hollows and ridges in the morphology of poverty. Furthermore, since localities tend to be segregated into clusters of similar income groups with some schools serving poorer districts and others serving richer, the factors of parental pride and child embarrassment should

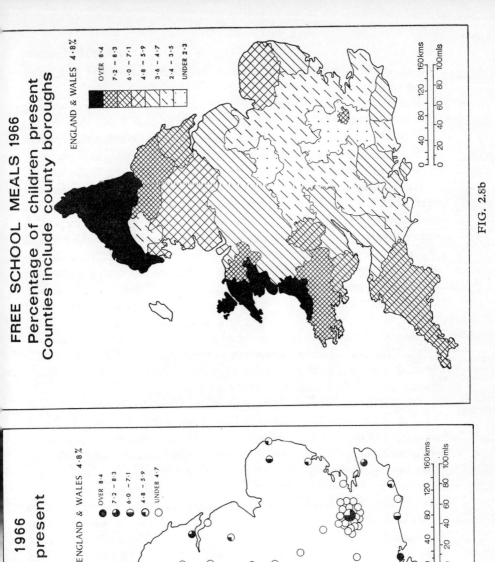

FREE SCHOOL MEALS 1966
Percentage of children present
County Boroughs only

ENGLAND & WALES 4·8%

● OVER 8·4
◐ 7·2 – 8·3
◑ 6·0 – 7·1
◒ 4·8 – 5·9
○ UNDER 4·7

0 20 40 60 80 100mls
0 40 80 120 160kms

FIG. 2.8a

FREE SCHOOL MEALS 1966
Percentage of children present
Counties include county boroughs

ENGLAND & WALES 4·8%

■ OVER 8·4
▨ 7·2 – 8·3
▧ 6·0 – 7·1
▤ 4·8 – 5·9
▒ 3·6 – 4·7
╱ 2·4 – 3·5
· UNDER 2·3

0 20 40 60 80 100mls
0 40 80 120 160kms

FIG. 2.8b

be effectively smoothed out of causal relevance by the scale of framework used here.[1]

Thus we consider that our maps come very close to the truth in showing the broad features of the morphology of poverty, and clearly the evidence presented earlier on taxable incomes tends strongly to confirm this opinion.

Fig. 2.8a shows the percentage of children present who were receiving free school meals in the county boroughs of England and Wales and in Inner London[2] on a given day in 1966. Four grades above the mean and one grade below it are used to indicate variation. A core area in which provision is less than the mean is discernible at once. Inner London excepted, it encompasses all outer London boroughs and the county boroughs enclosed by a line from Southend via Derby, Wolverhampton, Worcester, Oxford, Reading, Croydon and back to Southend. Much of this area is within that of above-average incomes shown in fig. 2.2c. The exceptions are Derby and Northampton which have less child poverty than fig. 2.2c would lead one to expect, and Gloucester, Newport and Bristol which have rather more. Moreover, Greater London considered as a whole was below the mean in 1966. This close apparent agreement between figs. 2.2c and 2.8a provides mutual corroboration of the satisfactory quality of the data, from two separate sources, upon which both maps are based.

Outside the core area an outward gradation is visible. On Merseyside and in Lancashire and Yorkshire–Humberside there are six boroughs below average, five over 8·4 per cent and twenty-three in intermediate grades. On balance, therefore, these seem to be intermediate areas.[3] South Wales has two boroughs over 8·4 per cent and two intermediate, and in north-east England no borough is better than intermediate and five out of eight are worse. Poverty, therefore, seems to be greater in both these areas than in the Lancashire–Yorkshire–Humberside combination. The four worst boroughs in England and Wales were all in the north-east: Newcastle upon Tyne (14·7 per cent); Gateshead (11·1); Middlesbrough (10·8); and Sunderland (10·3).

Data for Scotland and Northern Ireland for 1966, but not mapped here, give the following returns for the major cities there: Aberdeen 3·9 per cent; Dundee 7·5; Edinburgh 8·9; Glasgow 14·1; Belfast 10·0; and Londonderry 16·9.

By amalgamating data for the administrative counties and county boroughs in England and Wales an even better measure of the spatial variation of family poverty can be obtained. The findings are presented on fig. 2.8b, which shows

---

[1] Social Science Research Council, *Research on Poverty*, 1968
[2] The Inner London Education Authority is responsible for education in what was the County of London
[3] They were investigated as 'intermediate' or 'grey' areas in other respects by the Hunt Committee, *The Intermediate Areas, Report of a Committee under the Chairmanship of Sir Joseph Hunt*, Cmnd 3998, 1969

a very marked outward gradation indeed from south-eastern and midland England. From the standpoint of social welfare this map indicates a morphological surface and a spatial trend of great importance. In absolute terms it probably understates the extent of poverty but as a sample of reality it is probably very close to the truth discernible at a medium-scale framework of analysis.[1]

In Scotland, no directive from the Scottish Department of Education was in operation in 1966, and consequently the policies of local education authorities probably varied. The mean, 7·74 per cent, was considerably higher than in England. In Northern Ireland the mean was 16·48 per cent, ranging from 33·9 per cent in County Londonderry to 9·35 per cent in Antrim (excluding Belfast).

Poor people and poor places cannot pay as much tax as rich people and rich places. This obvious fact applies even more to direct (i.e. income) tax than to other kinds of revenue. One would, therefore, expect a map of the yield

TABLE 2.2

Economic Planning Region	Income tax £ per cap. 1964–65
South East	64
West Midlands	55
United Kingdom	50
South West	42
Yorkshire and Humberside	40
North West	39
East Midlands	39
Scotland	39
East Anglia	38
Wales	33
Northern England	32
Northern Ireland	24

of income-tax *per capita* to portray approximately, the converse of a map of poverty. Available data will not allow this hypothesis to be tested. The closest approach that can usefully be made is to divide the tax-yield in 1964–5 for each economic planning region by the estimated total of the population in 1965. The results are ranked in table 2.2, but it should be remembered that one is dividing incomes according to place of work by population according to place of residence.

Natal environment is not open to choice by the child, but it greatly affects his subsequent scope for opportunity in many ways, not least in income and thus also in material welfare. The south-eastern child is likely to earn more and thus pay more in tax when he becomes adult than are children elsewhere.

[1] Chapter 11, p. 292

Conversely, more of the latter are likely to have poor parents and so to need free school meals. There is no other solution to this fundamental injustice arising from place of birth and upbringing than to develop effectively the resources, natural, man-made, and man himself, of those areas where it is presently disadvantageous to be born. The only environmental limitation of any real economic significance upon development within any region of the United Kingdom is that the resource structure of the locality should be sufficient to permit the attainment of adequate economies of scale. And within the resource structure the most important component is an adequate supply of labour.

If this component is not properly taken up or if it is locally too small for adequate economies of scale to be achieved, some of the population will move away in search of work or higher incomes. In so far as it is the young and abler people who move rather than the old and less enterprising, the area that they leave finds it increasingly hard, as time goes on, to restore its fortunes and even to maintain its economic vitality. So it is important that few young people should have to move far to find the opportunities they need. There is, therefore, a strong case, wherever local viability is in doubt on grounds of inadequate potential economies of scale, for the establishment of growth points at which improved opportunities are accessible to people in the surrounding area.

The supply of labour and the availability of good opportunities for employment are crucial economic and social issues. Thus in the next chapter we shall examine certain aspects of employment and the supply of labour during the post-war period in Britain. The findings presented about incomes – how they vary from place to place; how their spatial variations have changed since 1950, and how the structure of incomes so markedly favours the south-east – should be borne in mind throughout the next and succeeding chapters.

3
Employment: Total, Secondary and Tertiary

Personal incomes are one useful guide to the economic and social geography of Britain, employment is another; but it is far more complex, and cannot be measured by a single yardstick as can income. Data for employment are, however, more detailed and plentiful than those for income.

There are two major sources, namely, the industry tables of the censuses of population since 1921, and returns collected by the Department of Employment and Productivity and its predecessor, the Ministry of Labour. The latter are not published for areas smaller than the Economic Planning Regions and unpublished local returns are subject to certain disadvantages for geographical analysis, so census data only are used in this chapter.[1]

Fig. 3.1 portrays broad aspects of employment in absolutes by counties for 1961. The total employment (fig. 3.1a) corresponds closely, but not exactly, to the distribution of population for four reasons: first, the statistics refer to place of work rather than place of residence which is the normal basis for the mapping of population;[2] secondly, areas such as Wales and north-east England have relatively few women at work while Lancashire, for example, has considerably more than the national mean;[3] thirdly, officially recorded unemployment is far higher in Northern Ireland than elsewhere;[4] fourthly, there is a larger proportion of retired people in some counties, notably those along the south coast of England, than in others.

The main purpose of fig. 3.1a is not, however, to map employment for its own sake but to provide a comparative base for discussion of fig. 3.1b and c, for it is in these that the nub of regional variation is to be found. It is

---

[1] The industry tables of the 1966 (sample) census were not published when this chapter was in preparation. Findings from these data are used in the *Hunt Report*, 1969. The 1966 census is, however, unsatisfactory as a means of ascertaining either absolute numbers or change through time

[2] In Northern Ireland employment data are allocated in the census to place of residence

[3] This topic is discussed further in chapter 5, pp. 108–21

[4] The maps in this chapter do not include the numbers of those who are classed as unemployed

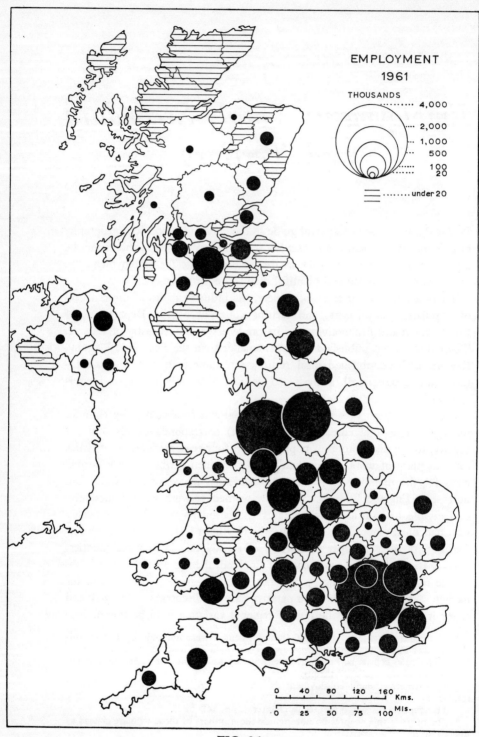

EMPLOYMENT
1961

THOUSANDS

········ 4,000

··· 2,000

··· 1,000

··· 500

··· 100
    20

········ under 20

0   40   80   120 160 Kms.

0   25   50   75   100 Mls.

FIG. 3.1a

essential to note that the maps of service employment[1] (fig. 3.1c) and manufacturing employment (fig. 3.1b) have the same scale for the proportional
symbols, but that this has been enlarged in relation to the scale used on
fig. 3.1a to facilitate visual, proportional comparisons. For instance, Warwickshire on fig. 3.1a and c has symbols equal in size for total employment and
for services respectively, and since Warwickshire has an unusually small
proportion of employment in services (fig. 3.1d) a visual exaggeration is
contrived that is helpful for analysis.

While it must be borne in mind that the county framework with its dis-
parate areal units is a rather unsatisfactory analytical device, the following
major features can be discerned on these maps.

Total Employment (fig. 3.1a)

The populous and highly urbanized region[2] of England that is said to stretch
from Kent, Sussex and Hampshire north-westwards to Lancashire and the
West Riding presents its largest symbols in the north-west and towards the
south-east. The latter has London as a compact core, while the former is more
diffuse, more a coalescence of cities and towns, a multiplicity of central places
without a multi-functional and all-powerful metropolis to give it functionally
dynamic cohesion. It is a diffuse amalgam of conurbations linked more by
ribbons of settlement than by centralized flows of people, goods and services.
In contrast, London is without doubt a multi-functional, cohesive and
centralized metropolis with minor appendages and outliers. It is in effect an
enormous unitary city rather than a conurbation.

There were, so the late C. B. Fawcett[3] used to assert in his lectures, more
people living within thirty-five miles of Manchester town hall in 1891 than
within the same distance from Charing Cross, a fact never before and never
since recorded in any census of population. Even today, however, there is
less difference in employment between Lancashire and the West Riding,
together comprising 4,220,000 on the one hand, and London, Middlesex
and the contiguous counties of Kent, Surrey, Bucks., Herts. and Essex
together comprising 6,120,000 on the other, than is commonly appreciated.

---

[1] Service employment is taken here to comprise Main Orders XVII to XXIV in the
Standard Industrial Classification. Manufacturing comprises Main Orders III to
XVI. See chapter 4, pp. 77–8, for full list of Main Orders

[2] (i) Taylor, E. G. R. (and others), 'Discussion on the geographical distribution
of industry', *Geogr. J.*, **92**, 1938, 22–29

(ii) Smailes, A. E., 'The urban mesh of England and Wales', *Trans. Inst. Brit.
Geog.*, **11**, 1946, 85–101

(iii) Baker, J. N. L., and Gilbert, E. W., 'The doctrine of an axial belt of industry
in England', *Geogr. J.*, **103–4**, 1944, 49–73

[3] Professor of Geography, University College, London, 1928–49

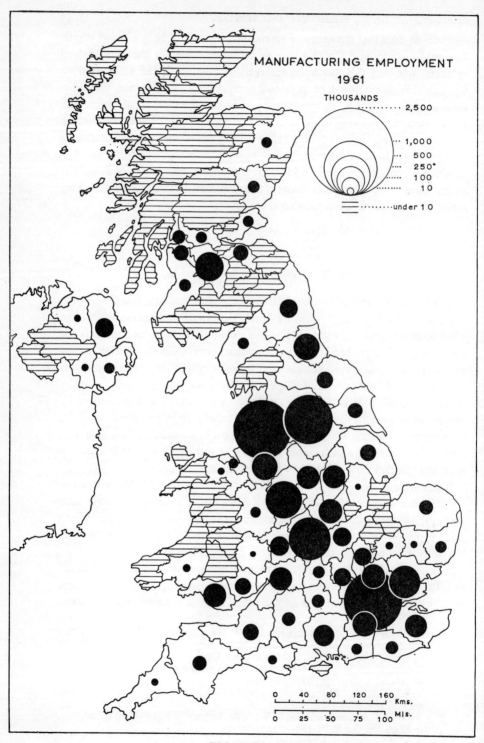

MANUFACTURING EMPLOYMENT
1961

THOUSANDS
2,500
1,000
500
250
100
10
under 10

0   40   80   120   160
Kms.

0   25   50   75   100
Mls.

FIG. 3.1b

Moreover, the northern counties have the twofold handicap of a smaller area and a larger proportion of virtually uninhabitable upland.

This comparison serves to correct impressions gained about the dominance in population and employment of the south-east that result from the use of statistics for Economic Planning Regions within the framework of which the South East Region is very large while the West Riding and Lancashire are separated as parts of two much smaller regions for statistical purposes.[1] But if the statistical distortions inherent in the use of a county framework were removed and if a systematic medium-scale framework were applied instead,[2] then the emphasis that has been placed on the two great concentrations of employment in the 'Axial Belt' would be seen to be justified. Together they contain almost half the employed population of England and Wales and about 43 per cent of that of the United Kingdom as a whole.

Manufacturing Employment (fig. 3.1b)

The pattern of manufacturing employment diverges from that of employment as a whole. In general outline it is clearly more concentrated upon the London–Manchester axis, away from which most counties make a comparatively poor showing. Moreover, the emphasis shifts within the so-called 'axial belt'. London and Middlesex are slightly less important than Lancashire, whilst the central south-eastern counties[3] have only slightly more employment in manufacturing (2,022,000) than Lancashire and the West Riding combined (1,868,000) to which, on the basis of continuity of built-up area, the population of parts of Cheshire should be added. The midland counties, especially Stafford and Warwick gain greatly in importance when compared with their showing on fig. 3.1a. There is thus a far stronger case to justify an 'axial belt' of manufacturing as a significant descriptive generalization than there is for employment as a whole, and the conventionally accepted dominance of the south-east, already in doubt on fig. 3.1a, is even less apparent on fig. 3.1b.

[1] There is no doubt, however, of the dominance of London and the south-east in income. In 1965–6, there were 7·4 million tax cases with incomes over £275 in the South East compared with 4·4 million in the North West and Yorkshire–Humberside Economic Planning Regions combined. The disparity in tax yield was strikingly greater:

South East Region   £1,436 million
North West and Yorkshire–Humberside Regions combined   £570 million

[2] See (i) Forbes, Jean and Robertson, Isobel M. L., 'Population enumeration on a grid square basis', *Cart. J.*, 4, *1*, 1967, 29–37
   (ii) Lloyd, P. E. and Dicken, P., 'The data bank in regional studies of industry', *T. Pl. Rev.*, 38, *4*, 1968, 304–316
The meaning and relevance of 'systematic, medium-scale framework' are indicated in chapter 11
[3] London, Middlesex, Kent, Surrey, Buckinghamshire, Hertfordshire and Essex

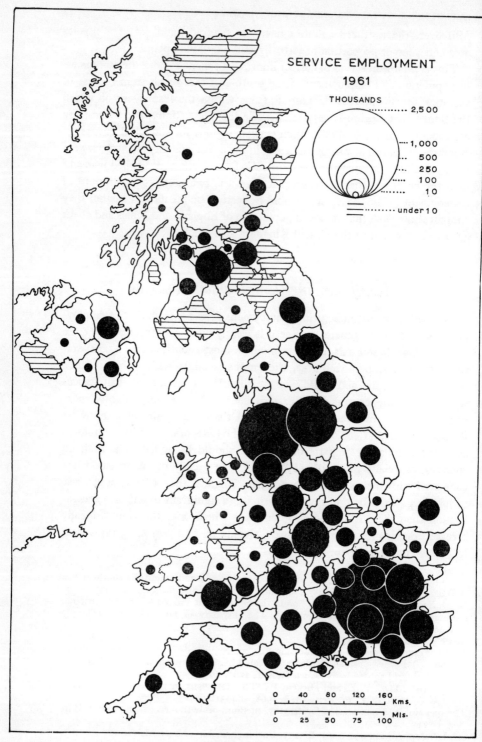

SERVICE EMPLOYMENT
1961

THOUSANDS

·········· 2,500

·····— 1,000

·· 500

····· 250

····· 100

········ 10

········· under 10

0   40   80   120   160
Kms.

0   25   50   75   100
Mls.

FIG. 3.1c

Service Employment (fig. 3.1c)

Here the 'axial belt' as a regional generalization breaks down completely. There are still two major concentrations of employment, Lancashire and the West Riding on the one hand and south-east England on the other. But there is no doubt whatsoever which is dominant,[1] or that many counties outside the 'axial belt' are quite well endowed with employment in services.

Manufacturing versus Service Employment (fig. 3.1d)

The grades of shading used on fig. 3.1d summarize the spatial variation and regional imbalance of the two major sectors of the national employment structure. Counties where manufacturing employment exceeds that in services are clearly well out of balance, though less significance should be attached to the figures for Bedford, Renfrew and Clackmannan than to those for the midland counties of Stafford, Warwick, Northampton and Leicester, which as a group are far more self-contained so far as employment is concerned since commuting to major centres of service employment outside the group-area is not feasible for their inhabitants.

Areas with employment in services more than 3.2 times that in manufacturing are well out of balance in the opposite direction. Most of these are rural counties with a high proportion of employment in agriculture which is not represented on fig. 3.1d, and they contain many communities that are isolated in the sense that daily journeys to alternative employment elsewhere are out of the question. To seek alternatives means migration in most instances. Between these extremes of great dependence respectively on manufacturing or on services is to be found the greater part of the United Kingdom. But the range from 1.0 to 3.1 in the ratio of the two major sectors of employment is wide when compared with a national ratio of 1.6. Not only are there sizeable inter-county differences as between West Sussex 2.9, Surrey 2.2, Cumberland 1.9 and the West Riding 1.1, but there are internal variations within individual counties which are especially important where daily commuting to correct imbalance is impossible.[2]

Absolute Changes in the Decade 1951-61

The three aspects of employment – total, manufacturing, services – did not remain static between 1951 and 1961.[3] The absolute quantitative changes

[1] Lancashire and the West Riding has only 2,120,000 employed in services compared with 3,970,000 for the London, Middlesex and adjacent counties group

[2] Lawton, R., 'The journey to work in Britain: some trends and problems', *Regional Studies*, **2**, *1*, 1968, 27–40

[3] Smith, D. M. 'Recent changes in the regional pattern of British industry', *Tijdschrift voor Economische en Sociale Geografie*, **56**, 1965, 133–144

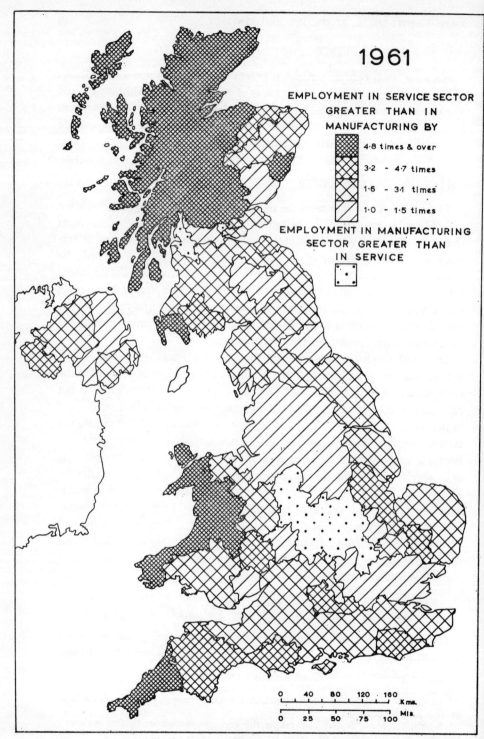

1961

EMPLOYMENT IN SERVICE SECTOR GREATER THAN IN MANUFACTURING BY

4·8 times & over

3·2 - 4·7 times

1·6 - 3·1 times

1·0 - 1·5 times

EMPLOYMENT IN MANUFACTURING SECTOR GREATER THAN IN SERVICE

0   40   80   120   160   .Kms.

0   25   50   .75   100   Mls.

FIG. 3.1d

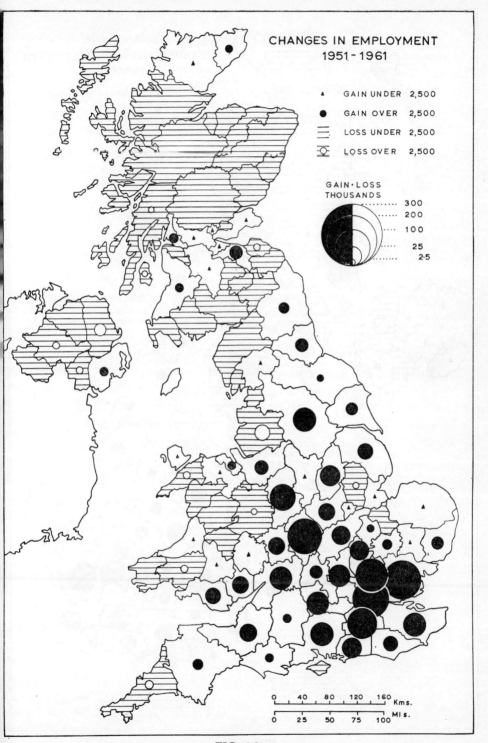

CHANGES IN EMPLOYMENT
1951 - 1961

▲ GAIN UNDER 2,500

● GAIN OVER 2,500

≡ LOSS UNDER 2,500

⊖ LOSS OVER 2,500

GAIN · LOSS
THOUSANDS
·········· 300
······ 200
······ 100
····· 25
····· 2·5

0   40   80   120 160 Kms.

0   25   50   75   100 Mls.

FIG. 3.2a   E

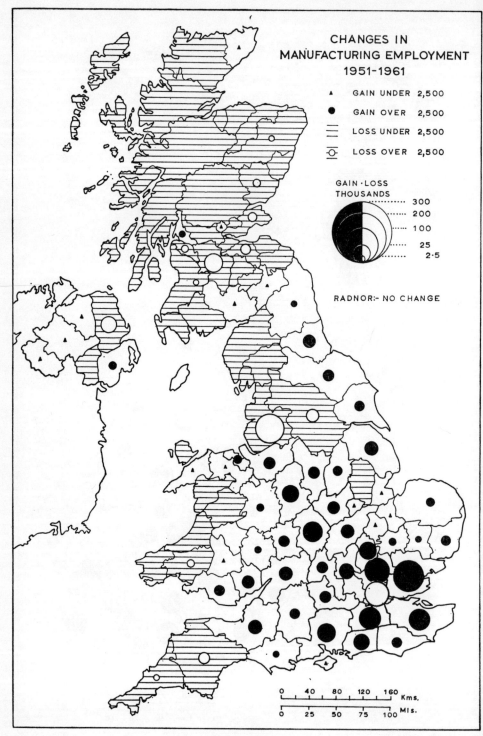

CHANGES IN
MANUFACTURING EMPLOYMENT
1951-1961

▲ GAIN UNDER 2,500
● GAIN OVER 2,500
≡ LOSS UNDER 2,500
⊖ LOSS OVER 2,500

GAIN · LOSS
THOUSANDS
········ 300
········ 200
········ 100
········ 25
········ 2·5

RADNOR:- NO CHANGE

0   40   80   120   160 Kms.
0   25   50   75   100 Mls.

FIG. 3.2b

in each aspect are shown on fig. 3.2. A glance back to fig. 3.1a and its comparison with fig. 3.2a gives immediate and irrefutable proof of a major trend in action. Employment in the United Kingdom increased by nearly 1·2 million of which most was in the south-east and parts of the Midlands. Essex, Hertfordshire, London and Middlesex, Surrey and Warwickshire together expanded by 490,000, over 40 per cent of the net national increase. If the counties contiguous with the six named above are added to them, the 490,000 is increased to about 925,000, leaving only about 260,000 extra jobs for the rest of the United Kingdom. It should be noted that the largest increase in any one county was 121,000 in Essex; that the increase was greater around London (including Middlesex) than within it; that Monmouth and Glamorgan together gained more than Northumberland, Durham and the North Riding, and that Lancashire lost 20,000, a larger absolute decrease than in any other county. Above all else, a shift in the emphasis of employment towards the south-east concentration and away from its rival (noted on fig. 3.1a) in Lancashire and the West Riding occurred during the decade.

Employment in primary production (agriculture etc., fishing, mining and quarrying) declined by 420,000 in the United Kingdom between 1951 and 1961. Thus manufacturing and services must have been jointly responsible for the net increase shown on fig. 3.2a. Manufacturing (fig. 3.2b) was by far the smaller contributor of the two. It provided a net increase for the United Kingdom of only 354,000. Scotland ($-56,000$), Northern Ireland ($-15,000$), Lancashire ($-64,000$), the West Riding ($-13,000$), Devon ($-9,000$), Glamorgan ($-8,000$), and London with Middlesex ($-49,000$), were among the areas that suffered a decrease in manufacturing employment. Of the net increase (354,000), 206,000 was in Essex, Hertfordshire, Kent and Surrey, to which might be added a further 93,000 increase in Bedfordshire, Berkshire, Buckinghamshire, Hampshire and West Sussex, the total being more than enough to offset the decrease in the inner metropolitan area of London and Middlesex. Clearly growth was broadly peripheral to London. It is noteworthy too that north-eastern England (including the North Riding) did rather better than South Wales in manufacturing, thus reversing the relationship apparent for employment as a whole.

The growth in services (fig. 3.2c) during the decade shows a closer approximation than manufacturing to both employment as a whole in 1961 (fig. 3.1a), and employment in services 1961 (fig. 3.1c). The increase amounted to 1,560,000 in the United Kingdom as a whole. Few areas actually declined, and the one sizeable decrease, in Shropshire, resulted largely from the closure of a defence establishment. But although all major populous areas gained substantially in service employment, fig. 3.2c is by no means a mirror image of fig. 3.1c. On a wider regional scale the south-east is clearly a major recipient with 290,000 in London and Middlesex, Essex, Surrey, Hertfordshire and Berkshire. London and Middlesex alone received 140,000, so the increase in

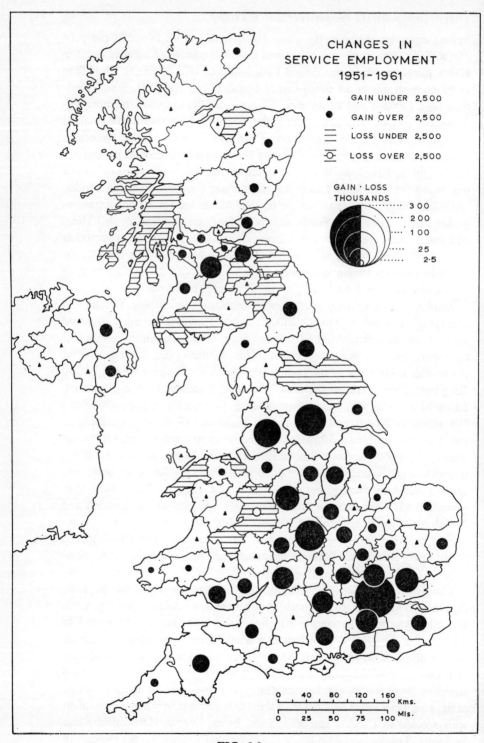

CHANGES IN
SERVICE EMPLOYMENT
1951-1961

▲   GAIN UNDER 2,500

●   GAIN OVER   2,500

≡   LOSS UNDER 2,500

⊖   LOSS OVER   2,500

GAIN · LOSS
THOUSANDS
300
200
100
25
2·5

0   40   80   120   160
Kms.

0   25   50   75   100
Mls.

FIG. 3.2c

this instance was clearly central and not peripheral to London. Among other populous counties Stafford and Warwick had substantial increases. But although the West Riding did better than Lancashire, this northern pair fared much less well than the Midlands and the south-east. In effect, however, a major national trend is less well-marked for services than for either total employment or manufacturing when mapped in absolutes as in this section. Further trends are discerned in the next section of this chapter when proportional mapping is used.

Density and Proportional Change in Total Employment

By 1961 there was a mean density of employment per square mile of 257 in the United Kingdom, as compared with 244 in 1951. All counties cross-shaded in fig. 3.3a had densities above the national mean. The largest area of cross-shading stretched in a great, widening crescent from Glamorgan to Lancashire and the West Riding, and with 9,154,000 people in employment had an overall density of 662 per square mile. Separated from this huge populous area by Wiltshire, Oxfordshire and Northamptonshire was the next largest group centring on London. This south-eastern employment region had 7,324,000 and a density of 787 per square mile.[1]

Since about half this number worked in the counties of London and Middlesex, over 4,000,000 must have worked in Greater London as defined and restricted by the green belt. Seen in this fashion, undesirably imprecise as it has to be with the serious shortcomings of the county-based measuring system, the south-east appears, once more, less dominant than current, so-called regional thinking would have us believe. London is easily the foremost compact concentration of employment in Britain, but the south-east is not the paramount 'regional' concentration even when assessed on the restrictive basis of aggregating the contiguous counties with densities above the national mean.[2]

It is, of course, impossible to discern truly measured regions of any sort at all clearly on a county, or on any other, basis currently available to us, as the remaining areas with more than average density of employment show. Central Scotland contains the third group of above average counties and County Durham stands out alone as the fourth and least extensive in the class. Their appearance on the map tells us little of interest except that

---

[1] Ratio $\frac{\text{south-east}}{\text{crescent}}$ = 1·19, i.e. density of total employment in the south-east (the sum of the south-easterly counties cross-shaded on fig. 3.3a) was only 19 per cent greater than the density in the crescent

[2] Density in the south-east, excluding London and Middlesex, reached only 424 per square mile

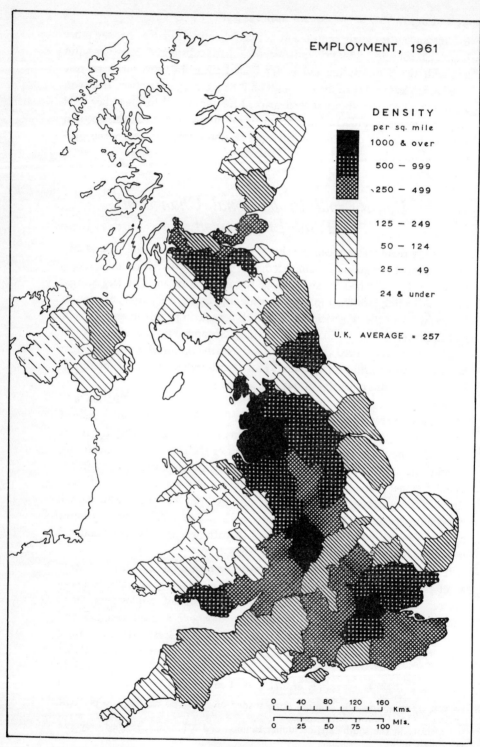

FIG. 3.3a

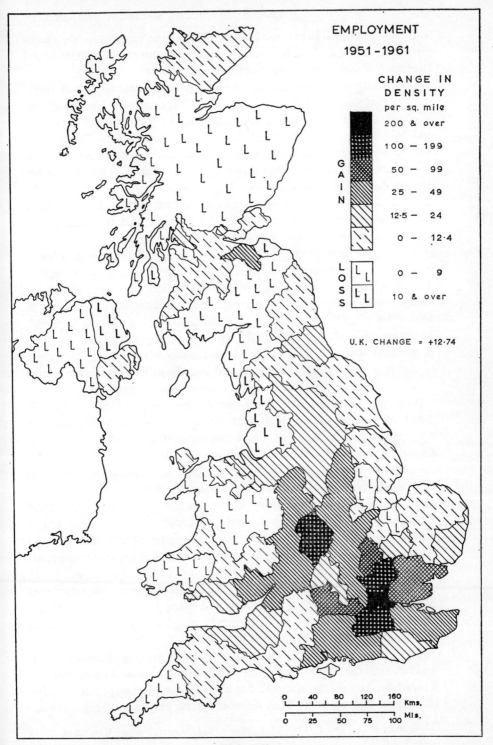

EMPLOYMENT
1951–1961

CHANGE IN
DENSITY
per sq. mile
200 & over
100 — 199
50 — 99
25 — 49
12·5 — 24
0 — 12·4

GAIN

LOSS   0 — 9
        10 & over

U.K. CHANGE = +12·74

0   40   80   120   160 Kms.
0   25   50   75   100 Mls.

FIG. 3.3b

neither of them is large in comparison with either the 'crescent' or the south-east. Scotland as a whole had fewer people employed than Lancashire, and Durham had fewer than either Surrey or Staffordshire.

The density of employment increased between 1951 and 1961 in all counties that had more than average density in 1961, except for Lancashire and Renfrew. But the outstanding growth shown on fig. 3.3b occurred in London and Middlesex, Essex, Hertfordshire, Surrey, Warwickshire, Bedfordshire and Berkshire. In all these the density of employment rose by more than 50 per square mile. This is a large increase, not significantly different from the average density of population over the land surface of the world as a whole. The increase of over 200 per square mile in London and Middlesex (actually 308 per square mile) is one reason for the allegation that the south-east is a congested region. It is not, but London assuredly is.

What fig. 3.3b achieves otherwise is to provide confirmation of a 'drift' into south-eastern and midland England; to indicate the depletion of employment in certain rural counties, the reduction of congestion of employment in Lancashire by nearly 11 per square mile, and a notably different increase in Midlothian of 42 per square mile when compared with the rest of Scotland. It also reveals such curiosities as the effect on employment of ventures such as that at Dounreay in the sparsely peopled county of Caithness. The pattern of change in density should be compared with the pattern of absolute change shown on fig. 3.2a from which it differs in emphasis in certain respects.

Percentage changes reveal yet another different pattern (figs. 3.4a and b). Total employment rose by 5·2 per cent between 1951 and 1961. The counties with percentages around and above that amount are shaded in fig. 3.4a. Caithness, with over 36 per cent, stands out alone in the far north. Otherwise the major percentage growth occurred in a band of counties from Hertfordshire to Berkshire. West Sussex also stands out, largely one assumes as a result of the new town at Crawley. There was also appreciable growth from Kent through Surrey to Hampshire and from Cambridge through Northamptonshire and the South Midlands into Gloucestershire, Monmouth and Somerset. Lindsey, Nottinghamshire and East Suffolk also seem to have made considerable proportional headway.

The horizontally shaded areas on fig. 3.4b suffered proportional decreases in employment. Most of them are rural and sparsely peopled, with densities (fig. 3.3a) of less than 124 per square mile except for Antrim. The greatest county decrease was 34 per cent in Bute.[1]

The stippled areas on fig. 3.4b and the lowest percentage category on fig. 3.4a represent the fairly stagnant and slightly declining areas for employment. Lancashire, Lanark, the North Riding and Durham are grouped in the same class (stippled on fig. 3.4b). They recorded a worse percentage change between

[1] Storrie, M. C., and Jackson, C. I., *Arran 1981; 2,021?*, Scottish Council of Social Service, 1967

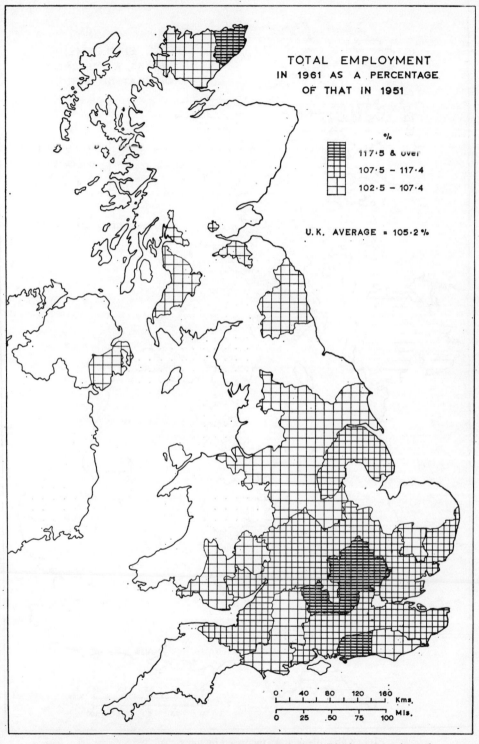

TOTAL EMPLOYMENT
IN 1961 AS A PERCENTAGE
OF THAT IN 1951

%
117·5 & over
107·5 – 117·4
102·5 – 107·4

U.K. AVERAGE = 105·2 %

FIG. 3.4a Increase around and above the national mean. Blank areas registered either an increase of less than 2·5 per cent or a decrease

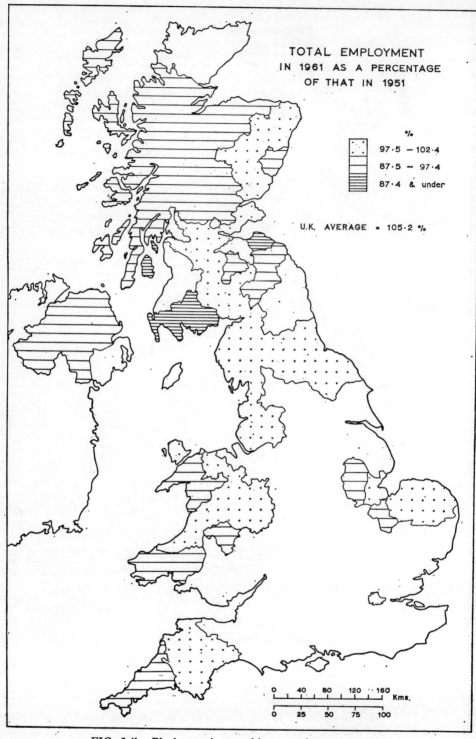

FIG. 3.4b Blank areas increased by more than 2·5 per cent

TOTAL EMPLOYMENT
IN 1961 AS A PERCENTAGE
OF THAT IN 1951

%
97·5 — 102·4
87·5 — 97·4
87·4 & under

U.K. AVERAGE = 105·2 %

0   40   80   120   160
                        Kms.
0   25   50   75   100

1951 and 1961 than did Glamorgan, Staffordshire, Derbyshire, the West Riding, Northumberland and Ayrshire, for example. Yet in 1961, and when the data upon which these maps were based saw the light of day in 1966, these nine counties were by no means receiving similar benefits under the distribution of industry policy of the Board of Trade, a policy based more on unemployment data of dubious value than on trends in employment.

Density and Proportional Change in Manufacturing Employment

The mean density of employment in manufacturing in 1961 was 92 per square mile, a much lower figure than that for employment as a whole. The pattern of areas above the mean (fig. 3.5a) clearly differs from that for total employment shown on fig. 3.3a. The major differences are: (a) the linking together above the mean of the 'crescent'[1] and the metropolitan high density area to make a continuous band of counties with a higher than average density extending from Kent to Lancashire and from the West Riding to Glamorgan;[2] (b) East Sussex, Hampshire and Berkshire do not attain the mean density on fig. 3.5a whereas Northamptonshire does; (c) since Fife and West Lothian fail to reach the average, the manufacturing area of central Scotland is smaller than that for employment as a whole. Another noteworthy difference is the very poor showing of south-west England in manufacturing.

Changes in the density of manufacturing employment between 1951 and 1961 are shown in fig. 3.5b. Predominantly vertical shading indicates a gain, horizontal shading a loss. Areas suffering great losses were London, Lancashire and Lanarkshire. The major growth area surrounded London and extended from Kent to Severnside and from Hampshire to Staffordshire. County Durham, Flintshire and Dunbartonshire also achieved appreciable growth in manufacturing.

Fig. 3.6a shows where the proportional change in manufacturing employment was positive but greater than 2·5 per cent. Counties that recorded a positive change less than 2·5 per cent or suffered a decrease are left blank. Small absolute increases register strongly on fig. 3.6a, as in Caithness, Breconshire and Fermanagh, but when augmented by comparison with either the absolute or the density maps (figs. 3.2b and 3.5b respectively) there can be little doubt where proportional increase was most strongly felt. The largest area with an increase greater than 17·5 per cent conforms quite closely to the South East Economic Planning Region.

[1] See chapter 3, p. 55
[2] Rawstron, E. M., 'Industry', chapter 16 in Watson J. W., and Sissons, J. B., *The British Isles*, 297–317, 1964. *N.B.* The densities shown in the figures in chapter 16 take the whole of Ireland into account. They are not, therefore, exactly comparable with the densities mapped in the present chapter

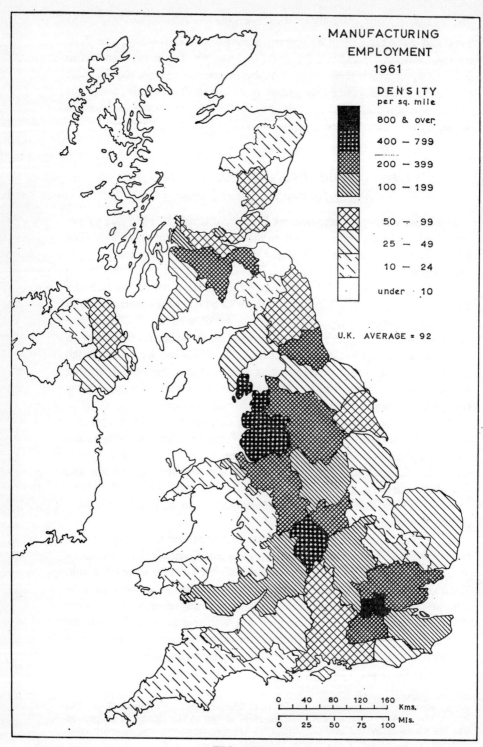

MANUFACTURING
EMPLOYMENT
1961

DENSITY
per sq. mile

800 & over
400 — 799
200 — 399
100 — 199

50 — 99
25 — 49
10 — 24
under 10

U.K. AVERAGE = 92

0 40 80 120 160 Kms.
0   25   50   75 100 Mls.

FIG. 3.5a

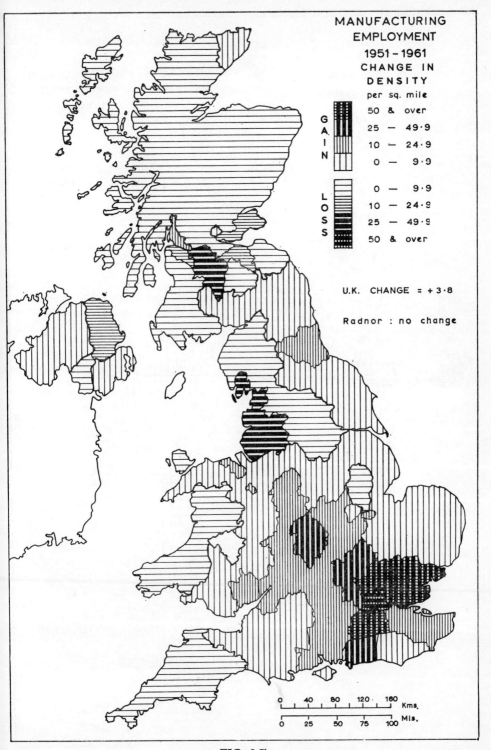

MANUFACTURING
EMPLOYMENT
1951 - 1961
CHANGE IN
DENSITY
per sq. mile
50 & over
25 — 49·9
10 — 24·9
0 — 9·9

0 — 9·9
10 — 24·9
25 — 49·9
50 & over

GAIN

LOSS

U.K. CHANGE = + 3·8

Radnor : no change

0   40   80   120   160
                          Kms.
0   25   50   75   100
                          Mls.

FIG. 3.5b

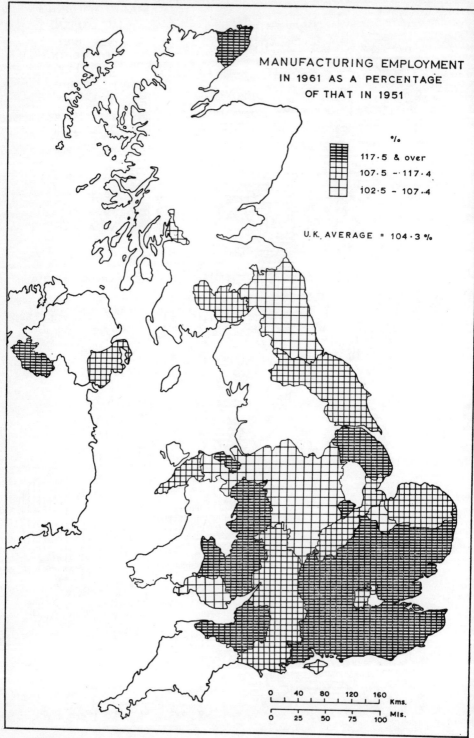

MANUFACTURING EMPLOYMENT
IN 1961 AS A PERCENTAGE
OF THAT IN 1951

%
117·5 & over
107·5 - 117·4
102·5 - 107·4

U.K. AVERAGE = 104·3 %

0   40   80   120   160
Kms.
0   25   50   75   100
Mls.

FIG. 3.6a   Increase around and above national mean. Blank areas registered either
an increase of less than 2·5 per cent or a decrease

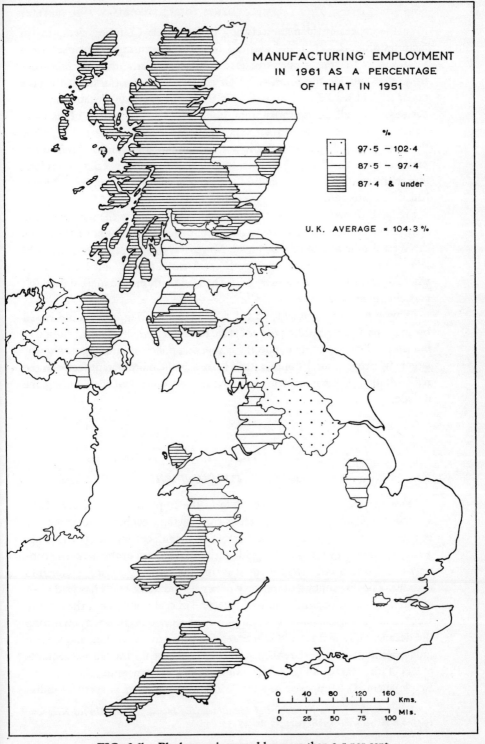

MANUFACTURING EMPLOYMENT
IN 1961 AS A PERCENTAGE
OF THAT IN 1951

%
97·5 — 102·4
87·5 — 97·4
87·4 & under

U.K. AVERAGE = 104·3 %

0 40 80 120 160 Kms.
0 25 50 75 100 Mls.

FIG. 3.6b   Blank areas increased by more than 2·5 per cent

In the expansion of manufacturing in the Home Counties, decanting of factories from London and starting new manufacturing enterprises from scratch were the major operative forces rather than any drift of enterprises from areas outside the south-east.[1] Of course, there must also have been a major drift of workers south-eastwards from other parts of Britain and from overseas[2] as well as outwards from London. The distribution of industry policy since the war has been attempting to reduce inter-regional drift, while the aim of the policy of creating new towns around London has been to improve conditions within the south-east. The two policies came, therefore, into conflict with each other, and fig. 3.6a shows which of them, by and large, had won up to 1961.

Fig. 3.6b shows the degree to which areas clearly below the national mean were deficient. Mostly these are sparsely populated areas, but not Lancashire, the West Riding and central Scotland. Moreover, these three areas performed less well during the decade than both north-east England and South Wales where the distribution of industry policy had evidently proved more successful, particularly in South Wales.

As with total employment, so too with manufacturing, doubts are raised by figs. 3.6a and b regarding the scientific basis upon which the distribution of industry policy was applied, and the competing policy of building new towns largely in a ring around London itself is seen as the more potent factor in the redistribution of manufacturing employment on a national scale during the decade.

Density and Proportional Change in Service Employment

Manufacturing is not the major item in the employment structure of the United Kingdom. Services, including construction, comprised over 55 per cent of the total or 1·6 times the number in manufacturing in 1961 (see fig. 3.1d), and no policy intended to guide the spatial pattern of the national economy can function effectively without taking the tertiary (service) sector into account. The distribution of industry policy has not done so. It has paid close attention to manufacturing and to the decline in coal-mining, but the tertiary sector and the expansion of office employment received little attention during the decade. Only in 1965 did offices receive legislative attention, and service industries in general have remained unrestricted save for the normal requirements of physical planning and the influence of a fiscal measure, the Selective Employment Tax, imposed in 1966. Moreover, the latter is spatially indis-

[1] Howard, R. S., *The Movement of Manufacturing Industry in the United Kingdom 1945–65*. H.M.S.O., 1968, paragraphs 45–53
[2] See chapter 6

criminate in the service sector except for rural hotels in Development Areas. So it is desirable now to examine patterns of service employment which, as they developed spatially during the decade, very largely obeyed principles of *laissez-faire*.

Except for West Sussex and differences in central Scotland, fig. 3.7a shows a similar pattern of above average density of employment in services in 1961 to that for employment as a whole (fig. 3.3a). The crescent from Glamorgan to Lancashire had a density overall of 323 per square mile in service industries while the above-average group of counties centring on London[1] reached 524 per square mile. The density ratio of the south-east in relation to the crescent was 1·62. Expressed otherwise, this means that the south-east had a density of service employment 62 per cent greater than that of the crescent, whereas for total employment the south-east was only 19 per cent higher. But if London and Middlesex are excluded from the calculations, the density in the rest of the south-east registers only 272 per square mile, which is less than that in the crescent. The emphasis in the south-east as a whole, therefore, is clearly upon services rather than manufacturing, and so far as density is concerned, upon Greater London rather than the south-east as a whole. If these findings are accepted as even broadly correct, it would seem a more apt planning policy to attempt to redistribute and disperse services from the metropolis than (*a*) to restrict the growth of manufacturing there and (*b*) to disperse what is proportionately a scarce component in the economy of London, notwithstanding that in absolute terms manufacturing there is very important indeed.[2]

Whereas the density of manufacturing employment increased by only 3·8 per square mile in the United Kingdom from 1951 to 1961, employment in services rose by over 12 per square mile. Similar trends in favour of services are apparent in most advanced countries. Thus few areas in Britain registered a decrease (fig. 3.7b). Increases occurred in all major populous areas but, apart from Midlothian and Warwickshire, the highest gains were in the south-eastern counties of London and Middlesex, Surrey and Berkshire.

Fig. 3.8 presents the same data on a proportional basis in relation to a national growth of 9·3 per cent. Here it was the turn of the Home Counties north of London and those in the southern part of the West and East Midlands to record the greatest increase. The exclusion of Glamorgan, Lancashire,

---

[1] Chapter 3, p. 55, footnote 1

[2] (*i*) Martin, J. E., *Greater London, an Industrial Geography*. 1966. Contrast our opinion with Martin's that (p. 60) 'Greater London is the first manufacturing region of the nation by any yardstick'. Moreover, employment in manufacturing has continued its decline absolutely and proportionately to that in services during the 1960s in Greater London

(*ii*) Fullerton, B., 'The localization of service industries in England and Wales', *Tijdschrift voor Economische en Sociale Geografie*, 1963, 126–135

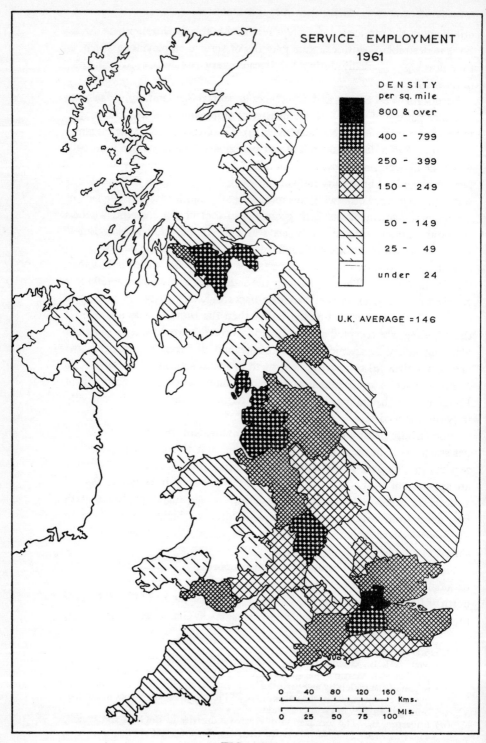

SERVICE EMPLOYMENT
1961

DENSITY
per sq. mile

800 & over

400 - 799

250 - 399

150 - 249

50 - 149

25 - 49

under 24

U.K. AVERAGE = 146

0   40   80   120 160
Kms.
0   25   50   75   100
Mls.

FIG. 3.7a

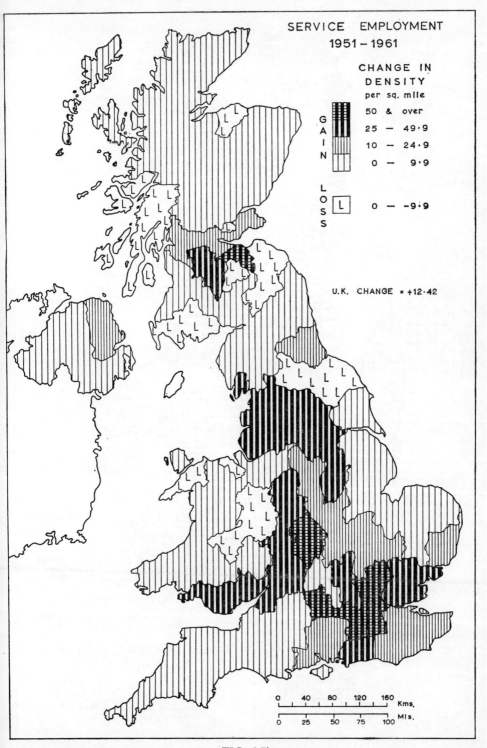

SERVICE EMPLOYMENT
1951 – 1961

CHANGE IN
DENSITY
per sq. mile

GAIN
50 & over
25 — 49·9
10 — 24·9
0 — 9·9

LOSS
L   0 — −9·9

U.K. CHANGE = +12·42

0   40   80   120   160   Kms.

0   25   50   75   100   Mls.

FIG. 3.7b

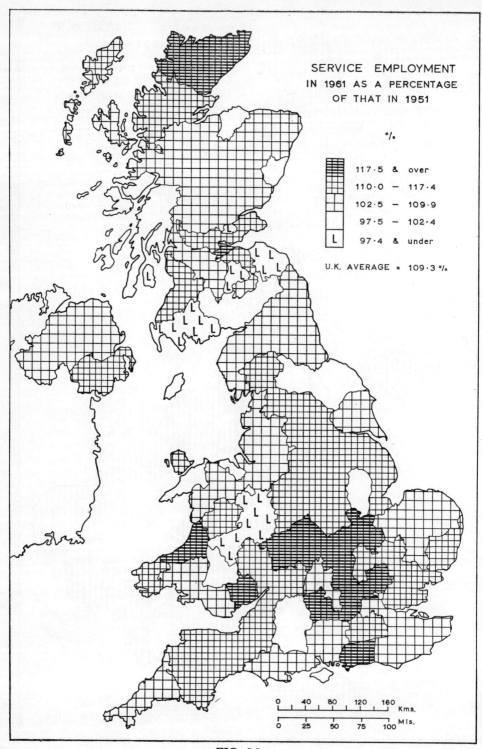

SERVICE EMPLOYMENT
IN 1961 AS A PERCENTAGE
OF THAT IN 1951

%

117·5 & over
110·0 — 117·4
102·5 — 109·9
97·5 — 102·4
L   97·4 & under

U.K. AVERAGE = 109·3 %

0   40   80   120   160   Kms.
0   25   50   75   100   Mls.

FIG. 3.8

Northumberland, Durham and the North Riding from the area where the proportional change exceeded the national rate is significant particularly when compared with the changes indicated on figs. 3.4a (total employment) and 3.6a (manufacturing employment). Glamorgan and Northumberland registered similar growth on all three maps; Durham increased in manufacturing and services but not in total, largely on account of the decline in coalmining; the North Riding grew appreciably in manufacturing but insignificantly otherwise; but Lancashire had to make do with a mediocre growth in services alone. One can readily infer from these three maps that a balancing regional planning policy was not being effectively followed during the decade. No doubt this inference is correct, but these maps can do no more scientifically than give a strong but imprecise indication of the complexity of regional change and demonstrate the urgent need for proper spatial measurement as a foundation for informed regional planning decisions. This contention is discussed further in chapter 11.

4

Employment: the Diversity of Change

Examination of the major sectors of the employment structure provides generalizations which fail to reveal a multitude of changes among individual industries. Some of these are declining; some are stagnating; and some show the desirable quality, growth.[1] It is upon the last-named category that increasing national prosperity depends, provided always that management of the national economy, especially with reference to the balance of payments and the achievement of a competitive edge in overseas markets, is geared to encourage economic growth. Choice of location can assist or hamper growth. The protagonists of *laissez-faire* would say that entrepreneurs know best where to locate their enterprises for the greatest profit on their own and the nation's account. Social planners, however, would argue that areas with a preponderance of declining industries need to develop and acquire growth industries not only for humanitarian reasons, but also to make effective use of labour (including brain-power) and of the existing man-made fabric of local environments, and thereby to enhance national prosperity. A telling additional argument is that many entrepreneurs do not find location a critical factor for profitability in a country as small as the United Kingdom.

Neither profitability of the firm nor social profitability can yet be measured spatially. Thus no decisive case in pounds, shillings and pence can be made for either school of thought. It is on the one hand quite without any justification in the supposedly hard facts of accountancy for non-planners to plead that national prosperity is best served either by entrepreneurs having a completely free choice of location or by 'giving South-East England its head' and allowing unfettered development there. On the other hand it is equally unjustifiable in terms of hard cash for social planners to plead the contrary. The only reasonably acceptable evidence is to be found in existing patterns of employment and recent spatial changes therein for individual industries.[2]

[1]   (i) Humphrys, G., 'Growth industries and the regional economies of Britain', *District Bank Review*, *144*, 1962, 35–36
　　(ii) Smith, David M., 'Growth industries in Britain', *Geography*, *49*, 1965, 288–293
[2]   An industry may be largely concentrated in a particular region, perhaps south-east England or the west Midlands, yet the existence and evident profitability of plants located elsewhere, but in the same industry, is a denial of the economic need to locate in a particular region. Nor is the existence of a regional concentration proof that the optimum has been found

It is unfortunate that for regional economic management reliance has to be placed upon measurement of the input of a single factor of production, labour, rather than upon spatial measurements made in monetary terms of supply, demand, costs, prices and profits. Satisfactory statistics even of physical output are lacking. So to glimpse the spatial diversity of economic change one must have recourse to analytical case-studies of employment in selected industries.[1]

Two Growth Industries

1 ELECTRICAL ENGINEERING AND ELECTRICAL GOODS

Electrical engineering and electrical goods (Minimum List Headings 361 to 369 in the Standard Industrial Classification) comprise one group of industries that showed considerable growth (36 per cent, i.e. at least eight times the rate for manufacturing as a whole) between 1951 and 1961. Employment in this group is certainly unevenly distributed spatially (fig. 4.1a) in comparison with manufacturing as a whole (fig. 3.1b). The outstanding feature shown on fig. 4.1a is the emphasis upon London, Middlesex and adjacent counties. This area had 280,000 workers in the group or 37 per cent of the total for the United Kingdom in 1961, which proportion compares very favourably with its share of only 24 per cent in the whole manufacturing sector. The second largest concentration of electrical industries is in Lancashire, and like the south-east, it has a favourable ratio of 16 per cent in electricals to 13 per cent in all manufacturing. The West Riding especially is poorly represented but the West Midlands, north-east England, South Wales, some Scottish counties and many other localities are quite well represented on fig. 4.1a.

A distribution balanced in relation to detailed patterns of population or employment is neither to be expected nor to be desired, for economies of scale demand a measure of concentration and tend thereby to create sizeable local pockets of specialized employment. The major implication of fig. 4.1a is simply that the electrical industries are not obliged to concentrate in and around London. They are successful in Lancashire and can in all probability make very adequate and growing profits wherever a sufficient number of suitably qualified or trainable workers can be assembled for at least one plant to achieve tolerable economies of scale. If Plymouth, Londonderry, Inverness, Barnsley or Millom, for example, are found to satisfy these not so stringent requirements, then there is little to impede the early success of an electrical goods factory set up in the near future in these towns.

Fig. 4.1b shows where the increase in employment (36 per cent or 203,000

[1] Chisholm, M., 'Must we all live in South-East England?', *Geography*, 49, 1964,

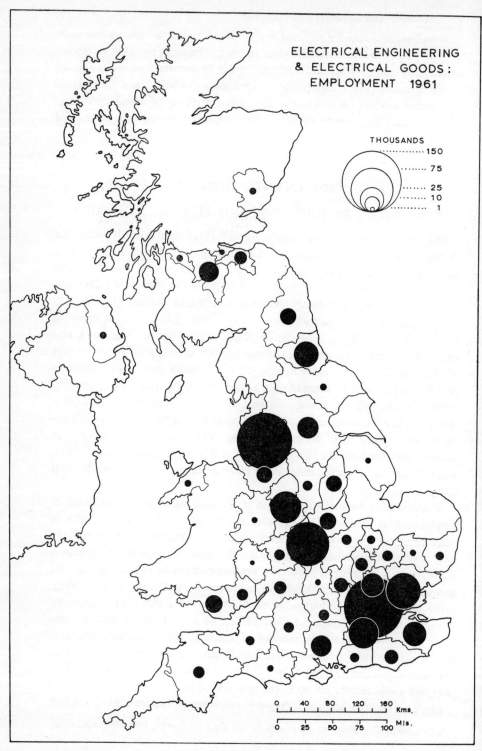

ELECTRICAL ENGINEERING
& ELECTRICAL GOODS:
EMPLOYMENT 1961

THOUSANDS
150
75
25
10
1

0   40   80   120   160   Kms.

0   25   50   75   100   Mls.

FIG. 4.1a

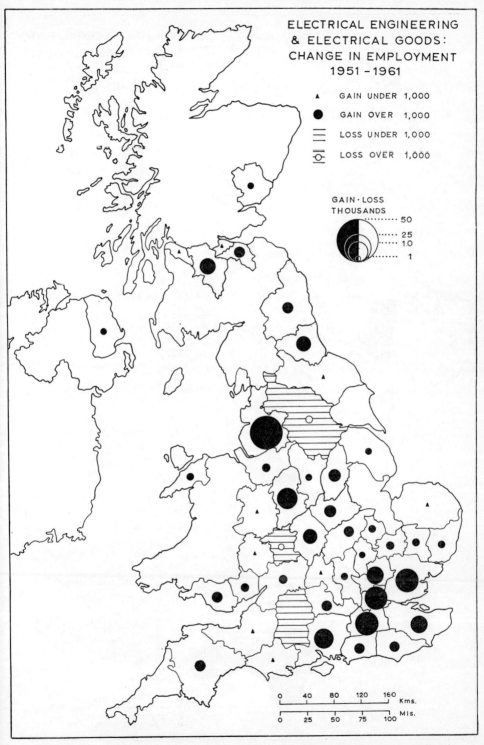

FIG. 4.1b Symbols have been omitted for counties with fewer than 1,000 employed

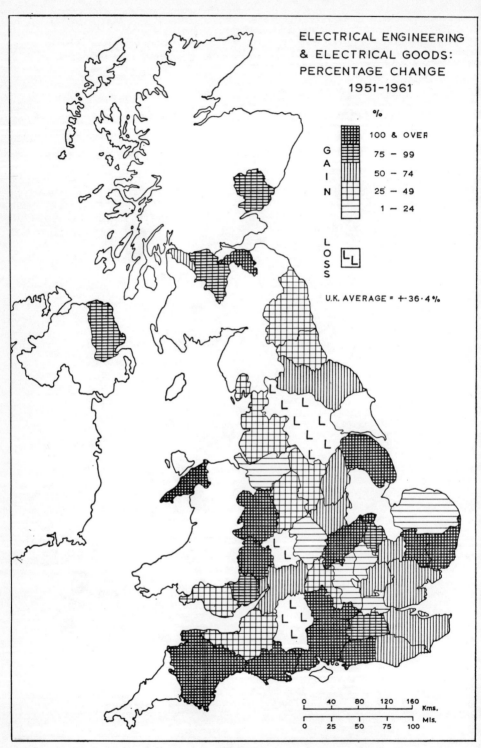

ELECTRICAL ENGINEERING
& ELECTRICAL GOODS:
PERCENTAGE CHANGE
1951–1961

%

GAIN
100 & OVER
75 – 99
50 – 74
25 – 49
1 – 24

LOSS

U.K. AVERAGE = +36·4%

0   40   80   120   160   Kms.
0   25   50   75   100   Mls.

FIG. 4.1c

workers) occurred between 1951 and 1961. The pattern is not greatly different from that of fig. 4.1a. The south-east and Lancashire are the dominant areas but there is a wide scatter demonstrating again the locational tolerance of this industry. If any new preference can be detected, it is for locations in the south of England, notably in Sussex, Hampshire and Devon. Areas where small decreases occurred have no major significance.

Fig. 4.1c provides an index of proportional change. Areas marked 'L' declined. Areas left blank employed too few to warrant proportional analysis. The distribution of positive proportional change has, however, significantly little regional regularity in relation to the national index of 136 (a 36 per cent increase during the decade). Certainly proportional change presents no evidence of a marked preference for the south-east.

The conclusions to be drawn from these three maps may be: (a) for economic success to be achieved it is not imperative for these industries to concentrate in any particular region, and (b) in so far as entrepreneurs prefer the south-east, and clearly by no means all of them do, their choice is personal, imitative or expedient in the short-run rather than the result of careful analysis aimed at maximizing profits by optimizing location. Probably the so-called optimum theory of industrial location has little relevance for this group of industries.

2 CHEMICAL AND ALLIED INDUSTRIES

'Chemicals and Allied Industries' (minimum list headings 261 to 277[1]) make up another group that grew considerably during the decade. The index

---

[1] The Standard Industrial Classification used in official statistics of employment is divided into 24 Main Orders as follows:

I Agriculture, forestry, fishing
II Mining and quarrying
III Food, drink and tobacco
IV Chemicals and allied industries
V Metal manufacture
VI Engineering and electrical goods
VII Shipbuilding and marine engineering
VIII Vehicles
IX Metal goods not elsewhere specified
X Textiles
XI Leather, leather goods and fur
XII Clothing and footwear
XIII Bricks, pottery, glass, cement, etc.
XIV Timber, furniture, etc.
XV Paper, printing and publishing
XVI Other manufacturing industries
XVII Construction
XVIII Gas, electricity and water
XIX Transport and communication
XX Distributive trades
XXI Insurance, banking and finance
XXII Professional and scientific services   [Footnote continued overleaf.

of employment stood at 115 in 1961, an increase of 15 per cent since 1951. Like electrical goods, chemical manufacturing is quite widespread with major concentrations in the London area and in north-west England (fig. 4.2a). But there are chemical plants in County Derry, Cumberland and even in Merioneth, and there is no marked development along the south coast of England. There is a preponderance of heavy chemical manufacture (alkalis and heavy acids) in Lancashire and Cheshire, and in north-east England, while light chemicals tend to be better represented in south-east England. But there is nothing exclusive or economically compelling about these tendencies, except for those parts of the industry which employ large amounts of salt from the Cheshire salt field and anhydrite from County Durham. The wide scatter of plants owned by I.C.I., the presence of Fison's on Humberside, Monsanto's plant at Ruabon, Boot's at Nottingham and in Ayrshire, and many other large and small examples indicate the locational tolerance and freedom of much of this industry.

The changes in employment between 1951 and 1961 (fig. 4.2b) present no evidence seriously to question the truth of this conclusion. The only major item of interest arising from fig. 4.2b is the widespread tendency for the industry to decline in central Scotland during the decade. Otherwise local rather than regional changes were taking place. Similarly fig. 4.2c, showing proportional change, reveals no special provincial preference. There is no drift to the south-east as shown for manufacturing as a whole on figs. 3.6a and b. The pattern is clear evidence of locational tolerance.

Since neither the electrical goods nor the chemical industries followed the

---

XXIII Miscellaneous services
XXIV Public administration and defence

Most main orders are further divided into Minimum List Headings (M.L.H.). For example, Main Order X, Textiles, is divided as follows:
  411 Production of man-made fibres
  412 Spinning and doubling of cotton, flax, and man-made fibres
  413 Weaving of cotton, linen and man-made fibres
  414 Woollen and worsted
  415 Jute
  416 Rope, twine and net
  417 Hosiery and other knitted goods
  418 Lace
  419 Carpets
  421 Narrow fabrics
  422 Made-up textiles
  423 Textile finishing
  429 Other textile industries

There were some 142 Minimum List Headings (many of them subdivided) used in the Industry Tables of the 1961 Census. Unfortunately the many alterations that were made in 1958 to the M.L.H. classification used in the 1951 Census preclude comparative analysis of an appreciable amount of the data published for the two Censuses.

The Censuses for 1931 and 1921 also have industrial classifications, but these are far from identical and differ from those used in 1951 and 1961

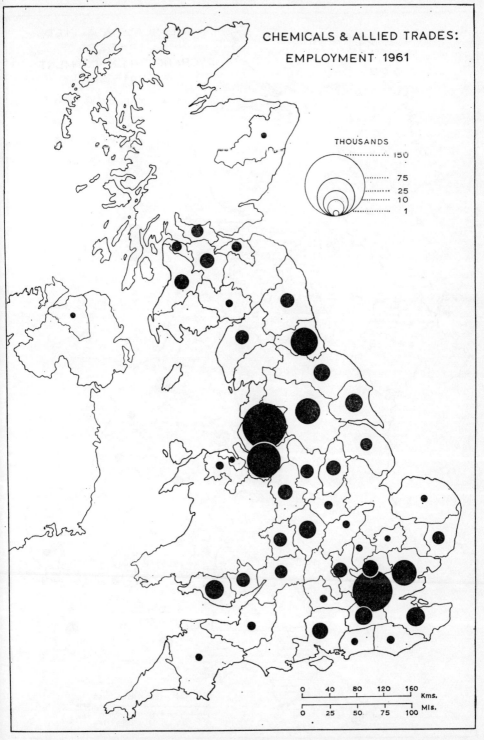

CHEMICALS & ALLIED TRADES:
EMPLOYMENT 1961

THOUSANDS
150
75
25
10
1

0   40   80   120 160
Kms.
0   25   50   75   100
Mls.

FIG. 4.2a Symbols have been omitted for counties with fewer than 1,000 employed

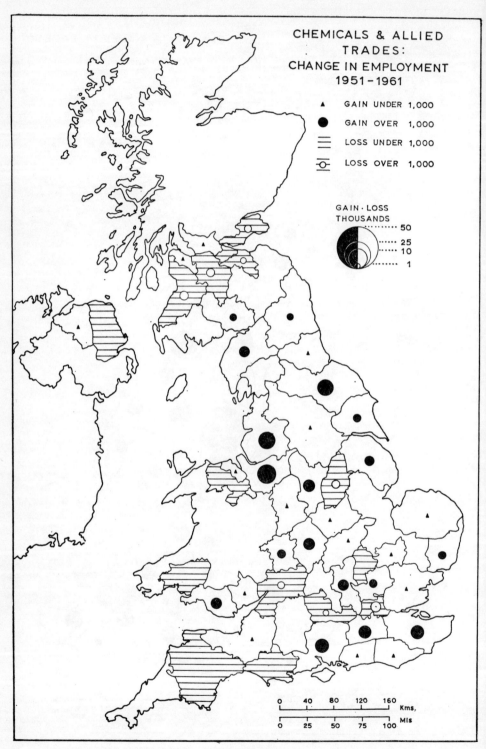

CHEMICALS & ALLIED
TRADES:
CHANGE IN EMPLOYMENT
1951–1961

▲ GAIN UNDER 1,000
● GAIN OVER 1,000
☰ LOSS UNDER 1,000
⊖ LOSS OVER 1,000

GAIN · LOSS
THOUSANDS
.... 50
.... 25
.... 10
.... 1

0   40   80   120   160
                              Kms,
                              Mls
0   25   50   75   100

FIG. 4.2b

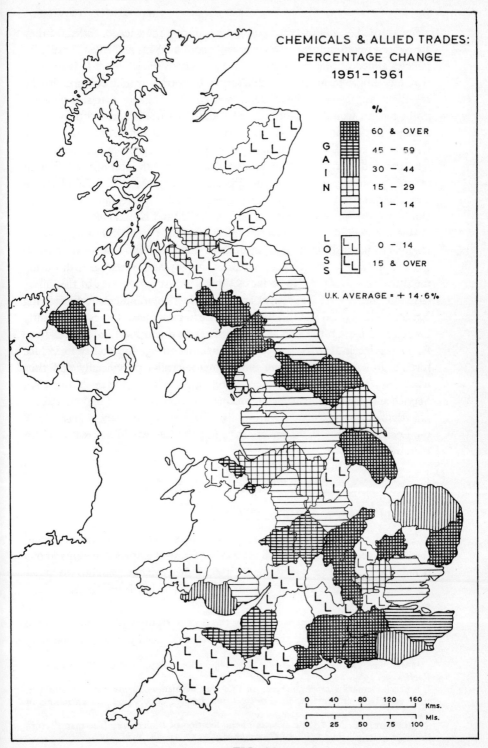

CHEMICALS & ALLIED TRADES:
PERCENTAGE CHANGE
1951–1961

%

GAIN
60 & OVER
45 – 59
30 – 44
15 – 29
1 – 14

LOSS
0 – 14
15 & OVER

U.K. AVERAGE = + 14·6 %

0   40   80   120   160 Kms.

0   25   50   75   100 Mls.

FIG. 4.2c

regional trend of manufacturing in general during the decade, and since they are major growth industries, they provide both a means and a justification for policies aimed at redistributing industry to satisfy social need. It is unlikely that any single group of manufacturing industries would conform to the regionally expressed national trend, and equally unlikely that any standard profit motive would promote it. The locational needs and attitudes of industries and of the managements of individual firms differ, and many of the differences are idiosyncratic and personal, hence the irregular mosaics of figs. 4.1c and 4.2c. 'Growth industries demand growth locations' is a dictum of little positive relevance when applied to many sectors of the electrical and chemical industries. Probably these would tolerate, and succeed in, almost any adequately populated part of the United Kingdom.

It is not possible in this chapter to examine the patterns of other growing manufacturing industries. Nor, even more unfortunately, can we yet analyse the sub-sections of the tertiary sector of employment where growth during the fifties was so rapid.[1] In so far as service industries are part of the 'infrastructure' making for an efficient and convenient environment for both living conditions in general and thriving enterprise in particular, studies are urgently needed to ascertain the size and scale of regional and local imbalance. In so far as service industries possess, like manufacturing, the ability to induce further growth of wealth and employment locally, provincially and thus nationally, such studies are even more urgent.[2] The growth of the Civil Service and efforts to disperse its routine departments from London, and the growth of office employment with similar efforts at dispersal now being made by the Location of Offices Bureau are cases in point that would be greatly helped thereby.

Two Stagnant Industries

1   KNITWEAR MANUFACTURING

The knitwear industry increased roughly threefold in employment during the first 50 years of the twentieth century, and in 1951 employed nearly 130,000 people in the United Kingdom. By 1961 it had declined slightly to about 126,000. The distribution of this industry to 1951 has been discussed elsewhere.[3]

Fig. 4.3a shows the changes during the decade from 1951 to 1961. Though stagnant in employment the industry was not wholly static in location.

---

[1] Manners, G., 'Service industries and regional economic growth', *Town Planning Review, 33,* 1963, 293–303

[2] Service enterprises comparable in this way to manufacturing are, for example, airports, tourist enterprises, mail order firms, finance houses and concentrations of offices

[3] Rawstron, E. M., 'Some aspects of the location of hosiery and lace manufacture in Great Britain', *East Midland Geographer, 9,* 1957, 16–28

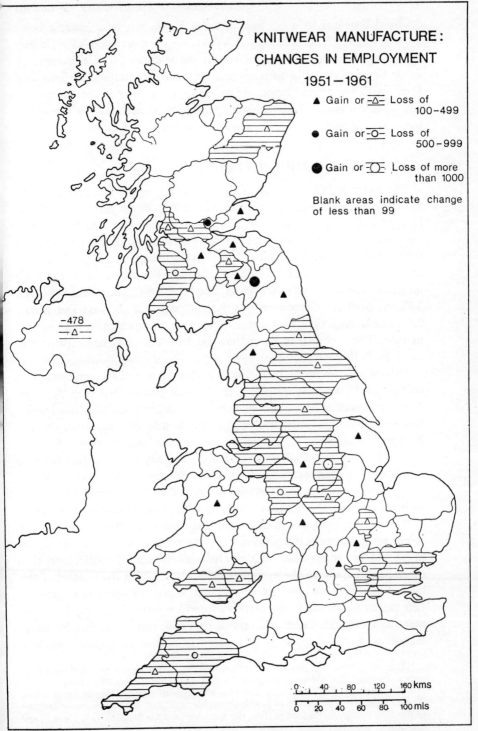

KNITWEAR MANUFACTURE:
CHANGES IN EMPLOYMENT
1951–1961

▲ Gain or ⁻△⁻ Loss of
100–499

● Gain or ⁻○⁻ Loss of
500–999

⬤ Gain or ⁻○⁻ Loss of more
than 1000

Blank areas indicate change
of less than 99

−478
⁻△⁻

0   40   80   120   160 kms

0   20   40   60   80   100 mls

FIG. 4.3a   An open circle to show a loss of 1,600 has been omitted for Middlesex

Scotland benefited by a net gain of 2,500, the largest local increase being 2,100 in Roxburgh. In England and Wales there was a net loss of 5,800, largely in Nottinghamshire, Cheshire, Lancashire and Middlesex. These changes may safely be ascribed to the fortunes and comparative enterprise of individual firms, including rationalization of production, rather than to the operation of any locational factor.[1] From the standpoint of social need the loss of employment in Lancashire and Devon was undesirable.

2 FOOTWEAR MANUFACTURING

The footwear industry is almost the same size as the knitwear industry, though it declined rather more during the decade. Employment was 128,000 in 1951 and 119,500 in 1961. Very little of this industry is to be found in Scotland, Northern Ireland and Wales. There are large concentrations of footwear manufacture in the East Midlands (Northamptonshire and Leicestershire) and in Lancashire (Rossendale district), but the industry is locally important too in several other places, notably Norwich, London, Somerset, Tilbury, Stafford, Gloucestershire, Kendal, west Cumberland and Mansfield. Leeds was a significant centre of footwear manufacture in 1951 but not in 1961. The evolution of the pattern has been described and explained in detail by P. R. Mounfield.[2]

Although employment in footwear declined more than employment in knitted goods manufacture, fig. 4.3b shows a greater shift than fig. 4.3a. There were notable increases in Somerset, Lancashire and Cumberland which partially offset substantial decreases in the leading manufacturing district, Northamptonshire and Leicestershire, and in other localities such as London, Leeds, Norwich and Stafford. It is unlikely that any one locational factor or standard group of factors could explain these changes. Detailed knowledge of the policies, products and fortunes of individual firms would be needed, including policies of rationalization that may have been introduced as a result of the extensive mergers and take-overs that have occurred in this industry in recent years. Vigorous competition from imported footwear in certain sectors of the trade is another factor that may have affected some localities more than others. Indeed, one of the major difficulties in studying the location of this kind of industry, and there are many like it, is non-homogeneity of product. One cannot expect the manufacturers of products that differ, notwithstanding that they are classified under the same M.L.H., to be identical in their locational behaviour. Fortunately choice of location in relation to optimum profit or

[1] But see Johnston, W. B., 'The East Midlands and post-war development in manufacturing', *East Midland Geographer*, 1, 4, 1955, 3–18, especially 12–13
[2] Mounfield, P. R., The Location of Footwear Manufacture in England and Wales, Ph.D. thesis, 1962, University of Nottingham. Mounfield, P. R., *The Footwear Industry of the East Midlands*. Reprinted from the *East Midland Geographer*, 3, 6, 7 and 8, and 4, 1 and 3, 1964 to 1967

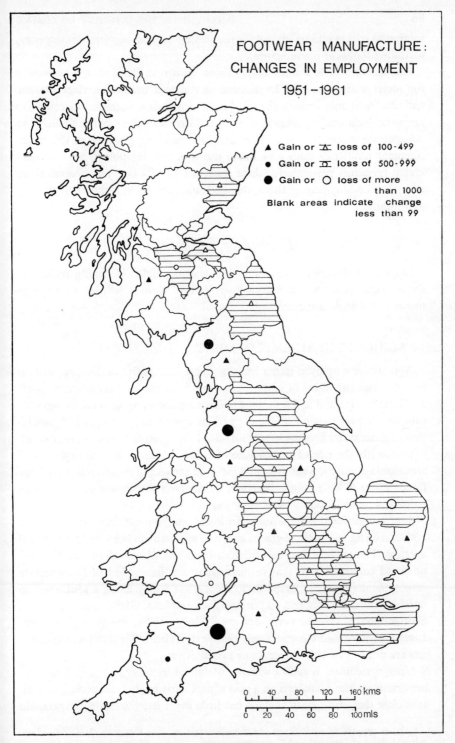

FOOTWEAR MANUFACTURE:
CHANGES IN EMPLOYMENT
1951–1961

▲ Gain or △ loss of 100-499
● Gain or ▢ loss of 500-999
⬤ Gain or ◯ loss of more
                        than 1000
Blank areas indicate change
                        less than 99

0 40 80 120 160 kms

0 20 40 60 80 100 mls

FIG. 4.3b

minimum cost is seldom crucial for the success of most economic enterprises, including footwear manufacture.

But changes in locational emphasis as shown on fig. 4.3b are important for social welfare at local levels even in stagnant industries, since a static national figure may conceal sizeable local changes. It is necessary therefore, to keep the locational behaviour of such industries in view and not simply to concentrate attention upon those that are markedly growing or declining. Stagnant industries cannot be much use as a tool for policy, but they can create problems particularly where areas are heavily dependent upon them and when employment in them, though static nationally, is mobile regionally and locally.

Declining Industries

Stagnant industries show the amber warning light. Declining industries show bright red. In this section three industries in which labour requirements fell sharply are examined.

1 AGRICULTURAL EMPLOYMENT

Agriculture employed rather less than 4 per cent of the working population in 1961, and the index of employment fell from 100 in 1951 to 78 in 1961. In Northern Ireland it fell to 72. Unlike manufacturing or services, agriculture does not correspond at all closely to the distribution of towns and population in general. Its greatest input and need is land rather than labour or capital, consequently the size of a county and its endowment of agricultural land of reasonable quality is a fundamental factor in the size of its agricultural labour force. There is little point, therefore, in mapping the pattern of agricultural employment on a county basis.[1]

The proportional decline in agricultural employment from 1951 to 1961 is shown on fig. 4.4 in three grades arranged approximately around the national average. The pattern is quite different from any discussed so far. There is no trend comparable to that in manufacturing (figs. 3.6a and b) or service employment (fig. 3.8). Major decline occurs not only along a south-east to north-west axis in England and in populous Durham, Glamorgan and central Scotland, but also in the peripheral areas, North Wales, Pembroke, Cornwall, Inverness, Ross and Cromarty and Northern Ireland. The intervening counties are either just below average or just above it.

Since agriculture is such a widely distributed industry and since land is so important an input, analysis on a grid square basis might be especially useful. It is clear that our county analysis has little more use than as a cartographic

[1] Other aspects of agriculture are more interesting. See Coppock, J. T., *An Agricultural Atlas of England and Wales*, 1964

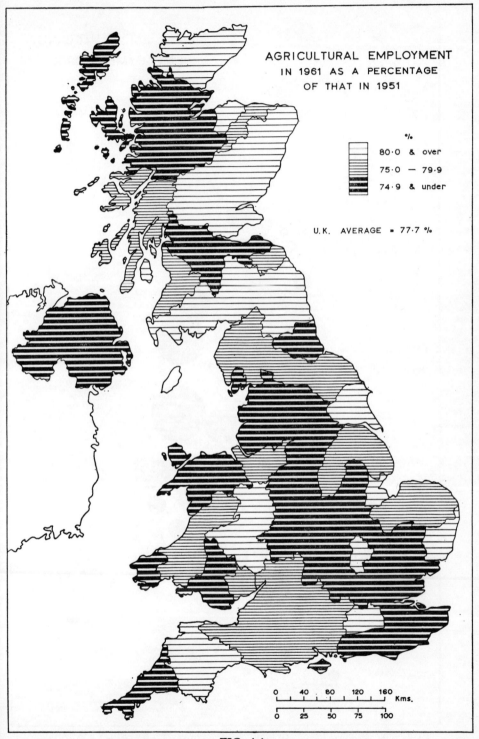

AGRICULTURAL EMPLOYMENT
IN 1961 AS A PERCENTAGE
OF THAT IN 1951

%
80·0 & over
75·0 — 79·9
74·9 & under

U.K. AVERAGE = 77·7 %

0 40 80 120 160
                    Kms.
0 25 50 75 100

FIG. 4.4

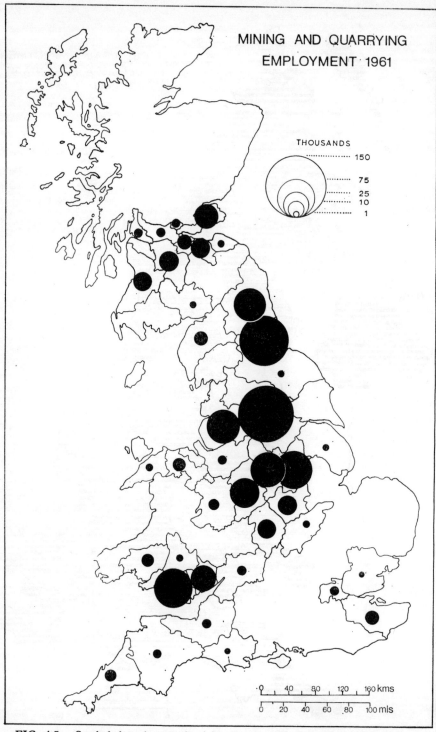

MINING AND QUARRYING
EMPLOYMENT 1961

THOUSANDS
150
75
25
10
1

FIG. 4.5a Symbols have been omitted for counties with fewer than 1000 employed

exercise, except that it indicates marked spatial variations worthy of the more refined and intricate analysis suggested above.

2 EXTRACTIVE INDUSTRIES

Employment in the extractive industries (840,000 in 1951 and 723,000 in 1961) declined proportionately and absolutely rather less than in agriculture, but the fall was substantial and must have been much greater since 1961 in view of the huge decrease in coal-mining which comprises so large a part of the extractive industries (table 4.1).

TABLE 4.1 *Coal-mining in Great Britain* Mean Annual Manpower 1950–68

Year	Thousands employed	Year	Thousands employed
1950	691	1960	602
1951	693	1961	571
1952	710	1962	551
1953	707	1963	544
1954	702	1964	517
1955	699	1965	491
1956	697	1966	456
1957	704	1967	419
1958	693	1968	391
1959	658		

The rapid decrease of manpower in coal-mining began in 1958–9

Fig. 4.5a shows the pattern of employment in extractive industries. Inevitably, it bears a close relationship to the distribution of coal-fields. But it is worth noting that both the West Riding and Durham had more workers in mining in 1961 than either Scotland or South Wales, and worth remembering too that the productivity of mining varies considerably from field to field, so the relationship is imprecise. It does not vary directly either with the output of coal or with the extent of coal-bearing strata marked on a geological map.

Inevitably, since minerals cannot be extracted where they do not exist, coal-mining creates pockets both large and small of specialized employment, and since the mineral cannot be extracted twice, a decline in a highly localized industry such as this creates in turn severe local stress.[1] Drift from the mines is a problem of a different order from drift to the south-east. It is fragmentary,

[1] (i) House, J. W., and Knight, E. M., *Pit Closure and the Community*, Papers on Migration and Mobility in Northern England, No. 5, 1967
(ii) Knight, E. M., *Men leaving Mining, West Cumberland 1966–67*, Papers on Migration and Mobility, No. 6, 1968

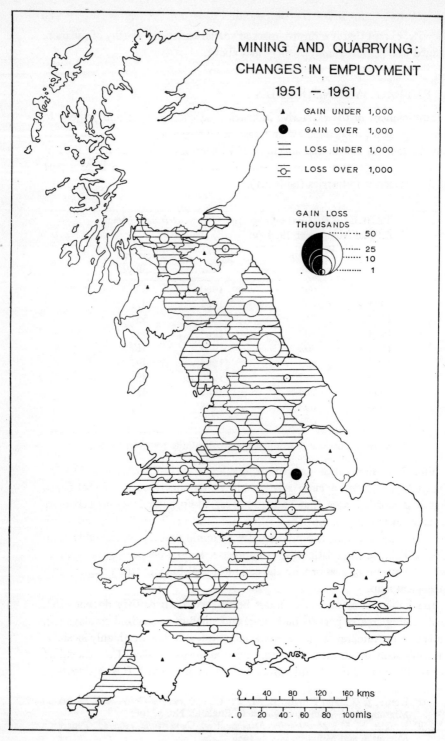

MINING AND QUARRYING:
CHANGES IN EMPLOYMENT
1951 — 1961

▲ GAIN UNDER 1,000
● GAIN OVER 1,000
≡ LOSS UNDER 1,000
⦶ LOSS OVER 1,000

GAIN LOSS
THOUSANDS
50
25
10
1

0 40 80 120 160 kms
0 20 40 60 80 100 mls

FIG. 4.5b

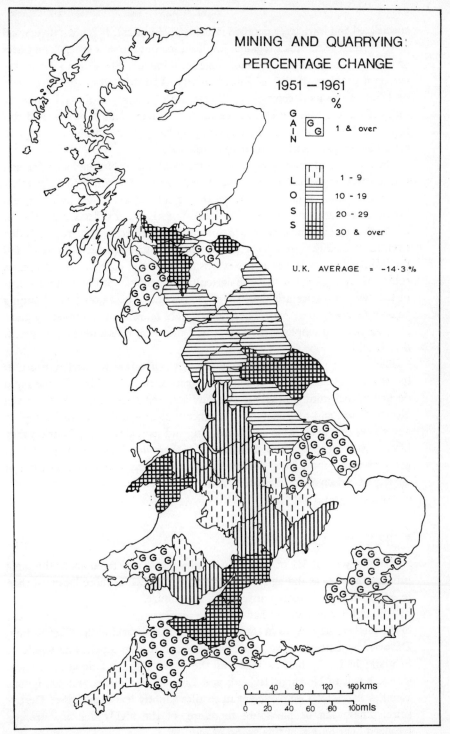

MINING AND QUARRYING:
PERCENTAGE CHANGE
1951 – 1961
%

GAIN   1 & over

LOSS   1 - 9
        10 - 19
        20 - 29
        30 & over

U.K. AVERAGE = –14·3%

40 80 120 160 kms
20 40 60 80 100 mls

FIG. 4.5c

specialized and intricately detailed in the spatial context. It is not a diversified general trend with broad regional implications but rather a specialized series of local events often with an immediate local impact. The drift to the south-east is a problem of the urbanized society. The drift from the mines is a problem of the local community. There are of course, as fig. 4.5a implies, more of these communities in some parts of Britain than in others, and this fact should be borne in mind when studying fig. 4.5b, which shows change in extractive employment between 1951 and 1961.

Only four coal-mining counties, Ayr, Midlothian, Nottinghamshire and Carmarthen, registered an increase. Small increases in other counties relate to the extraction of clay for brickmaking, sand and gravel for building, and limestone for cement making. The increase in London reflects expansion of head-office staffs. The area in which significant decreases occurred extended over most counties from central Scotland through northern England and the Midlands into Wales and Severnside. In some counties the decreases substantially augmented those in agriculture. Examples af the combined loss in the two industries are Durham 21,000; Lancashire 24,000; West Riding 30,000; Glamorgan 18,000. These losses were more than recouped by gains in other fields of employment except in Lancashire where total employment decreased by 20,000 (fig. 3.2a).

The map of proportional change (fig. 4.5c) like that for agriculture uses too coarse a mesh to reveal much of interest except for picking out the rapid decline of coal-mining in Gloucestershire and Somerset, of slate and stone in North Wales, and of ironstone and other minerals in the North Riding. It also shows that in so far as south-east England has extractive industries, they have mostly prospered and they have not, therefore, hindered its growth in prosperity or imposed any burden upon its economy save that a measure of anxiety has arisen about the future of the small Kent coal-field and the reserve of sand and gravel supplies.

3 TEXTILE EMPLOYMENT

Nationally the index of change in textiles (79·5) registered about the same proportional loss as did agriculture. Yet the loss was far more localized than in either mining, or more particularly, agriculture.

Although many counties had over 500 textile workers in 1961, 64 per cent of the total employed was in the five counties of Lancashire, the West Riding, Derbyshire, Leicestershire and Nottinghamshire (fig. 4.6a). The whole of Scotland had only half as many as the West Riding; Leicestershire was almost equal to Northern Ireland; and London, Middlesex and contiguous counties had a total employment in textiles slightly less than that of Derby-shire. There can be no doubt therefore, of the highly uneven, strongly localized distribution of this group of industries.

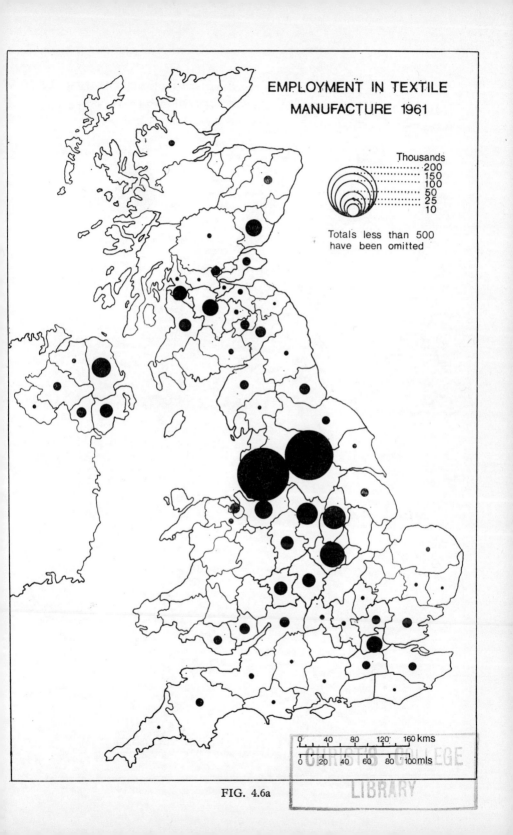

EMPLOYMENT IN TEXTILE
MANUFACTURE 1961

Thousands
200
150
100
50
25
10

Totals less than 500
have been omitted

0   40   80   120   160 kms
0 20 40 60 80 100 mls

FIG. 4.6a

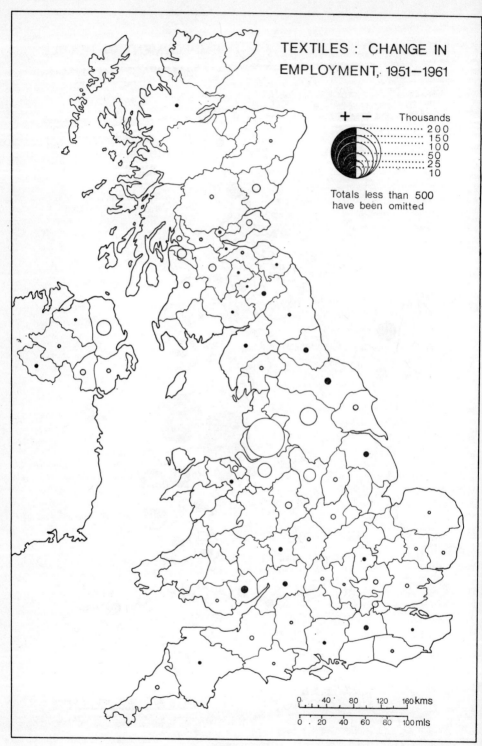

TEXTILES : CHANGE IN
EMPLOYMENT, 1951–1961

+ −   Thousands
.... 200
.... 150
.... 100
.... 50
.... 25
.... 10

Totals less than 500
have been omitted

0   40   80   120   160 kms

0   20   40   60   80   100 mls

FIG. 4.6b

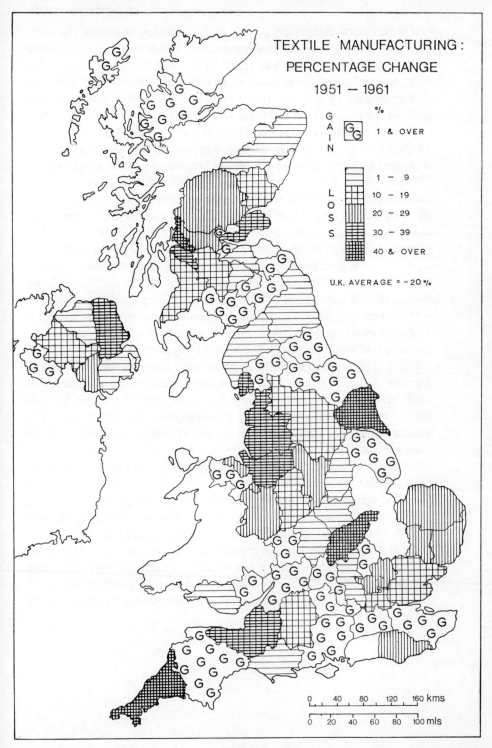

TEXTILE MANUFACTURING:
PERCENTAGE CHANGE
1951 — 1961

GAIN
%
G G   1 & OVER

LOSS
1 — 9
10 — 19
20 — 29
30 — 39
40 & OVER

U.K. AVERAGE = -20%

0   40   80   120   160 kms

0   20   40   60   80   100 mls

FIG. 4.6c

The pattern of change from 1951 to 1961 was even more uneven (fig. 4.6b). Over half (121,000) the national net decrease (217,000) occurred in Lancashire. The next largest loss was 24,000 in the West Riding. Lancashire lost over one-third of its employment in textiles during the decade. The West Riding declined by just over 11 per cent. In Durham there was an increase of 1,100 (18 per cent) and in Monmouth 6,060 (64 per cent).

The three declining industries discussed here brought about a decrease of 145,000 jobs or 5·8 per cent of total employment in Lancashire in 1951, compared with 20,000 or 3·4 per cent in Durham, 18,000 or 3·7 per cent in Glamorgan, and 3,200 or 1·8 per cent in Monmouth. Notwithstanding that Lancashire had and still has a more diverse economic structure than, notably, the West Riding, it must have been subjected to a stress of destructive change during the decade greater than occurred in any other industrialized and urbanized county in Britain. It was saved from disaster largely by its diversity, by the brakes applied by the Government to the decline of the cotton industry, by the enterprise of its people and organizations, by the feasibility of converting disused cotton mills to other uses – something which cannot be done with disused coal-mines – and by the traditional willingness of its women as well as its men to go out to work. Had the calamity of cotton struck wool, far greater stress would have beset the West Riding during these ten years.

Fig. 4.6c shows proportional changes between 1951 and 1961. Even during a general decline in textiles some areas benefited from increases. These were small, scattered, and largely concerned with the expanding sector, i.e. synthetic fibres. To understand better what happened spatially in the textile industry an analysis item by item among the Minimum List Headings of the Standard Industrial Classification would have to be undertaken.[1] Our examination earlier of the knitwear industry indicated the desirability of this more detailed study, but the broad examination of the Main Order Heading 'Textiles' brings out the massive change in Lancashire, a change resulting mainly from the decline in employment in cotton manufacture in England and Wales of 149,000 of which 80,000 occurred in Lancashire.

Other declining, stagnant and expanding industries, including those in the service sector could be examined, but for many of them changes in the Standard Industrial Classification between 1951 and 1961 make an acceptable degree of accuracy impossible to achieve. This fact, in large measure, explains the selection made here.

[1] See p. 77, footnote 1

5

Female and Male Employment

There are several reasons why particular emphasis should be given to female employment.[1] First, if there is a major reserve of labour that might quite quickly be tapped to the benefit of the national economy, it is 'womanpower'. The spare capacity here is far greater than the official unemployment statistics indicate, and it is very unevenly distributed over the country in relation to the male labour force. Lancashire is a case in point. In 1961 no fewer than 120,000 more women were employed there than would have been if Lancashire had conformed to the national rate adjusted to allow for the age-structure of the resident female population of the county.[2] In London and Middlesex together the excess was 233,000 calculated on the same basis. In Northumberland, Durham and the North Riding there was a combined deficit of 78,000, and one of 58,000 in Glamorgan and Monmouth. Thus there is a sound practical reason for devoting considerable space in this chapter to female employment. Secondly, most men whether married or single can commute considerable distances to work if they wish or need to. They can even work away from home, returning at weekly or less frequent intervals, for they do not have primary responsibility for the day-to-day running of the home and care of children. Conversely many women cannot commute far for family reasons, and must have jobs near at hand or even use the home itself as a workshop or office. Female employment is thus more severely restricted than male employment by distance and accessibility, which are integral parts of the study of geography. Geographical analysis is likely, therefore, to be even more pertinent to the solution of problems of female employment than those of male employment. Thirdly, because manpower is the foundation of the active work force, its pattern tends more closely than that of female employment to reflect the pattern of population itself. Of course, there are local anomalies but their amplitude is less for men than for women, many of whose roles outside the home tend to be ancillary rather than basic, supplementary rather than essential.

Analyses of population distribution and changes therein between censuses are often used to draw conclusions about patterns and changes in the economy

---

[1] Hunt, Audrey, *A Survey of Women's Employment.* H.M.S.O., 1968
[2] But see Rodgers, H. B., 'The Hunt Report: prospects for Pennine England', *Area* (Inst. Brit. Geog.), *3*, 1969, 1–9

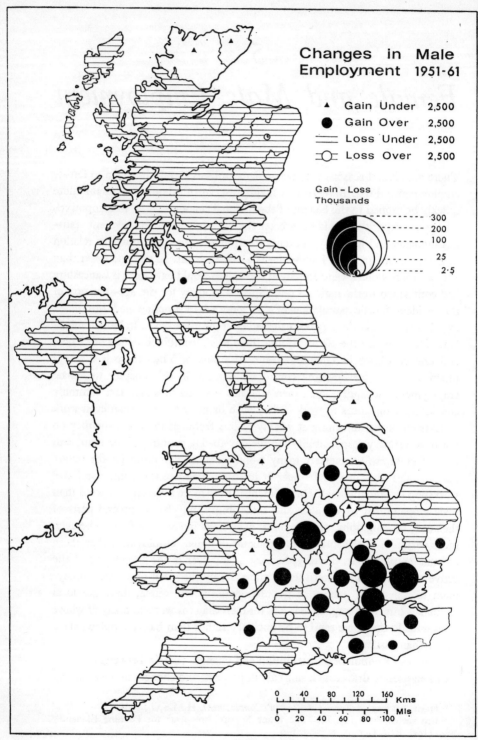

Changes in Male
Employment 1951-61

▲ Gain Under 2,500
● Gain Over 2,500
— Loss Under 2,500
⊖ Loss Over 2,500

Gain – Loss
Thousands

-------- 300
-------- 200
-------- 100

-------- 25
-------- 2·5

0   40   80   120   160
                        Kms
                        Mls
0   20   40   60   80   100

FIG. 5.1a

and sociology of Britain. Like the official unemployment figures, so closely watched month by month as a barometer of the economic weather over the country, such analyses are defective, for they paint a picture in shades of only one 'colour' and to a predominantly masculine perspective. Many other 'colours' are used in this book, and the present chapter provides an opportunity to add a feminine perspective to the canvas.

The first set of maps (figs. 5.1a, b and c) show changes between 1951 and 1961 in the employment of males, females and married women respectively. The pattern of change in male employment shows a midland and south-eastward tendency similar both to that for employment as a whole (fig. 3.2a) and to that for manufacturing (fig. 3.2b). But there are important differences. First, the area of declining male employment was far greater than the areas of decline shown on figs. 3.2a and b. Secondly, there was a gain in male employment in London and Middlesex but a loss in manufacturing. Thirdly, the growth in male employment in the midland counties of Leicester, Northampton, Nottingham, Stafford and Warwick was greater than the increase in manufacturing employment (fig. 3.2b). Nevertheless, even if one examined all the differences in detail, the salient feature would remain that the shift in male employment underpins that in total employment. Men were moving to jobs in the south-east and the Midlands.

So were the women, but far less strongly (fig. 5.1b). Very few counties experienced an absolute decline in female employment. Those that did suffer a loss were mostly rural, and the worst affected area was Northern Ireland. Confirmation of the movement of women workers in a south-easterly direction is clearly made by a comparison of fig. 3.1a with fig. 5.1b. But there were interesting shifts in detail too. In Scotland, Midlothian (Edinburgh) gained most. The increase in female employment there (12,000) was virtually the same as the increase in total employment (13,000). In Scotland as a whole, however, the number of women workers increased by 44,000 while total employment rose by only half as much. Without the female increase Scotland would have suffered an overall decline equal to that of Lancashire, the two work-forces being about the same size. But the use of women workers in Lancashire must be close to saturation whereas in Scotland the female 'activity rate'[1] is lower and there is clearly ample scope for an increase. In Lancashire only 10,000 more women found jobs, and with a loss of 30,000 males from the employed population an overall decrease occurred. Not so in the West Riding, where a puny increase of only 4,000 in male workers was heftily augmented by bringing 40,000 more women into employment. North-east England (Durham, Northumberland and the North Riding) and South Wales (Glamorgan and Monmouth), in both of which women formed a substantially smaller proportion of the employed population in 1961 than in the United Kingdom as a whole, had increases of 40,000 and 29,000

[1] See p. 112   H

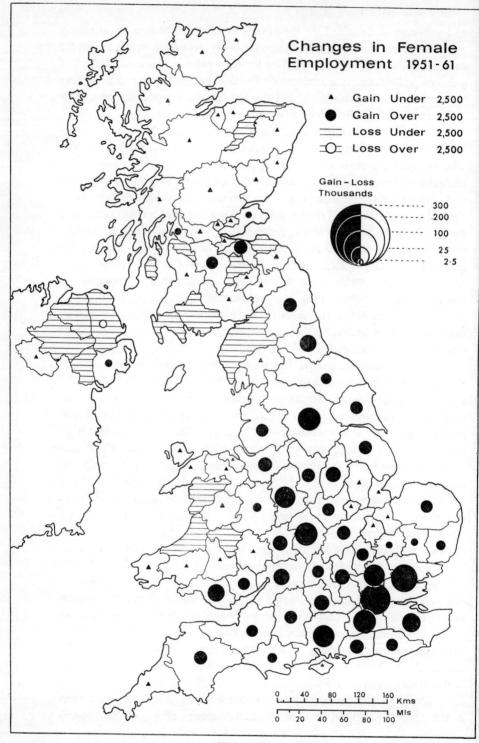

Changes in Female
Employment 1951-61

▲ Gain Under 2,500
● Gain Over 2,500
Loss Under 2,500
○ Loss Over 2,500

Gain - Loss
Thousands
300
200
100
25
2·5

0   40   80   120   160 Kms
Mls
0   20   40   60   80   100

FIG. 5.1b

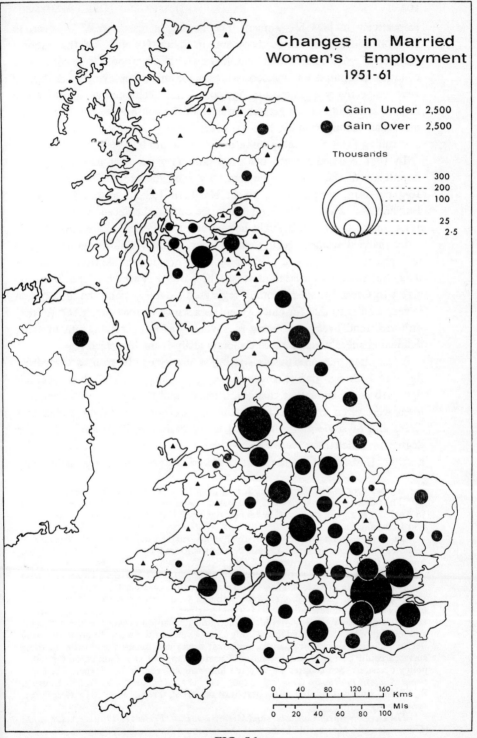

Changes in Married
Women's Employment
1951-61

▲ Gain Under 2,500
● Gain Over 2,500

Thousands

300
200
100

25
2·5

0   40   80   120 160
Kms
Mls
0   20   40   60   80   100

FIG. 5.1c

respectively in jobs for women. The largest increases were, however, in London and Middlesex (67,000) and in Essex (51,000). Of the national increase of 764,000 in female employment, the metropolis and contiguous counties accounted for 234,000, whereas for male employment the figures were respectively 422,000 and 237,000. These comparative figures are a further indication of the greater strength of the south-eastward drift among men than among women, thus both confirming observations made earlier and calling for a close comparison of figs. 5.1a and b.

In 1951 married women made up only 11·7 per cent of the employed population of the United Kingdom.[1] By 1961 the proportion had risen to 16·3 per cent, ranging from 9·3 in Northern Ireland to 16·9 per cent in England and Wales.[2] The overall increase during the decade was 1,237,000. What proportions of this might be ascribed to (a) earlier marriage, (b) more older married women seeking employment as their children grew up, and (c) a greater availability of part-time jobs[3] is not discernible from the census data. But there was a large increase, the pattern of which is shown on fig. 5.1c.[4] In Great Britain no county registered a decrease, and the distribution is very similar to that for employment as a whole in 1961 (fig. 3.1a). A fairly uniform trend over the country as a whole was in operation, thus masking detailed changes which a more elaborate analysis might reveal.

A less close but nevertheless striking similarity can be seen by comparing fig. 5.1c with fig. 3.2c (changes in service employment).[5] Taken together, figs. 5.1b and c show that changes in female and married women's employment were often important in sustaining the economies of the Development Areas and of some of the so-called 'grey' or intermediate areas.[6] But the degree to which they were effective varied considerably from one area to another. Had female employment not been sustained or increased in many

---

[1] 6·3 per cent in Northern Ireland, 12·4 per cent in England and Wales

[2] The percentage for Wales was well below that for England. It ranged from 6·8 in Anglesey to 13·1 in Brecon. The highest figures in England were: Leicestershire 29·0 and Lancashire 20·0

[3] In so far as data on part-time female employment published for the censuses is reliable, the increase in Great Britain between 1951 and 1961 was only about 100,000 less than that for married women all told

[4] No county data for married women were published for Northern Ireland for 1951

[5] A remarkable progression inwards upon the south-east can be seen by looking in succession at figs. 5.1c, 3.2c, 5.1b, 3.2a, 3.2b and 5.1a. This sequence is clear evidence of the existence of several so-called 'trend surfaces' or major generalizing features reflecting processes of demographic erosion and deposition at work in the economic and social morphology of the United Kingdom. Given a grid system as both a collecting device and a framework for analysis, the broad slopes and detailed sinuosities of these surfaces could be found, interpreted and usefully applied as a foundation for sound policy decisions. See chapter 11, and the following references: (i) Haggett, P., *Locational Analysis in Human Geography*, 1965, 153–182. (ii) Chorley, R. J., and Haggett, P., 'Trend surface mapping in geographical research', *Trans. Inst. Brit. Geogr.*, 37, 1965, 47–67

[6] *The Development of Lancashire and Merseyside; Past, Present and Future*, L.A.M.I.D.A. (Lancashire and Merseyside Industrial Development Association), 1963

'black' and grey counties, the relative economic deterioration in these areas during the decade would have been very much worse.

That the economic health in Northern Ireland was worse than in any other province is in keeping with the failure of female employment to increase there. It barely held its own, and although 15,000 more married women were at work in 1961 than in 1951, representing an increase from the very low level of 6·33 to 9·30 per cent of the labour force, a huge reserve of married women remained unemployed. Moreover, women in general were unable through lack of opportunity to compensate for the overall loss of jobs. Central Scotland did rather better, for in every county (except Angus which is 'borderline' central) the increase in the proportion of married women at work was above the level for the United Kingdom (46 per cent). West Lothian, Dunbarton, Midlothian and Lanark registered 103, 95, 91 and 65 per cent respectively. Without these huge increases no white band across central Scotland would show up on fig. 3.2a.

Similar feminine support was given in the north-east of England, in Glamorgan and Monmouth (the last-named recorded an increase of 102 per cent in the employment of married women), and in Wiltshire, Dorset and Devon. Otherwise these areas too would have been shaded on fig. 3.2a.

Among present Development Areas in England, Cumberland fared worst. There the women were unable to compensate for the decline in male employment notwithstanding an increase of 60 per cent in the number of married women at work. But Cumberland set in the national perspective is a small item. The frequent mention of Lancashire in recent pages implies that a bigger problem exists there. Yet Lancashire as a whole has never been a Development Area, although it has been ailing persistently with the decline of coal-mining since 1907, cotton since 1918, and its male labour force during the 1950s.

Lancashire has a larger employed population than Scotland, and like the latter it should preferably be examined in internal detail. This cannot be done for Lancashire, because no appropriate subdivision of a county can be derived from the published employment data of the 1961 Census. Even without examination of internal details,[1] however, a comparison of employment in Lancashire with that in Scotland as a whole is worth while.

The populations of the two areas are virtually the same, yet Lancashire had about 320,000 more in employment in 1951, though the gap had narrowed to some 280,000 in 1961. Whereas the employment of males in Lancashire was only 80,000 greater than in Scotland in 1961, the former had almost 200,000 more women employed. Both areas declined in male employment

[1] (i) The North-West, a Regional Study, 1965. See especially pp. 25–44
(ii) Smith, D. M., 'Identifying the "grey" areas', Regional Studies, 2, 2, 1968, 183–193; The North West, 1969

during the decade, but Scotland drew upon its female reserves, whereas Lancashire had few reserves left. More married women in Scotland would probably go out to work if jobs were available, for in Dundee and in the county of Selkirk, at least, the employment of married women exceeds the national level in the United Kingdom. Edinburgh, however, compares unfavourably with London in this respect.

So Scotland has large untapped reserves of labour and space for economic expansion while Lancashire, considered as a whole, has congestion, near saturation especially of the female work-force and less scope for econogeographical manoeuvre. Furthermore, Scotland in 1951 had considerable, albeit old-fashioned, economic diversity, whereas Lancashire carried the huge burden of nearly 350,000 workers in a largely moribund textile industry to which other sectors of its economy were closely linked for their prosperity. Scotland is rightly designated a Development Area so far as employment is concerned, because it has unused resources awaiting the opportunity to add to the national product and to the wealth of its own people. It is an underdeveloped land. Lancashire, in contrast, should be designated a *Re*-development Area. It has shown the ability to accept and generate change, but the need now is for more help to rearrange its powerful, vigorous work-force to its own and the national benefit. Its development is full but maladjusted for future prosperity.

As already noted,[1] the second largest concentration of people and employment in Britain is the regional combination of Lancashire and the West Riding. The economic well-being and increasing vitality of this region is, therefore, very important indeed for the future prosperity of the country as a whole. So having devoted considerable space to Lancashire some reference should now be made to the West Riding, where employment was just under three-quarters that of Lancashire in 1961, and where male employment and manufacturing employment both stagnated during the preceding decade.

Considered as a whole, the West Riding suffered less during the decade than Northern Ireland, Scotland and Lancashire, but scrutiny of figs. 3.2a, b and c, 5.1a, b and c shows the West Riding's performance to have been at most only slightly better than that of either the north-east, or South Wales. Like Scotland, however, the latter two areas had a clearly underdeveloped work-force, whereas that in the West Riding was more fully used though neither to the same level nor probably as evenly as in Lancashire.[2] The West Riding is, however, less generally diverse and sub-regionally more specialized than Lancashire. But it has not carried as heavy a burden of declining textiles and ancillary trades, and its coal industry expanded during the twentieth

---

[1] Chapter 3, p. 45

[2] (i) Coates, B. E., and Hunt, A. J., 'Sheffield and the Don basin conurbation in relation to the new Economic Planning Regions', *East Midland Geographer*, 3, 7, 1965, 358–372, especially figure 2, p. 363

(ii) Fraser, L. N., *A Growth Policy for the North*, 1966, Appendix II, Table 12

century up to 1957. Even in Yorkshire, however, coal is now causing growing anxiety, and this coupled to the lack of diversity in the West Riding must make for instability in the future.[1] As in Lancashire, Re-development Area status and economic rearrangement of resources are needed, but congestion is less and scope for econo-geographical manœuvre is greater in the West Riding. As coal-mining declines there will be not only a need but also a great opportunity to redeploy the male labour force of the present active coal-field; to expand Doncaster; to diversify industry, and to bring a large number of married women, no longer restricted by the exigencies of male shift-work and the narrow opportunities for employment characteristic of many colliery settlements, into the active work-force.[2]

The West Riding is not yet dangerously 'grey', but certain parts of it could quickly become so and change to 'black' if close watch is not kept and early action taken when needed.[3] How to improve surveillance is outlined and discussed in chapter 11.

Proportional Change

The proportional changes in male and female employment in the United Kingdom are illustrated by figs. 5.2a and b, respectively. Apart from increases in Ayrshire, Caithness and Dunbarton, proportional change in male employment grades outwards from the south-east.[4] Between the major growth area (from the Trent to the Channel and from Severnside to the Humber) and Scotland there is a large neutral band comprising 8 out of 9 northern counties of England (fig. 5.2a). London and Middlesex, Glamorgan, and much of central Scotland too, are neutral. The outward gradation from the south-east is most rapid towards North Wales and into the Fenland counties and Norfolk.

To what extent the pattern would have been different without new towns around London and without an official green belt, no one can tell precisely. But it is certain that what is shown in the south-east on this map is mainly the result of the outward spread and overspill of London as a multi-functional and cohesive magnet for growth, to which men were drawn also from many other parts of the country and from overseas during the decade. Growth in the south-east was engendered by London, notwithstanding that the greatest proportional increases were in new towns and elsewhere beyond the green

[1] Coates, B. E., and Lewis, G. M., *The Doncaster Area*, British landscapes through maps, No. 8 (ed. K. C. Edwards), 1966
[2] *Hunt Report*, 1969. Paragraphs 187–193
[3] Rodgers, H. B., *op. cit.*, 1969. See pp. 6 and 7
[4] Increases above the national mean (2·7 per cent) were experienced only in the following counties: Bedford, Berkshire, Buckingham, Cambridge, Essex, Gloucester, Hertford, Huntingdon, Leicester, Lindsey, Middlesex, Northants and Peterborough, Nottingham, Oxford, Rutland, Somerset, Stafford, East Suffolk, Surrey, West Sussex, Warwick, Worcester, Flint, Monmouth and Caithness

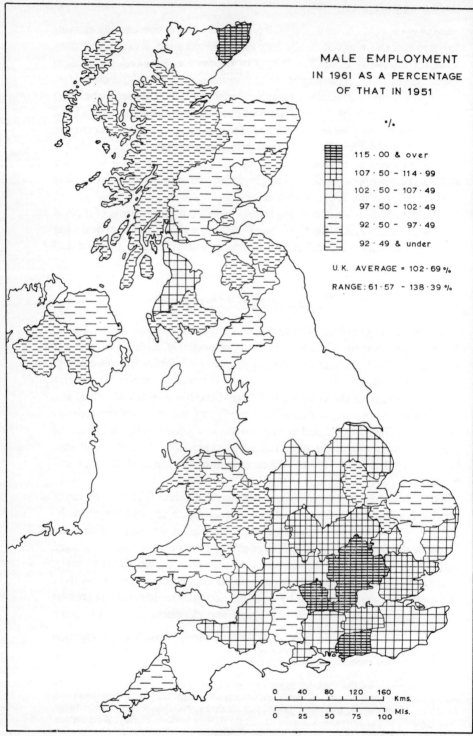

MALE EMPLOYMENT
IN 1961 AS A PERCENTAGE
OF THAT IN 1951

%

115 · 00 & over
107 · 50 – 114 · 99
102 · 50 – 107 · 49
97 · 50 – 102 · 49
92 · 50 – 97 · 49
92 · 49 & under

U. K. AVERAGE = 102 · 69 %

RANGE : 61 · 57 – 138 · 39 %

0   40   80   120   160
Kms.

0   25   50   75   100
Mls.

FIG. 5.2a

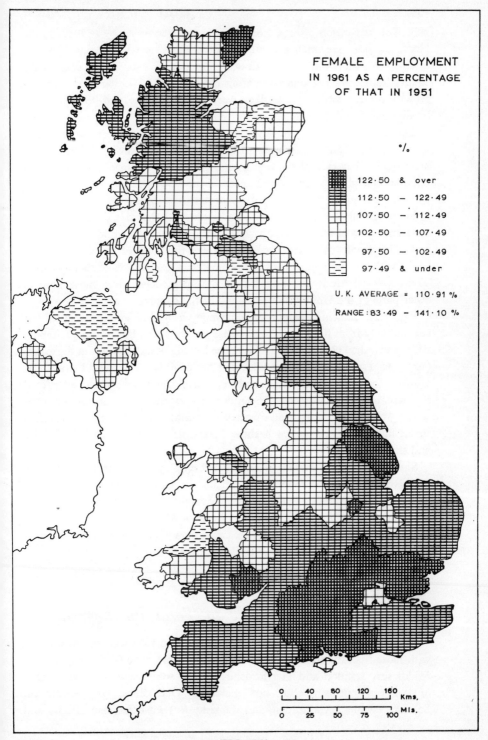

FEMALE EMPLOYMENT
IN 1961 AS A PERCENTAGE
OF THAT IN 1951

%

122·50 & over
112·50 — 122·49
107·50 — 112·49
102·50 — 107·49
97·50 — 102·49
97·49 & under

U. K. AVERAGE = 110·91 %

RANGE : 83·49 — 141·10 %

0   40   80   120   160   Kms.

0   25   50   75   100   Mls.

FIG. 5.2b

belt. This expansion around London is picked out on fig. 5.2a because the
Home Counties are small and subdivide the area over which a unitary force,
that of London, is functioning. In other parts of the country the scale of the
county framework is too large to allow discernment of similar trends around
growth centres which themselves were much smaller and less powerful
locally than London.

The question remains, however, would expansion in the south-east have
been so great without London's attractive ring of new towns? There can be
little doubt that this physical planning policy which focused its attention
upon certain physical and social needs of the South East Region, conflicted
with the economic planning policy for the distribution of manufacturing
industry throughout the country as a whole, and that the absence between
1951 and 1961 of any national policy relating to the distribution of services
and office employment further strengthened the hand of physical planners
to act without due regard for the regional economic effects of their policies.
The supposed needs of London thus took precedence over those both of
other parts of the United Kingdom and of the country as a whole.

Fig. 5.2b showing proportional change in female employment differs
substantially from fig. 5.2a. The increase for women is larger and even more
widespread than choice of intervals in the key might indicate, for in the grade,
(107·5 to 112·49) which straddles the national mean (110·9) Derbyshire,
Down, Northumberland, Staffordshire, Stirling and Sutherland all exceed
it. Increase above the national mean does not extend, however, into counties
where women have long been markedly committed to working in manufacturing industry, e.g. Angus, Cheshire, Lancashire, Leicester, Peebles, Selkirk
and the West Riding.

Since women tend more typically to seek employment in services, increase
in this sector may be found to underpin the pattern shown on fig. 5.2b.
Sector by sector[1] analysis of female employment has not yet been attempted,
however, so the relationship to services cannot be properly tested. Comparisons of fig. 5.2b with figs. 3.6a (increase in manufacturing) and 3.8 (changes
in service employment) are necessarily inconclusive.

Proportion of Female to Total Employment

Almost one-third of the employed population in 1961 were women. Areas
with more than the national mean by place of work were (i) Sussex, Surrey,
Middlesex, London and Hertfordshire in the south-east; (ii) a great ring
of counties enclosing but not including Derbyshire; (iii) Roxburgh,
Selkirk, Peebles, Midlothian and Lanark; (iv) Clackmannan, Perth and

[1] Primary, secondary and tertiary at least

Angus; (v) Armagh and Antrim in Northern Ireland, and (vi) Bute (fig. 5.3a). The highest proportion was in Selkirk, the lowest in Fermanagh. Among the coal-mining counties those in South Wales, northern England (Cumberland, Durham and Northumberland), several in Scotland (Fife, West Lothian and Ayrshire), and Derbyshire were absent from the top two categories. Fife, Durham, Derbyshire, Glamorgan and Monmouth were particularly low. The major agricultural counties of England, and sparsely peopled counties of Highland Britain were also low, and in some of them women made up less than a quarter of the employed population. Counties with large textile industries often figure in the highest category (Lancashire, Leicestershire, Selkirk and Angus).

It is clear, however, that no one determinant, certainly no single trend, governs the pattern shown on fig. 5.3a. It is a mosaic designed and laid by a different combination of forces in different areas. The mix of the economy, as in London, Surrey and Leicester, favours high female unemployment, whereas a dominant specialization may favour, as in Bute and Selkirk, or retard, as in many agricultural and mining districts. Traditional social behaviour is probably another factor. But to explain this pattern fully would require detailed local and historical analysis and would doubtless reveal important variations over quite short distances.

Nor is the map of the proportion of married women in employment (fig. 5.3b) open to a straightforward unitary explanation but it makes a thought-provoking comparison with fig. 5.3a. Here is an axial belt irrefutably aligned from south-east to north-west through England.[1] Apart from Derbyshire, all counties abutting a line from Beachy Head to Barrow in Furness have more than the national quota of married women in employment. Outside this axial belt only Selkirk, Clackmannan and Angus exceed the national norm.

No ready-made or simple explanation can be offered for this remarkably exclusive pattern. There are, however, some notable contrasts to be observed when figs. 5.3a and b are compared. In Northern Ireland women comprised 31·5 per cent of the employed population in 1961, almost reaching the national mean. Yet the proportion of married women was only 9·3 compared with the national mean of 16·3 per cent. In County Londonderry women and married women respectively were 30·8 and 6·9 per cent of the working population. In Scotland the respective figures were less divergent, 31·1 and 12·5 per cent, but still far apart. Durham (17·5 and 13·9), Glamorgan (27·6 and 13·0), and Monmouth (24·3 and 12·5) register parallel readings, a reduction in female employment below the national mean being accompanied by a nearly proportional reduction in the employment of married women.

[1] Taylor, E. G. R., op. cit., 1938

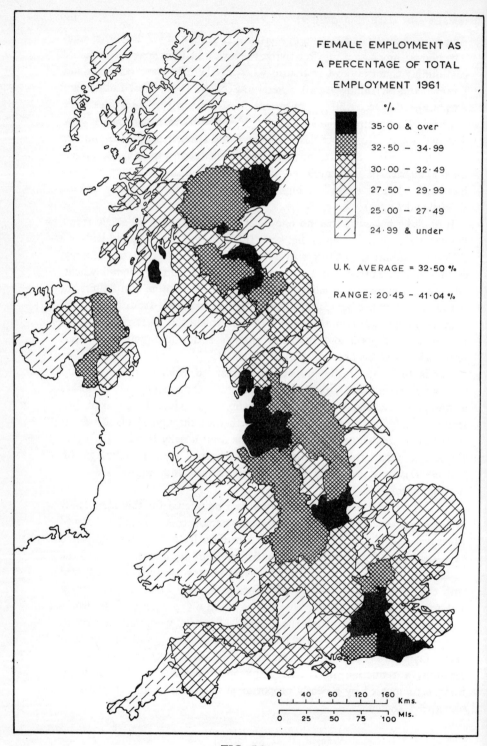

FEMALE EMPLOYMENT AS
A PERCENTAGE OF TOTAL
EMPLOYMENT 1961

%

35·00 & over

32·50 – 34·99

30·00 – 32·49

27·50 – 29·99

25·00 – 27·49

24·99 & under

U.K. AVERAGE = 32·50 %

RANGE: 20·45 – 41·04 %

FIG. 5.3a

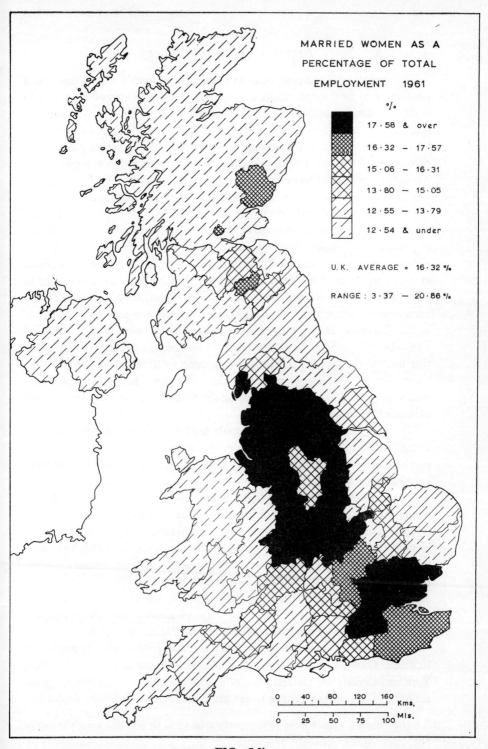

MARRIED WOMEN AS A
PERCENTAGE OF TOTAL
EMPLOYMENT 1961

%

17·58 & over

16·32 — 17·57

15·06 — 16·31

13·80 — 15·05

12·55 — 13·79

12·54 & under

U.K. AVERAGE = 16·32 %

RANGE : 3·37 — 20·86 %

0   40   80   120   160
                          Kms.
0   25   50   75   100
                          Mls.

FIG . 5.3b

Female Activity Rates

The foregoing discussion with its emphasis on female employment as a proportion of total employment is not a very good indicator of the extent to which available womanpower is taken into paid employment within the economy. The 'activity rate' is a device designed to overcome this defect at least in part. As applied to women it expresses the number employed as a percentage of the total female population over 15 years old in any given area. An upper age limit of 60 or 65 can be applied in making the calculations, but this restriction has not been imposed in preparing the maps that follow.

Official unemployment returns are reasonably accurate for men and reveal where reserves of male labour are to be found. The returns are quite inaccurate, however, as indicators of reserves of female labour. Female activity rates alone, therefore, are examined in this section. The data used are to be found in the occupation tables of the censuses and thus, unlike most other maps in this chapter which are based on the industry tables, they deal with female employment assessed specifically by place of residence and *not* by place of work. Moreover, it is useful here to distinguish between towns and rural areas. As defined here the latter, however, include 'urban areas' in England that have fewer than 50,000 people and those in Scotland with fewer than 10,000 people. The mapping criteria differ, therefore, between England and Wales on the one hand and Scotland on the other. Data for Northern Ireland have not been examined.

Fig. 5.4a shows the pattern of female activity rates in 1961 for towns in Great Britain. The mean for the country was 36·6 per cent, and three proportional grades are indicated on the map.[1] Towns with high activity rates are most frequent along the south-east to north-west axis in England. (London is examined separately on fig. 5.4b.) South Lancashire and West Yorkshire towns stand out clearly as pluses. Exceptions in Lancashire are Crosby, Southport and Blackpool, all on the coast, and Widnes. The solitary exception in the West Yorkshire conurbation is Wakefield. In the Midlands too, more towns register plus than zero, especially those in the Birmingham conurbation, and there are no minuses. The predominance of pluses recurs in the London area. The only towns in the Midlands, the North West, and the West Riding that register the lowest class of activity rate are Bebington, Rotherham and the Yorkshire coal-field towns, Doncaster and Barnsley.

Low rates are recorded in south Wales and also predominate in north-east England. Gloucester, Cheltenham, Worcester, Norwich, Oxford, Reading, York and Carlisle are marked plus, otherwise outside the axial belt the great majority of inland and coastal towns are marked zero or minus. Probably a

[1] *Hunt Report*, 1969. Figure 11 and paragraphs 58 to 60 take this topic forward to 1966

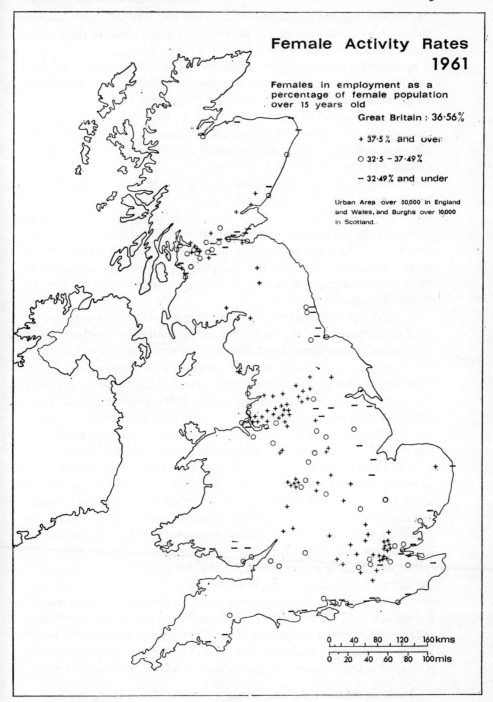

Female Activity Rates
1961

Females in employment as a
percentage of female population
over 15 years old

Great Britain : 36·56%

+ 37·5 % and over

O 32·5 – 37·49%

– 32·49% and under

Urban Area over 50,000 in England
and Wales, and Burghs over 10,000
in Scotland.

FIG. 5.4a

considerable number of the low-rated towns, and regional groups thereof, named above could substantially increase their contribution to the national product if more of their womenfolk could find employment.

Since the Scottish burghs have a different size range from towns in England and Wales on fig. 5.4a, they must be examined separately. Among the nine burghs with more than 50,000 people, five (Clydebank, Dundee, Edinburgh, Paisley and Glasgow) are marked plus. Nine smaller burghs[1] are in the same category but they are not concentrated in any particular locality of Scotland. The only localized group, including Paisley and Glasgow, is in the Clydeside district, but although Scotland as a whole has an activity rate nearly 2 per cent less than that for Great Britain and certainly far less than that for Lancashire and the West Riding (42 and 39 per cent respectively), it has a better rate than either south Wales or north-east England. The emphasis, however, of fig. 5.4a is more upon individual towns than upon regional groups thereof and it has practical value as an indication of the spatial reserve of urban womanpower that could be pin-pointed, assessed and brought into use if simple geographical techniques of analysis were applied properly by economic planners.[2]

Fig. 5.4b shows the urban pattern of female activity rates according to place of residence in and around London for 1961. All the former boroughs of the London County Council and Middlesex are represented as well as towns with more than 50,000 people in the surrounding area. The rate rises steadily inwards to reach a peak in Holborn (64 per cent), and the City (65 per cent). The lowest rate among L.C.C. boroughs occurs in Woolwich, and the lowest in Middlesex is at Southgate (38 per cent). Only four boroughs in Middlesex have less than 40 per cent. The two unnamed 'minus' urban areas are Gravesend which has predominantly male employing industries, and Epsom which is both wealthy and lacking in local opportunities for employment. It is, however, surprising that Esher, rather wealthier than Epsom to all appearances, has a clearly high activity rate for its female population. The explanation may be the presence of five mental hospitals with a total of about 3,500 female in-patients within the boundary of Epsom that add an unusual weighting to the statistics for the borough.

The very high figures in central London are probably a response to (a) the high proportion of young single women living there, (b) the family poverty that exists, paradoxically alongside wealthy institutions, in many central boroughs, and (c) the innumerable, wide-ranging opportunities for jobs that the metropolis presents, often close at hand. Poverty means that more married women especially will need to go out to work. Opportunity allows not only the poor to do so but it also entices those who are comfortably off to take employ-

---

[1] Dumfries, Forfar, Galashiels, Hamilton, Hawick, Irvine, Perth, Stirling and Dumbarton
[2] *The National Plan*, 1965. See pp. 36–39

Female Activity Rates:
London Area 1961

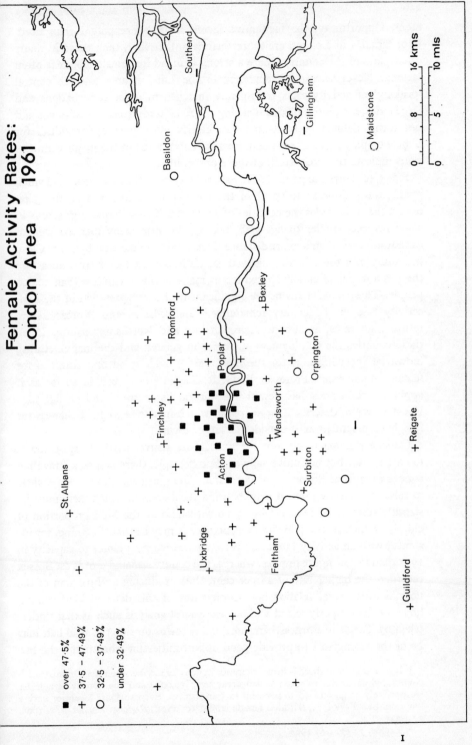

■ over 47·5%
+ 37·5 – 47·49%
○ 32·5 – 37·49%
| under 32·49%

St. Albans

Uxbridge

Finchley

Romford

Basildon

Southend

Acton

Poplar

Bexley

Gillingham.

Feltham

Wandsworth

Orpington

Surbiton

Guildford

Reigate

Maidstone

| 0   8   16 kms
| 0   5   10 mls

FIG. 5.4b

ment. Opportunity, the facilitative factor, is far more potent than need. Poor families in London are more fortunate, therefore, than those in many other parts of the country where a strong demand for female labour is often lacking. Nevertheless, the tendency in the London area towards central 'peaking' of activity rates is probably matched in other conurbations and large cities, for central places, meaning the retail trading centres of towns and not towns defined as built-up areas, clearly offer great opportunities for female employment. Census data for the central areas of the major conurbations indicate the likely truth of these observations.

Fig. 5.4c shows the pattern of female activity rates for rural areas and small towns, the residue so to speak of the country not considered on fig. 5.4a, except that it includes the counties of London and Middlesex. Fig. 5.4c is in some respects similar to fig. 5.3b, perhaps because many married women cannot go more than a short distance from home to take employment. Close proximity of a town is thus likely to be an important factor. In Lancashire there is a welter of closely spaced towns many of them with less than 50,000 people. These smaller towns are significant in the interpretation of the high activity rate in the county remainder.[1] Staffordshire and Worcestershire return high rates, as also do Leicestershire and Northamptonshire. In all these counties the employment structure in general and the manufacturing industrial specializations for the most part provide good opportunities for female employment. Professor E. G. R. Taylor's axial belt in so far as it applies to rural areas has slewed westward at its southern end on fig. 5.4c. But it serves to describe a large area in which moderate to good chances for female employment exist outside the larger towns.

Outside this axial belt jobs for women are scarce, partly because towns too are scarce, but not universally so. For example, there is now a straggling conurbation from Bognor to Seaford along the south coast but it does little to raise the activity rates of neighbouring rural areas in which there must be sizeable reserves of female labour, notwithstanding the high proportion of elderly women in the population structure. It may be that Worthing, for instance, with an activity rate of 23 per cent was working closer to capacity in 1961 than its low figure implies, whereas the county remainder of West Sussex recorded the higher rate of 28 per cent, thus producing an inversion of the normal urban-rural relationship. Conjectures of this detailed kind cannot, however, be properly tested without close local analysis such as that undertaken by Taylor in Furness.[2] In short, many towns outside the axial belt may be of the wrong sort to provide good opportunities for women and the raw

[1] It is notable that there is little difference in activity rate between the administrative county (which includes seven urban areas over 50,000) and the county remainder (respectively 40·44 and 40·36 per cent in Lancashire). Even so some localities have a low rate. See Taylor, J., 'Hidden female labour reserves', Regional Studies, 2, 2, 1968, 221–231

[2] Taylor, J., op. cit., 1968

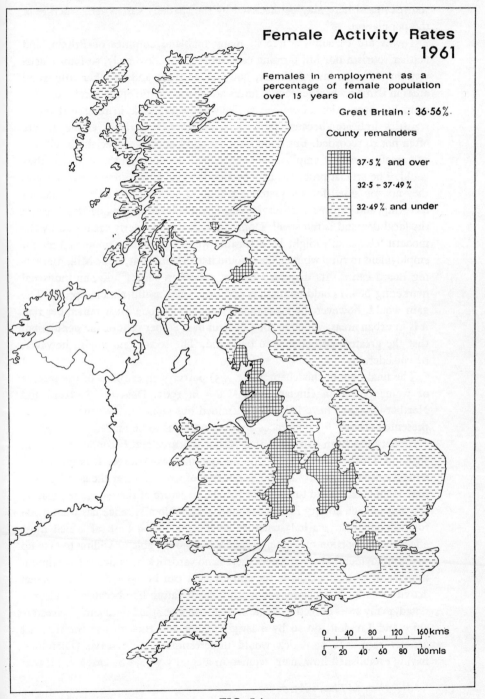

Female Activity Rates 1961

Females in employment as a percentage of female population over 15 years old

Great Britain : 36·56%

County remainders

37·5% and over

32·5 – 37·49%

32·49% and under

0   40   80   120   160 kms
0   20   40   60   80   100 mls

FIG. 5.4c

statistics used here may be distorted by the spatially varied age-structure of the population.

Towns are certainly scarce in many highland counties of Britain, and neither tourism nor hill farming can compensate adequately, so female activity rates remain low. Probably, however, in these and all other truly rural areas in Britain wherever family farms are characteristic of the rural economy, a smaller proportion of women is likely to be available in reserve than the statistics indicate, because farmers' wives though actively employed are often not so recorded. But there must be small pockets, especially in villages and small towns, of employable women who would gladly take jobs if they could. The crucial problems may be that the size of the groups is inefficient; they are too small for adequate economies of scale to be attained in manufacturing, and expansion of service employment is out of the question because the local demand is too small. Domestic industry, properly organized by the modern 'chapman', might be a feasible way of providing opportunities for employment to rural women. One would like to think that, if the Milk Marketing Board can do its dispersed task of collection successfully, an industrial marketing board could emulate it and bring in a useful national profit. The gain would, however, be economically modest for one must remember that it is in urban areas, which in total contain over 80 per cent of the population, that the greatest potential is to be found. The social gain might, however, be considerable.

The final map in this chapter (fig. 5.5) portrays an estimate of the reserve of womanpower in England and Wales in 1961. Data for Scotland and Northern Ireland have not been examined but sufficient evidence has been presented already for inferences about these areas to be made.

Anxiety has been expressed that labour is scarce and becoming scarcer in Britain.[1] This is substantially true for the male work-force. It is untrue for female employment. To assess the reserves of womanpower the activity rates have been recalculated to allow for the age structure of the female population resident in each county in England and Wales. No allowance has been made for differences in marital structure or income levels, both of which must affect the proportion of women in any area who are able or willing to take up paid employment. Unfortunately there is no yardstick by which the maximum number of women available for employment can be assessed. The national activity rate itself is clearly not a satisfactory datum line because, as already noted, many areas exceed it. Some of them, for example Lancashire, Leicestershire and London, do so by a large amount and thus to use the national activity rate as a yardstick would underestimate the reserve. Therefore, having established how many women in a county would be employed if that

---

[1]   (i) National Plan, 1965, p. 36
      (ii) Paradoxically, immigration which might have eased the scarcity of labour has been greatly restricted

county followed the national pattern of employment age-group by age-group, one must estimate how many women might be employed there if appropriate opportunities were available.

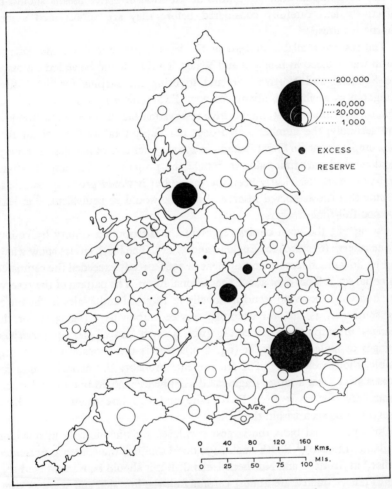

FIG. 5.5   Estimated reserve of womanpower, 1961

The estimate is based on a far lower level of attainment than that obtaining in London, where the highest activity rate of any county (33 per cent above the national rate) is to be found. To apply this level of attainment throughout the United Kingdom would yield a total reserve of at least 2,500,000 women. Furthermore, to use the excess reached in Lancashire (16 per cent), Leicestershire (17 per cent), Warwickshire or Middlesex (both 18 per cent) as a yardstick would also yield too optimistic a total. The level reached in three counties, Northamptonshire, Staffordshire and Worcestershire, has been adopted as a ceiling. These three exceed the national norm by a modest 8 per cent, the opinion being that this figure should be attainable if the economy were run with moderate regard for geographical efficiency within the general context of national economic management. Geographical efficiency here implies that the *spatial* distribution of scarce means should be effectively and carefully considered before they are apportioned among alternative uses.[1]

The reserve available in 1961 at the level 8 per cent above the national norm was 610,000 in England and Wales. To this should be added estimates for Scotland and Northern Ireland to bring the surplus for the United Kingdom as a whole to about 800,000. Two reservations should be noted about this estimate: first, the positive reservation that it could be far too low, and secondly, the number stated does not imply total availability for full-time employment. In Great Britain, in 1961, 25 per cent of females in employment worked part-time, almost double the proportion obtaining in 1951.[2] Part-time work has clearly been increasing but it would probably be safe to assume that the estimated reserve of 800,000 would be equivalent to at least 400,000 full-time workers.

On fig. 5.5 the open circles represent the distribution county by county of the reserve (610,000) for England and Wales. The black circles show where and by how much female employment in 1961 already exceeded the estimated potential set at 8 per cent above the national norm. The pattern of the reserve (open circles) shows no trend nationally in England and Wales in favour of the south-east as did, for example, service employment (fig. 3.1c) or the changes in employment structure (figs. 3.2a, b and c), or, *par excellence*, changes in male employment (fig. 5.1a). Nor is the opposite trend clearly visible, though elements of it are present. Probably the national trend increases away from a rather fragmented axial belt anchored upon London and Lancashire, for apart from Derbyshire and Cheshire there are no large reserves to be seen within the belt.

On a provincial basis the largest surpluses are undoubtedly in northern England (120,000),[3] South Wales (90,000)[4] and, on the evidence presented earlier,[5] in Scotland and Northern Ireland. But it should be remembered that the estimates quoted are almost certainly on the low side and serve as com-

[1] (i) Robbins, L., *An Essay on the Nature and Significance of Economic Science*, 1946, p. 16

    (ii) Hartshorne, R., *Perspective on the Nature of Geography*, 1959
If one combines Lord Robbins' definition of economics with Hartshorne's of geography, economic geography then becomes 'the study of the variable character from place to place over the earth's surface of human behaviour as a relationship between ends and scarce means which have alternative uses'. In the broad fields of national economic management and planning the findings that result from the study of economic geography can both clarify problems and guide the action needed for their solution
[2] In Scotland there were 17 per cent in 1961 and only 6 per cent in 1951
[3] Cumberland, Durham, Northumberland and the North Riding
[4] Brecknock, Carmarthen, Monmouth and Glamorgan
[5] See discussion of fig. 5.3a and b

parative indications of *relative* reserves rather than as measures of actual potential. Since they are probably low, however, there is little doubt that they could be realized in an effectively planned and expanding economy.

The Development Areas are not alone in having reserves. There were 37,000 in the East Riding and Lindsey combined, showing how Yorkshire and Humberside as an Economic Planning Region has internal variations which in turn must exist within the West Riding too.[1] And one can infer from these observations, apparent even at this large scale, that small-scale local analysis would reveal far larger reserves than are predicted here. Even in areas such as Lancashire[2] and the West Riding, which seem virtually saturated at a county level of analysis, substantial reserves would be found in some localities.

There are sizeable surpluses too in the 'grey' areas of East Anglia and the south-west,[3] and in the prosperous areas of the south and south-east, e.g. 59,000 in Devon, Somerset and Dorset; 44,000 in Hampshire; 33,000 in Gloucestershire and Wiltshire; 34,000 in Norfolk and East Suffolk; 27,000 in Essex, and 42,000 in Kent. The pinpointing of compact local pockets within these and other areas would be more significant than these county findings for the distribution of industry policy (formerly of the Board of Trade now of the Department of Trade and Industry) which, it is to be hoped, will before long be strengthened to apply to all branches of employment and not to manufacturing alone. But the county estimates suggest that present policy might beneficially be changed so that Industrial Development Certificates (I.D.C.) can be granted liberally to firms that will guarantee to employ many more women than men in appropriate places outside as well as within Development Areas.[4]

These findings with regard to the use of womanpower during the 1950s show that a state of full employment was never reached save in terms of a male-oriented and non-spatial model of the national economy. Spatial economic variations of the labour factor of production, especially those relating to the female labour supply, should be examined far more carefully as an aid to future national economic management than they have been in the past.

[1] Chapter 5, p. 104 and footnote 2
[2] Taylor, J., *op. cit.*, 1968
[3] *A Region with a Future*, South West Economic Planning Council, 1967, paragraphs 102–104
[4] The *Hunt Report*, 1969, recommends relaxation of I.D.C. control (paragraphs 482–491) on different grounds and for a different purpose

6

Newcomers: The Distribution of the Overseas Born

Immigration into the United Kingdom is a long-standing feature which has attracted particular attention since the mid-fifties. Interest has been heightened by both a change in the volume of migration and a change in the composition of immigrants. For more than 100 years prior to the 1930s the United Kingdom was a net loser by migration. In the case of England and Wales this trend was reversed from 1931 to 1946, then resumed up to the mid-fifties, when it was again reversed. Immigration prior to the mid-fifties was, however, on a substantial scale, with migrants mostly drawn from the continent of Europe.[1] Many of them entered the United Kingdom as refugees. Since 1955 the intake has exceeded the outflow and immigrants have been mainly from the New Commonwealth, particularly the West Indies, India and Pakistan, but also Cyprus, Malta and East and West Africa. For the first time, therefore, many immigrants were coloured. The Commonwealth Immigrants Act came into force on 1 July 1962 and since then immigration from the Commonwealth has consisted of fewer males of working age and an increasing proportion of women and children (table 6.1). The impact of the 1962 Act can also be judged from table 6.2 which reflects the great surge in immigration in 1961 and 1962, when many thousands of Commonwealth citizens attempted to 'beat the ban'.

Largely as a result of this most recent incursion, itself characterized by considerable numbers of coloured immigrants, the subjects of immigration into and of immigrants within the United Kingdom have become items of day-to-day interest and concern to politicians, educationalists, economists, sociologists, doctors and geographers. National and local politicians are concerned with the provision of services to newcomers drawn from widely

---

[1] See Isaac, J., 'British post-war migration', *National Institute of Economic and Social Research, Occasional Papers, XVII*, 1954, and Tannahill, J. A., *European Volunteer Workers in Britain*, 1958

TABLE 6.1* (a) Voucher holders arriving in the United Kingdom, 1962–7

From:	1962	1963	1964	1965	1966	1967	Total
India and Pakistan	1,040	21,890	7,120	6,310	3,150	2,930	42,440
Caribbean	1,600	1,390	820	280	60	30	3,220
All Commonwealth	5,120	30,130	14,705	12,880	5,460	4,930	73,270

(b) Dependants arriving in the United Kingdom, 1962–7

From:	1962	1963	1964	1965	1966	1967	Total
India	1,560	6,620	8,770	12,800	13,340	15,820	58,910
Pakistan	500	3,300	7,050	6,760	9,320	17,500	44,430
Caribbean	890	7,890	11,460	11,150	9,870	11,210	55,310
All Commonwealth	8,830	26,230	37,460	41,210	42,030	52,310	208,570

* After E. J. B. Rose, Colour and Citizenship, 1969, 86 and 88

TABLE 6.2† England and Wales: estimated net intake (+) or outflow (−) of categories of migrant, mid-1959 to mid-1964

Year ending 30 June	On foreign passports	On passports of overseas Commonwealth countries	By direct U.K. traffic with Irish Republic	From the rest of the U.K.	On U.K. passport beyond the U.K. and Irish Republic	Net migration ooos
1960	+30	+ 66	+32	+24	− 44	+108
1961	+20	+120	+35	+29	− 46	+158
1962	+20	+185	+32	+30	− 42	+225
1963	+20	+ 47	+30	+32	− 79	+ 50
1964	+30	+ 83	+28	+31	−120	+ 52

† Registrar General's Statistical Review of England and Wales 1963, Part III, Commentary, 1966, 35

124 NEWCOMERS: THE DISTRIBUTION OF THE OVERSEAS BORN

differing backgrounds, with the emergence of discrimination against coloured immigrants and with the feared backlash of the white electorate.[1] Educationalists are grappling with the many problems of training children drawn from very diverse backgrounds. Because of the particular distribution of the overseas born, the local education authorities are often handicapped by the Plowden-like environments in which many of the 'immigrant' schools are placed.[2] Economists are examining the contribution which the immigrants are making to the balance of payments and to the work-force, and their willingness to work shifts, long hours and, in many instances, to save hard in order to start their own businesses.[3] The concentration of immigrants in large numbers in relatively small areas of the country gives the sociologist an opportunity to examine how the pattern of life changes and how the conflicts, pressures and compromises are expressed in the community. Medical workers have a practical as well as academic interest in the morbidity patterns and health requirements of the immigrant population.[4] Geographers and others are studying the actual distribution of immi-

[1] There are several studies dealing with these topics. For instance, Deakin, N. (ed.), *Colour and the British Electorate 1964*, 1965; Deakin, N., 'The politics of the Commonwealth Immigrants Bill', *Political Quarterly*, **39**, 1968; Foot, P., *Immigration and race in British Politics*, 1965; Lester, A., and Deakin, N. (eds.), *Policies for Racial Equality*, 1967; Rex, J., 'The race relations catastrophe', in *Matters of Principle: Labour's Last Chance*, 1968, 'The social segregation of the immigrant in British cities', *Political Quarterly*, January–March 1968; Deakin, N. D. *et al.*, 'Colour and the 1966 general election', *Race*, July 1966; and Hindell, K., 'The genesis of the race relations bill', in Rose, R. (ed.), *Policy-making in Britain: a Reader in Government*, 1969

[2] The education of immigrant children has attracted particular attention in recent years. See, Department of Education and Science, *English for Immigrants*, Pamphlet no. 43, 1963; Hawkes, N., *Immigrant Children in British Schools*, 1966; Power, J., *Immigrants in School: a Survey of Administrative Policies*, 1967; Derrick, June, *English for the Children of Immigrants*, Schools Council Working Paper No. 13, 1967; Burgin, P. and Edson, P., *Spring Grove: the Education of Immigrant Children*, 1967; Beetham, D., *Immigrant School Leavers and the Youth Employment Service in Birmingham*, 1968; Bagley, C., 'The educational performance of immigrant children', *Race*, July 1968; and Butterworth, E., 'The presence of immigrant schoolchildren: a study of Leeds', *Race*, January 1967

[3] Published studies are also generally concerned with the subjects of discrimination and opportunity. See, for instance, Wright, P., *The Coloured Worker in British Industry*, 1968; Radin, B., 'Coloured workers and British Trade Unions', *Race*, October 1966; Patterson, S., *Immigrants in Industry*, 1968; Bayliss, F. J. and Coates, J. B., 'West Indians at work in Nottingham', *Race*, October 1965; Cohen, B. and Jenner, P., 'The employment of immigrants: a case study within the wool industry', *Race*, July 1968; and Mishan, E. J. and Needleham, L., 'Immigration: long-run economic effects', *Lloyds Bank Review*, January 1968

[4] See, for example, the following studies: British Medical Association, *Medical Examination of Immigrants: Report of the Working Party*, 1965; Wolstenholme, G. E. W. and O'Connor, M., *Immigration, Medical and Social Aspects*, 1966; Jones, K., 'Immigrants and the social services', *National Institute Economic Review*, August 1967; Waterhouse, J. A. H. and Brabban, D. H., 'Inquiry into fertility of immigrants: preliminary report', *The Eugenics Review*, April 1964; Yudkin, S., *The Health and Welfare of the Immigrant Child*, 1965; Parry, W. H., 'Immigration in Sheffield', *The Medical Officer*, 22 September 1966; Edgar, W., 'Tuberculosis among Pakistanis in Britain', *Race*, 6; and Kiev, Ari, 'Psychiatric illness among West Indians in London', *Race*, January 1964

grants, their degree of dispersal or concentration through time and the way in which these patterns are related to the socio-economic geography of the country.[1]

Data

By far the most important sources are the Censuses of Population of England and Wales, Scotland and Northern Ireland for the years 1951, 1961 and 1966, the latter being the first census taken in mid-decade and the first taken in its entirety on a sample basis. For this reason it is less reliable than the others, not because a statistically sound sample cannot be devised but rather because the enumerators are in practice so much freer to build in results which reflect their fallibilities. The 1966 Sample Census might be particularly vulnerable with regard to the enumeration of the overseas-born population and especially its coloured component. Given that the West Indian immigrants were so markedly under-enumerated in 1961[2] it would be surprising if the results of a 10 per cent sample were any better. In fact, it is thought that 35 per cent of the Pakistanis resident in England and Wales in 1966 were not enumerated.[3] Whether the extent of these and other under-enumerations are the same from place to place is not known. Enumeration is probably particularly bad among those whose housing conditions and working hours are unorthodox, and among those living in small households.

There are many deficiencies in the data. The most obvious is the variability in the data collected by the three Registrars-General, both in the same census year and between censuses. Comparison thus becomes difficult and at times impossible. A more important deficiency is the variability in the data given in the General and County Reports of the Censuses. For instance, the 1961 Census of England and Wales and the Census of Scotland recorded the number of males and females born outside the British Isles residing in each admini-

[1] For instance, Davison, R. B., 'The distribution of immigrant groups in London', *Race*, 5; Peach, G. C. K., 'Factors affecting the distribution of West Indians in Great Britain', *Transactions, Institute of British Geographers*, June 1966, 'West Indians as a replacement population in England and Wales', *Social and Economic Studies*, Sept. 1967, and *West Indian Migration to Britain*, 1968; Coates, B. E., 'The distribution of the overseas-born population of the British Isles', *Transactions, Institute of British Geographers*, April 1968; and Jones, P. N., 'The segregation of the immigrant communities in the City of Birmingham, 1961', *University of Hull, Occasional Papers in Geography*, 7, 1967

[2] Peach, G. C. K. in 'Underenumeration of West Indians in the 1961 Census', *Sociological Review*, March 1966, 73–80, suggests that low returns were made by the West Indians because of their desire to conceal the overcrowding in their living conditions from the authorities. After examining non-census material on migration, Peach concludes that the 1961 Census under-estimated the West Indian born population in the United Kingdom by at least 20 per cent

[3] See Rose, E. J. B. *et al.*, *Colour and Citizenship*, 1969, 774–775, and Appendix III, 4, where it is calculated that in 1966 the minimum under-enumeration was 16,800 'brown' Indians, 41,900 'brown' Pakistanis, 50,000 immigrants from the Caribbean and 7,100 British West Africans

strative area down to the level of the rural district (county district in Scotland). Yet the most detailed information relates only to those administrative areas which contained no fewer than 2,000 overseas-born residents.

There are more fundamental limitations. First, no census authority in the United Kingdom records information on the pigmentation and racial composition of its population. Consequently it is not known, for instance, how many indigenous West Indians, Indians or Pakistanis were resident in the United Kingdom at the time of the 1951, 1961 and 1966 Censuses. In 1961, for example, it would be incorrect to assume that the 188,172 persons then recorded as being born in India and Pakistan, but resident in England and Wales, were Indians and Pakistanis. In fact, Table 2 of the *Birthplace and Nationality Tables* (Census, 1961, England and Wales) reveals that no fewer than 81,748 of these persons were citizens of the United Kingdom and its Colonies 'by birth and descent'. By using such additional evidence on nationality, it would be possible to gain a more realistic picture of the spatial distribution of Indians and Pakistanis. Unfortunately, this particular evidence is available only for England and Wales together, though the aggregate of persons born in specified countries who were citizens of the United Kingdom and its Colonies (whether by 'birth or descent, by registration or marriage, by naturalization or by a mode of acquisition not stated') is given for the Standard Regions. Even if such information were available for counties, county and metropolitan boroughs and other administrative areas lower in the hierarchy, the use of nationality as a criterion for the definition of categories of persons born overseas would create formidable problems of interpreting the precise meaning of citizenship and complex constitutional relationships. For example, there were 100,051 Jamaican-born persons resident in England and Wales in 1961. Of these, 88,896 were classified as citizens of the United Kingdom and its Colonies, a further 11,021 failed to state their nationality on their returns, 52 were citizens of Commonwealth Countries and the Irish Republic, and only 82 were classified as aliens. In fact, there is little or no evidence in the 1961 Census to indicate how many of the immigrants were indigenous West Indians and how many were the offspring of 'white' parents born in the United Kingdom. Similarly, the composition of the immigrant population from India and Pakistan reflects the Indian-born offspring of a large number of British nationals involved in the administration and control of the Indian sub-continent before it was granted independence in 1947.

The second major structural weakness of the British census material is that the children born in these islands are naturally recorded as British born, irrespective of the birthplace, nationality or race of their parents. This means that it is impossible to accurately determine from the census either the actual size of a given 'immigrant group', that is that part of the overseas born from a particular country together with their British-born offspring, or the pattern of its distribution. It also follows that such important characteristics of the 'immigrant groups' as their age and sex structure, fertility and mortality rates, employment and occupations cannot be accurately ascertained from the census.[1] An important consequence is that the size of any particular group is a matter of speculation and it is not possible authoritatively to refute or confirm the guesses which are frequently made and reported in public. It is the Registrars-General who decide the form of the censuses. Some of the inadequacies noted above will, one hopes, be rectified, thus making possible a more thorough analysis of the immigrant population. In the meantime, the available census material must be used with care and its limitations understood in any attempt at interpretation. The following analysis is, therefore, restricted to a study of those persons born outside the British Isles (thus excluding the three-quarters of a million U.K. residents born in the Republic of Ireland), whatever their parentage or nationality might be, and thus *irrespective of colour.*

Distribution, 1951–66

Figs. 6.1, a, b and c show the distribution by geographical county of persons born overseas and resident in this country in 1951, 1961 and 1966. Visitors are excluded, as are those residents who failed to state their birthplace. Only counties with 1,000 or more overseas born are shown. By 1966 the Union

---

[1] *The Commonwealth Immigrant Tables*, 1969, of the *1966 Sample Census: Great Britain* contains demographic, social and economic information about residents in Great Britain who gave as their birthplace any Commonwealth country outside the British Isles. The tables distinguish between the 'Old Commonwealth', that is, Australia, New Zealand and Canada, and the 'New Commonwealth' which is all other Commonwealth countries. In a few of the tables those born in the following areas are treated separately – Australia and New Zealand, Canada, India, Pakistan, Hong Kong, British Caribbean, Cyprus, Malta, Kenya, Rhodesia, other Commonwealth countries in Africa, and all other Commonwealth countries combined. All but five of the eighteen tables cover everyone born in the Commonwealth outside the British Isles, including 'white' Indians and Pakistanis. In an attempt to discover how many children have been born in Great Britain to Commonwealth immigrants the other five tables cover all the people who were enumerated in households of which the head or the wife of the head was born in one of the countries specified above. Here, however, there is the curious situation where the children born to 'white' Indians and Pakistanis are included whereas people who were born in the specified countries but were in households where neither the head of the households nor the wife of the head was born in the specified countries are excluded.

One would expect *The Commonwealth Immigrant Tables* to be a gold-mine of information. But for anyone interested in the distribution of immigrants at the level of the counties and county boroughs they are very limited in their coverage. Only in one of the eighteen tables are data given at this level. Seven refer to Great Britain as a whole and there is no regional breakdown. Even at the conurbation level much of the information is missing – only in four tables are the recognized conurbations treated separately and eleven give data for the Greater London and West Midlands Conurbations. Though the latter are undoubtedly the most important immigrant areas within Great Britain, the lumping together of the other conurbations for statistical purposes seriously limits the usefulness of seven of the tables

of South Africa was a Republic and no longer a member of the Commonwealth. For purposes of comparison, therefore, South Africa has been transferred from the Commonwealth, Colonies and Protectorates list to the Foreign Countries list in both 1961 and 1951. It will be noted that the proportion of immigrants resident in London and Middlesex born in foreign countries is shaded differently. This is an attempt to give due visual weight to the importance of the proportional circles for London and Middlesex and the Home Counties.

1951 (fig. 6.1a)

2·1 per cent of the United Kingdom's population of just under 50·25 million was born overseas. The dominance of London and the South East is apparent. Forty per cent of all the overseas born were in the South Eastern Standard Region, which contained 22 per cent of the total population. London and Middlesex alone had more than one-quarter of all the immigrants in the United Kingdom. Outside the South East there are two sizeable outliers in Lancashire and the West Riding. Most English counties had several thousand immigrants. In 1951 there were more overseas born in Hampshire than Warwickshire, more in Essex than Wales and more in Lancashire than Scotland. In fact, many Welsh and Scottish counties had fewer than 1,000 immigrants.

In every county, except Hampshire, over half and often over threequarters of the overseas born were from foreign countries. In the United Kingdom as a whole there were 101,000 German-born, 37,000 Italians, 162,000 Poles, 81,000 Soviets and 64,000 Americans. The smaller numbers from the Commonwealth, Colonies and Protectorates included 55,000 Canadians, 46,000 Australians and New Zealanders, 119,000 Indians, only 16,000 Caribbean-born and a mere 12,000 Pakistanis.

1961 (fig. 6.1b)

By 1961 the overseas born top the $1\frac{1}{2}$ million mark and form 2·86 per cent of the United Kingdom's population. London and the South East were even more dominant than in 1951 with 830,000 overseas born in what is now the South East Economic Planning Region. The distribution in England was most uneven. There were fewer overseas born in County Durham (population $1\frac{1}{2}$ million) than in Huntingdonshire and the Soke of Peterborough (population 150,000).

The national increase in the proportion from the Commonwealth, Colonies and Protectorates was most marked regionally in those counties particularly attractive to recent immigrants. There were dramatic swings in Staffordshire, Warwickshire, London and Middlesex. On the other hand, there was rela-

DISTRIBUTION IN 1951,1961 & 1966 OF UNITED KINGDOM RESIDENTS WITH STATED BIRTHPLACE OUTSIDE THE BRITISH ISLES

TOTAL NUMBER OF OVERSEAS BORN RESIDENT IN

UNITED KINGDOM	1951 :	1,053,200
	1961 :	1,507,600
	1966:	1,876,300
LONDON & MIDDLESEX	1951 :	277,500
	1961 :	463,500
GREATER LONDON	1966:	684,800

OVERSEAS BORN FROM

FOREIGN COUNTRIES
[including Union of
South Africa] &
BORN AT SEA

COMMONWEALTH, COLONIES
AND PROTECTORATES
[excluding Union of
South Africa]

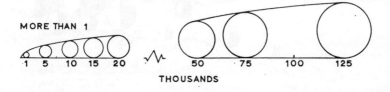

MORE THAN 1

1 5 10 15 20   50 75 100 125

THOUSANDS

FIG. 6.1

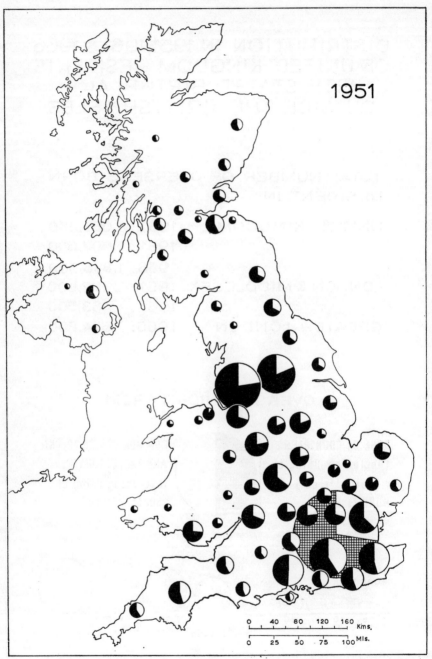

FIG. 6.1a

FIG. 6.1b

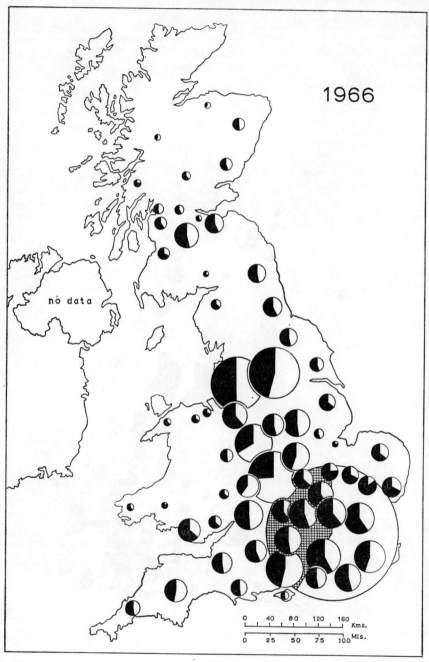

FIG. 6.1c

tively little change in the South West, east-coast counties and Scotland. Indeed, the swing in Norfolk and Suffolk was in the other direction.

1966 (fig. 6.1c)

3·5 per cent of the United Kingdom's population was born overseas.[1] Fifty-six per cent of the 1·88 million are in the South East, compared with its 32 per cent share of the total United Kingdom population. No other Economic Planning Region contains 10 per cent of the United Kingdom's overseas born and many counties still have fewer than 1,000 overseas born. The high degree of concentration in the South East and more especially in the Greater London Council area is illustrated by the following comparisons. There are more overseas born in the Metropolitan Boroughs of Brent or Camden or Lambeth than in Wales (37,400) or Northern (38,800); more in the Borough of Kensington and Chelsea than Surrey (45,500); more in Westminster than Staffordshire (50,100), and more in Westminster and Kensington and Chelsea than in Warwickshire, including Birmingham (95,600), or the West Riding (96,800) or the South West Economic Planning Region (99,800) and only 5,000 fewer than in Lancashire (106,700).

The proportion of the overseas born from foreign countries is now down to 48 per cent. It is less than one-half in Greater London, the West Riding, Worcestershire, Leicestershire, Hampshire and Kent, down to one-third in Staffordshire and as low as one-quarter in Warwickshire. For the most part districts where it is still more than one-half are those which have attracted relatively few immigrants from India, Pakistan and the Caribbean, e.g. Wales, the Northern Region, Scotland and East Anglia.

Change, 1951–66

Change in the proportion of the overseas born drawn from the Commonwealth, Colonies and Protectorates has been referred to above. Major changes in absolute numbers and in geographical distribution can be discerned from a comparative study of figs. 6.1a, b and c but they are shown more precisely on figs. 6.2a and b. It should be noted that the same scale and symbolization is used for 1951–61 and 1961–6 even though the time-scale is reduced by half.[2]

---

[1] The question on 'place of birth' was omitted from the 1966 Sample Census of Northern Ireland. There is no non-census evidence that suggests there was a great influx of immigrants into Northern Ireland in the 1960s

[2] London and Middlesex are combined in fig. 6.2a for cartographic reasons, whereas the G.L.C., Surrey and Kent are combined in fig. 6.2b owing to the creation of the G.L.C. in 1964 and the difficulties arising therefrom in attempting to compare data for 1966 with those for 1961

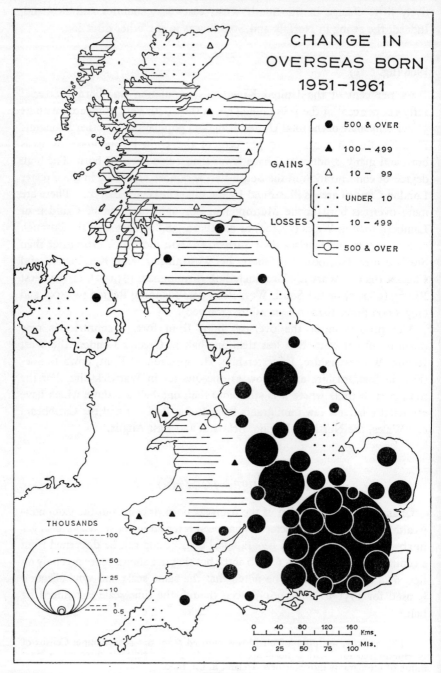

CHANGE IN
OVERSEAS BORN
1951–1961

GAINS
● 500 & OVER
▲ 100 – 499
△ 10 – 99
⋮ UNDER 10

LOSSES
— 10 – 499
⊖ 500 & OVER

THOUSANDS
100
50
25
10
1
0.5

0 40 80 120 160 Kms.
0 25 50 75 100 Mls.

FIG. 6.2a

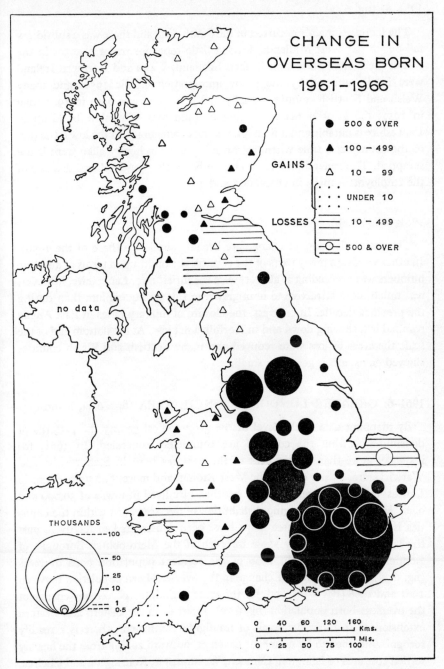

FIG. 6.2b   The G.L.C., Kent and Surrey are aggregated because of extensive boundary changes in 1964

1951–61 (fig. 6.2a)

The increases mainly occurred in the South-East and there was a subsidiary fall-out in the West Midlands, leaving little room for major changes in the rest of the United Kingdom. In fact, Scotland, Wales and Northern Ireland were hardly affected by the heavy immigration of the 1950s and many Welsh and Scottish counties actually had fewer overseas born in 1961 than in 1951; the greatest net loss being in Flintshire. The slow build-up in Lancashire is notable and it is an interesting commentary on the low attraction of the county at a time when cotton mills and machinery alike were being scrapped. The general pattern of change bears close resemblance to some of the employment maps in chapters 3 and 4.

1961–6 (fig. 6.2b)

The major elements of change are broadly similar to those of the 1950s. In other words, in many parts of the country the build-up in terms of absolute numbers was proceeding at almost twice the fifties' rate. Lancashire, however, was much more attractive to immigrants in this quinquennium than during the previous decade. In contrast, the closure of military bases in East Anglia resulted in a slowing down and in Norfolk a net loss. At the bottom end of the scale the areas of loss were reduced and many Scottish and Welsh counties showed gains, albeit generally small.

1961–6: GREATER LONDON COUNCIL AREA (figs. 6.3a, b and c)

By mapping data at the level of the geographical county the patterns of distribution within the counties are completely concealed. In 1961, for instance, more than 90 per cent of the overseas born in Staffordshire and Warwickshire, 85 per cent in the West Riding, and more than 75 per cent in Lancashire, Nottinghamshire and Bedfordshire lived in towns of 50,000 and over. Moreover, the changing distribution of overseas born within the counties is also concealed. Three maps have been constructed to rectify in part the latter weakness. They show for each of the Metropolitan Boroughs of London the percentage in 1966 of the resident population born overseas (fig. 6.3a), the magnitude of change in the overseas-born population between 1961 and 1966 (fig. 6.3b), and, for the same period, the percentage change of the overseas-born population (fig. 6.3c). Apart from the eastern and western extensions with their low levels of immigrant settlement, there is a readily recognizable, though by no means constant, outward zoning from the heavily settled core area of Islington, Camden, Westminster, Kensington and Chelsea, and Brent, each with an overseas-born component of between 15 and 25 per cent. Of these boroughs only Brent had a rate of increase between 1961 and 1966 higher than the Greater London Council average. In fact, as fig. 6.3c

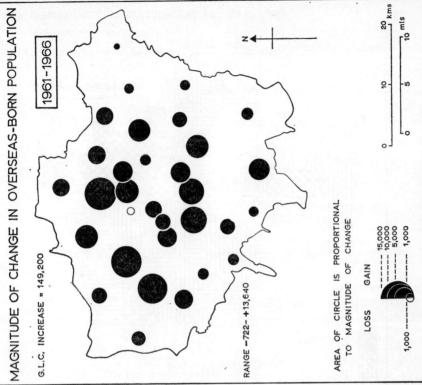

MAGNITUDE OF CHANGE IN OVERSEAS-BORN POPULATION

1961–1966

G.L.C. INCREASE = 149,200

RANGE −722 − +13,640

AREA OF CIRCLE IS PROPORTIONAL TO MAGNITUDE OF CHANGE

LOSS   GAIN

15,000
10,000
5,000
1,000

1,000

N

0   10   20 kms
0   5   10 mls

FIG. 6.3b   Boroughs of Greater London Council

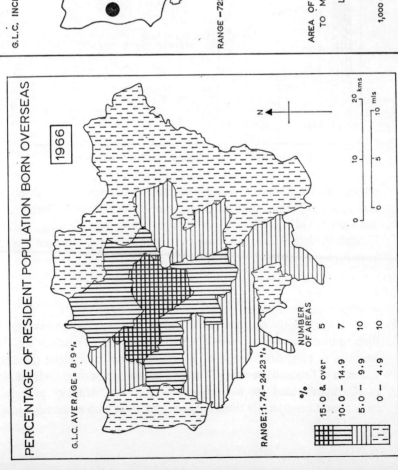

PERCENTAGE OF RESIDENT POPULATION BORN OVERSEAS

1966

G.L.C. AVERAGE = 8·9 %

RANGE: 1·74 − 24·23 %

%	NUMBER OF AREAS
15·0 & over	5
10·0 − 14·9	7
5·0 − 9·9	10
0 − 4·9	10

N

0   10   20 kms
0   5   10 mls

FIG. 6.3a   Greater London Council

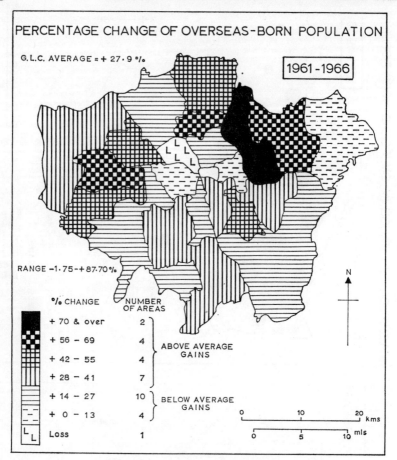

FIG. 6.3c   Greater London Council

shows, the highest rates of increase occurred to the west and north-east of the core area. In absolute numbers the increases were greatest in Haringey, Brent and Ealing, whilst the outermost boroughs, apart from Croydon, Barnet and Hounslow, were among those with the lowest increases. Camden was unique in returning a net loss.

Density, 1961 (fig. 6.4)

Well over half the counties of the United Kingdom have on average fewer than 10 immigrants per square kilometre. There are no counties with higher densities in Northern Ireland or Wales, only one in Scotland (Midlothian) and even in England the South West and the east-coast counties from Norfolk to Northumberland are extensive areas with low densities of immigrant settlement. Consequently there are only four areas with an average density of

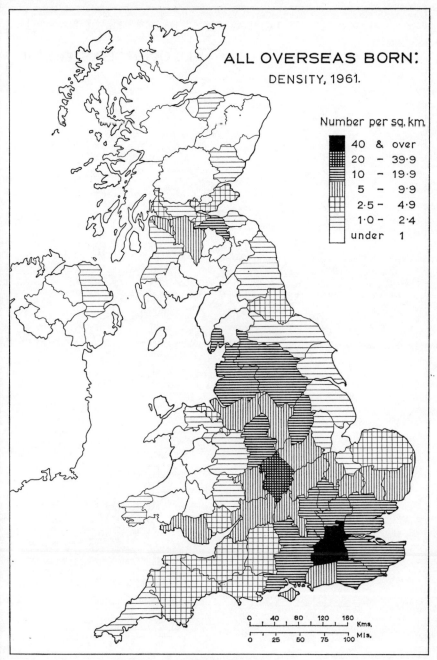

ALL OVERSEAS BORN:
DENSITY, 1961.

Number per sq. km.

40 & over
20 - 39·9
10 - 19·9
5 - 9·9
2·5 - 4·9
1·0 - 2·4
under 1

FIG. 6.4

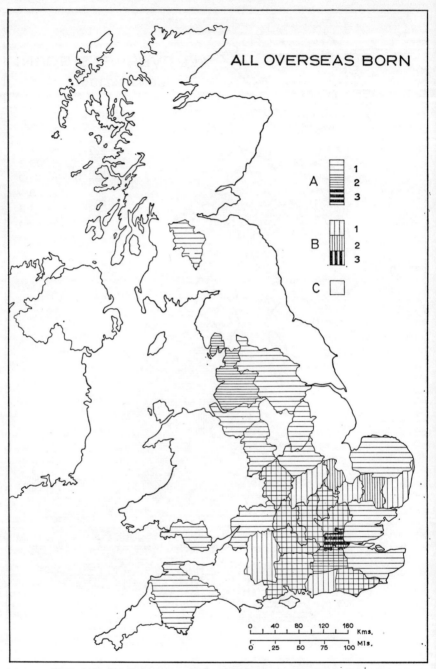

FIG. 6.5   See fig. 6.8, p. 158, for definition of categories A, B and C

10 and over – Midlothian; Lancashire, the West Riding and Nottinghamshire; Staffordshire and Warwickshire, and a block in the South East (excluding West Sussex). Parts of the two southern areas rise above 20 (Warwickshire) and above 40 (London and Middlesex and Surrey).

Dispersal 1961 (fig. 6.5)

The distribution of the overseas born is not simply a mirror image of the distribution of the total population. For instance, Durham contains 2·9 per cent of the total population of the United Kingdom but only 0·7 per cent of its overseas born; the proportions in Staffordshire are 3·3 and 2·4, in Glamorgan 2·3 and 1·2 and in Glasgow and Lanark 3·1 and 1·4. In contrast, London and Middlesex encompass 10·3 per cent of the United Kingdom's population and 30·7 of all its overseas-born residents. Only two other counties – Lancashire and Surrey – have more than 5 per cent of the overseas born and relatively few counties reach the 1 per cent level (A Areas). Most of the latter are in a belt from Lancashire and the West Riding to Hampshire and Kent. Even within this belt there are important gaps in Derbyshire, Northamptonshire and West Sussex.

Few counties enumerate a higher share of the overseas born than of the total population. All those that do so (B Areas) are to the east and south of Warwickshire: Essex and Kent are the only south-eastern counties with less than their proportional share of immigrants. This deficiency is compensated for by London and Middlesex, West Suffolk and Huntingdonshire (including the Soke of Peterborough) taking more than twice their proportional share.

SELECTED IMMIGRANT GROUPS

The proportion of a county's immigrants born in (a) the Commonwealth, Colonies and Protectorates and (b) Foreign Countries (figs. 6.1a, b and c) gives a very generalized statement of the composition of the overseas-born population in different parts of the country in 1951, 1961 and 1966. It is a crude index, for in group (a) New Zealanders, Australians, Indians, Canadians, West Indians and others are aggregated. Five of the largest immigrant groups have been selected in order to ascertain to what extent there are important differences in the geographical distribution of immigrants from different source areas, whether they are distributed within the United Kingdom in proportion to the indigenous population, and whether the changing distribution of the immigrant groups followed similar trends between 1951 and 1961. The five selected groups consist of residents who were born in the Caribbean, India and Pakistan, Germany, Italy and Poland.

Data for 1961 rather than 1966 are chosen because the latter are inadequate for this purpose, it being impossible to discern the number of immigrants from each of the five source areas resident in each county. Such information is available for countries and Economic Planning Regions: table 6.3, which is considered below, gives the number of people born in the five source areas and resident in each of these regions in 1961 and 1966. The 1961 data have been re-sorted in order to fit them as closely as possible to the Economic Planning Regions devised in 1965.

Distribution of Selected Immigrant Groups in 1961

NUMERICAL (figs. 6.6a, b, c, d and e)

In 1961 there were 1,507,600 residents of the United Kingdom who gave their birthplace as being overseas, i.e. outside the British Isles. Of these, 716,400 (47·5 per cent) were born in the five selected source areas. Figs. 6.6a–e show the county distribution of each immigrant group. Only counties with 500 or more immigrants from the stated area are considered.

Fig. 6.6a shows that the Caribbean born have settled almost exclusively in England. There are in fact far more of them in Nottinghamshire than in the whole of Wales, Scotland and Northern Ireland taken together. More than one-half of the total reside in London and Middlesex. The next most popular counties are a long way behind, e.g. Warwickshire (18,330), Staffordshire (8,130), the West Riding (7,770) and Lancashire (7,670). In effect the distribution is roughly coincident with the 'industrial coffin' and the immigrants are mainly to be found in its big towns and cities. In contrast, even the cities of north-west England, Merseyside and Humberside have not attracted many immigrants from the Caribbean and this is reflected in the county totals, except in the case of Lancashire with its multitudinous county boroughs. Rural areas are everywhere 'empty'.

Fig. 6.6b shows the Indian and Pakistani born to be more widely distributed and at the same time less concentrated in London and Middlesex, where less than one-quarter reside. There are, however, substantial numbers in the Home Counties and more than one-half of this group is in the South East. London and Middlesex are followed, in order, by Warwickshire (15,490), Surrey, the West Riding, Lancashire, Kent, Staffordshire and Essex (8,160). Most English counties are represented, except those in the extreme north-east and the Fenlands.

Fig. 6.6c shows the German born to be yet more evenly distributed, particularly in England. Less than one-quarter are in London and Middlesex. There are no outstanding concentrations outside the South East, though it is noteworthy that there are far more German born in Lancashire (6,750) and

DISTRIBUTION IN 1961 OF UNITED KINGDOM RESIDENTS BORN IN THE CARIBBEAN AREA, INDIA & PAKISTAN, GERMANY, ITALY AND POLAND

TOTAL NUMBER OF UNITED KINGDOM
RESIDENTS BORN IN:

CARIBBEAN AREA	173,700
INDIA & PAKISTAN	199,000
GERMANY	128,800
ITALY	87,500
POLAND	127,400

CROSS-HATCHED CIRCLES REPRESENT
THE NUMBER OF RESIDENTS OF LONDON
& MIDDLESEX BORN IN:

CARIBBEAN AREA	90,700
INDIA & PAKISTAN	48,300
GERMANY	31,300
ITALY	23,100
POLAND	36,200

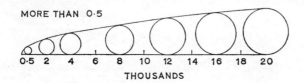

MORE THAN 0·5

0·5 2 4 6 8 10 12 14 16 18 20

THOUSANDS

FIG. 6.6

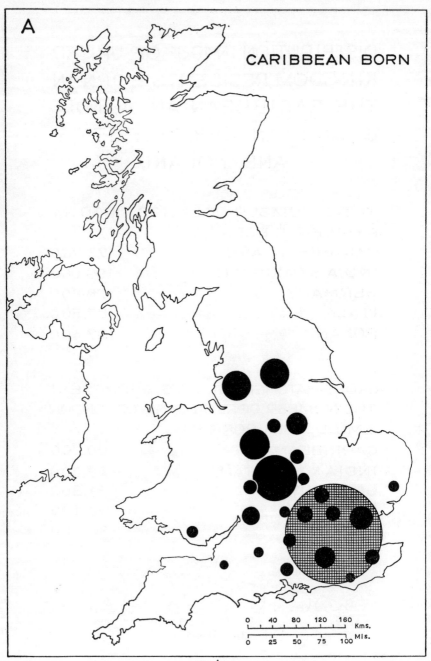

FIG. 6.6a

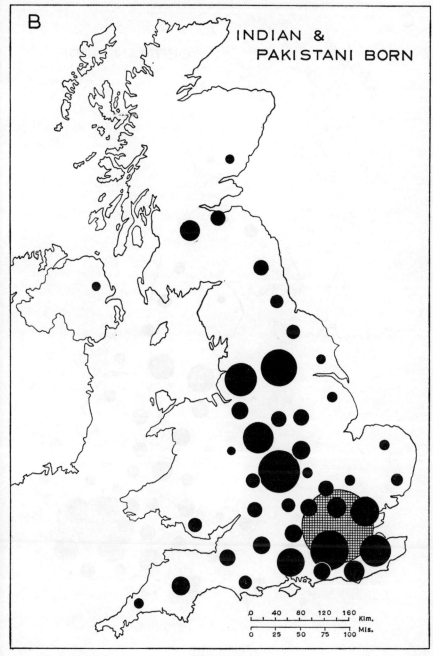

FIG. 6.6b

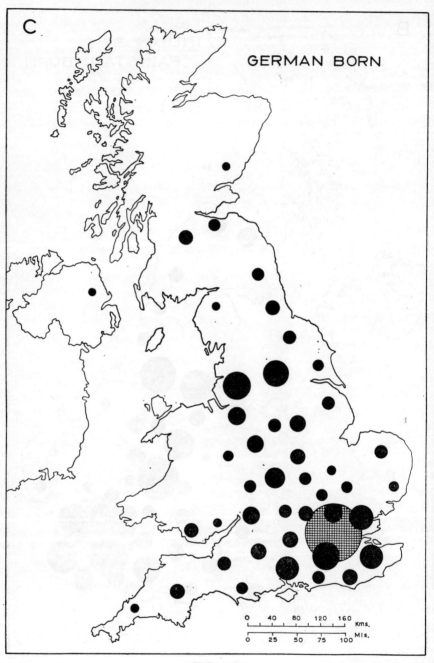

FIG. 6.6c

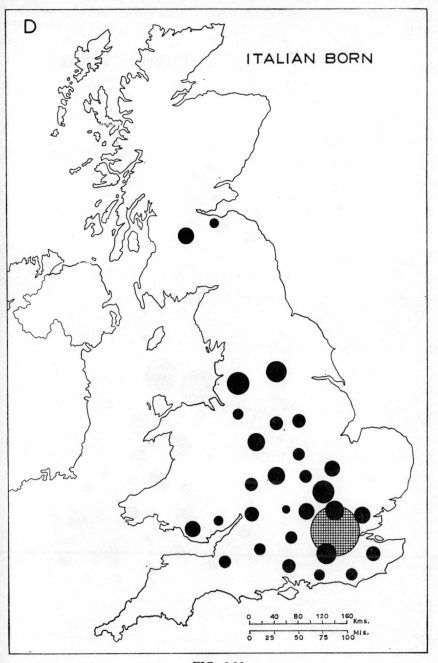

FIG. 6.6d

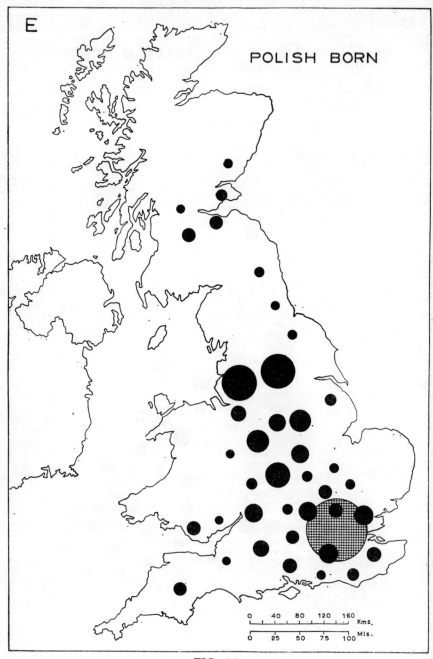

FIG. 6.6e

the West Riding (6,030) than in Warwickshire (3,700) and Staffordshire (2,310).

Fig. 6.6d (Italian born) bears some resemblance to 6.6c in that there is a relatively low concentration in London and Middlesex and the White and Red Rose counties are again more popular than West or East Midland counties. The high concentration of Italians working in the brick-fields of Bedfordshire (4,450) puts that county just ahead of its nearest rivals (Lancashire – 4,390 – and the West Riding – 4,060) in second place behind London and Middlesex.

Fig. 6.6e is similar to 6.6c in that both distributions in general terms tend to pre-date the 1950s when affluence and opportunity were so markedly increasing in south-east England and, to a lesser extent, in the West Midlands. As a result, the Polish-born group is unlike the other four in that more than one-half of its members are outside the south-east. Moreover, it is the only group with over 500 members in more than three Scottish counties and it shares with the German-born group the distinction of having more residents in both Lancashire and the West Riding than in Warwickshire and Staffordshire taken together. Even so, there are almost as many Polish born in London and Middlesex (36,160) as in the next five counties in the list – Lancashire (11,400), the West Riding (10,780), Warwickshire (5,530), Staffordshire (4,570) and Nottinghamshire (3,990).

DENSITY (figs. 7a, b, c, d and e)

County densities for each of the groups were calculated and categorized in an attempt to delineate both the most densely settled counties and the relatively minor but very important variations within the large areas with less than 100 immigrants per 100 sq. km. Fig. 6.7a-e does not, however, give due weight to London and Middlesex, which is at one and the same time one of the smallest unit areas and by far the most densely peopled. For this reason the relevant densities are given in the key. Elsewhere interest is focused upon the general pattern of distribution. The following points can be deduced from figs. 6.7a-e:

1   Only Warwickshire (twice – 7a and e) and Surrey (once – 7b) reach the top category.
2   On 7a, b and e three major groupings – around London, in the West Midlands and in the north – are separated from each other by lower densities in Oxfordshire and Northants in the south and Cheshire and Derbyshire in the north.
3   Only on 7b is there a very extensive area of high densities in the South East. In the case of the Indian and Pakistani born, each of the counties adjoining London, Middlesex and Surrey reach the third category; this is

DISTRIBUTION IN 1961 OF SELECTED IMMIGRANT GROUPS BY COUNTY

DENSITY:

NUMBERS   per 100 sq. kms.

1	OVER 400
2	200 - 399
3	100 - 199
4	50 - 99
5	25 - 49
6	10 - 24
7	UNDER 10

DENSITIES IN

LONDON & MIDDLESEX TOGETHER ARE:

CARIBBEAN BORN..........9990

INDIAN AND ⎫
PAKISTANI BORN⎰..........5320

GERMAN BORN.................3450

ITALIAN BORN.................2540

POLISH BORN..................3980

FIG. 6.7

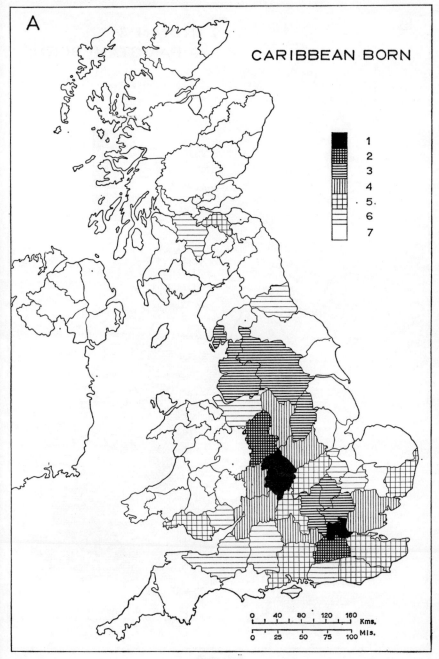

FIG. 6.7a

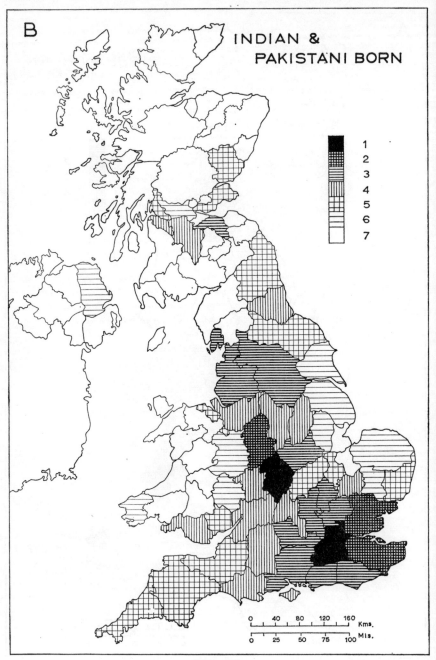

FIG. 6.7b

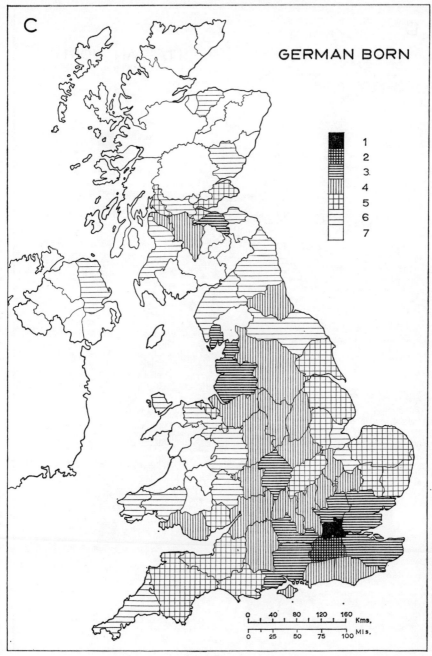

FIG. 6.7c

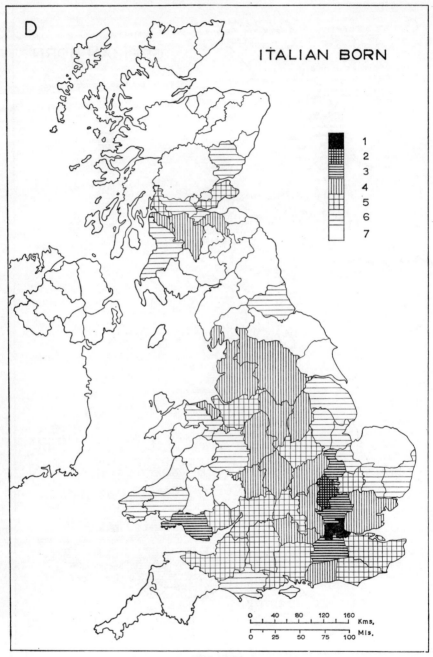

FIG. 6.7d

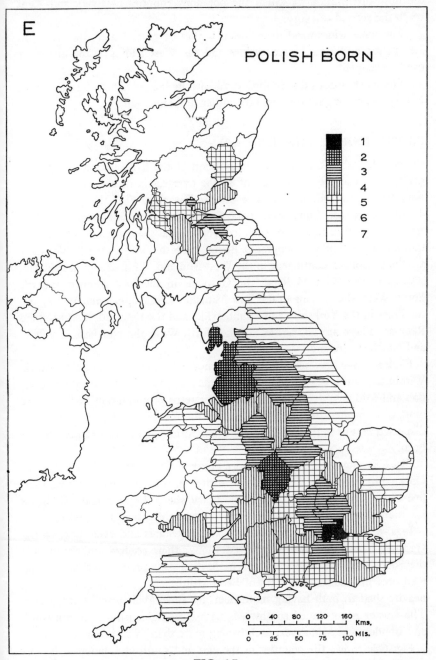

FIG. 6.7e

the only distribution in which the populous counties of Essex and Kent reach the second category.

4   The most widespread distribution is that of 7c and here the belt from Hampshire and Kent to Lancashire and the West Riding is the one most evenly occupied.

5   The most curious distribution is 7d with its belt of higher densities from Surrey to Huntingdonshire and its outlier in Glamorgan.

PROPORTIONAL SHARE (fig. 6.8)

Table 6.3 gives the regional distribution of the five selected groups, together with each region's share of all the overseas born and of the United Kingdom's total population. The outstanding feature of the geographical distribution is the dominance of the South East. This is so great that it is rare for any other region to reach its proportional share (that is, its share of the total population) of immigrants. Being so few the rarities are notable. They are the Caribbean contingent in the West Midland, the Indian and Pakistani settlers in the West Midland, the Germans in the East Anglian and the South West, the Italians in the East Midland, East Anglian and Wales, and the Poles in the Yorkshire and Humberside, and the East and West Midland Regions. There are no 'rarities' in the North West, the Northern, Scotland and Northern Ireland.

Figure 6.8a–e demonstrates the coarseness of the regional data framework. Within the South East Region, for instance, it shows the dominance of London and Middlesex and the contrasting patterns of immigrant dispersal: the most concentrated distribution is that of the Caribbean born and the most dispersed groups in the South East are the German, and Indian and Pakistani born.

Fig. 6.8a shows the Caribbean-born group to be by far the most restricted. Only a dozen counties, all English, have more than 1 per cent of the group and five of these have below their proportional share. London and Middlesex has more than five times its share and Warwickshire more than twice.

Figs. 6.8b and c show the Indians and Pakistanis and even more so the Germans to be more widely dispersed, though there are few counties outside the South East and Midlands with more than their proportional share. Fig. 6.8d presents the unusual sight of Bedfordshire and Huntingdonshire being heavily shaded, both having more than five times their proportional share. The cluster is continued southwards with Buckinghamshire, Hertfordshire and London and Middlesex, each having more than twice its share.

Fig. 6.8e shows the counties to the east and south of London to be unusually unattractive. The distribution is skewed to the Midlands and the North: this is the only instance where the West Riding has more than its proportional share. The other populous northern counties never do so.

TABLE 6.3 Percentage of (a) five selected immigrant groups, (b) all overseas born, and (c) total population of the United Kingdom, by country and region, 1961 (U.K. = 100). (Regional shares *below* that in the last column are in italics)

	West Indians	Indians and Pakistanis	Germans	Italians	Poles	All overseas born	Total U.K. population
England	98·08	93·08	90·73	87·68	91·02	91·87	82·45
Northern	*0·41*	*2·69*	*3·65*	*1·82*	*1·75*	*2·20*	*6·17*
Yorkshire and Humberside	*4·65*	*7·06*	*6·41*	*5·33*	*9·48*	*5·77*	*8·87*
North West	*4·70*	*6·16*	*7·20*	*6·40*	*10·51*	*6·88*	*12·46*
East Midland	*4·31*	*3·88*	*5·40*	*6·33*	*8·14*	*4·66*	*5·79*
West Midland	*16·27*	*13·21*	*6·46*	*7·56*	*9·54*	*7·94*	*9·03*
East Anglia	*0·91*	*1·81*	*3·39*	*3·78*	*1·88*	*3·78*	*2·78*
South East	*64·07*	*52·46*	*51·31*	*51·47*	*44·11*	*55·04*	*30·88*
South West	*2·76*	*5·81*	*6·91*	*4·99*	*5·63*	*5·60*	*6·47*
Wales	*0·81*	*1·48*	*3·17*	*5·27*	*2·80*	*2·29*	*5·02*
Scotland	*0·62*	*4·80*	*5·40*	*6·76*	*6·08*	*5·06*	*9·83*
N. Ireland	*0·49**	*0·64*	*0·70*	*0·29*	*0·10*	*0·78*	*2·70*

* This includes persons born throughout the Commonwealth, Colonies and Protectorates

DISPERSAL OF SELECTED IMMIGRANT GROUPS IN THE UNITED KINGDOM IN 1961

A. AREAS:

COUNTIES WITH MORE THAN ONE, FIVE AND TWENTY-FIVE PER CENT OF ALL U.K. RESIDENTS BORN IN STATED AREA.

A1   MORE THAN 1 PER CENT
A2   MORE THAN 5 PER CENT
A3   MORE THAN 25 PER CENT

B. AREAS:

COUNTIES WITH A HIGHER PROPORTION OF THE STATED IMMIGRANT GROUP THAN OF THE TOTAL U.K. POPULATION.

B1   MORE THAN PROPORTIONAL SHARE
B2   MORE THAN 2 TIMES PROPORTIONAL SHARE
B3   MORE THAN 5 TIMES PROPORTIONAL SHARE

C. AREAS:

COUNTIES WITH LESS THAN
(i)   ONE PER CENT &
(ii)   PROPORTIONAL SHARE OF THE U.K. RESIDENTS BORN IN THE STATED AREA

FIG. 6.8

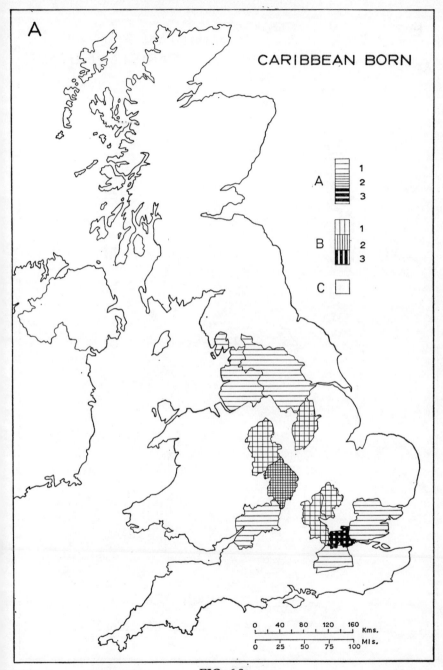

FIG. 6.8a

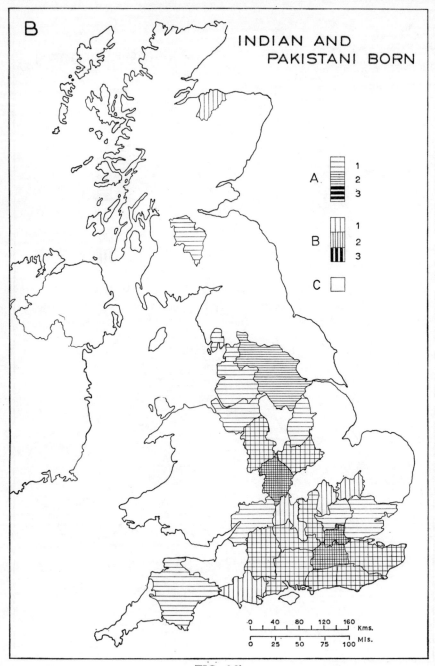

FIG. 6.8b

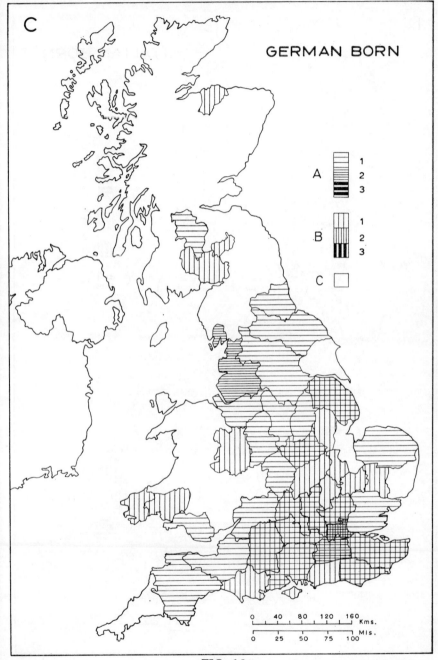

FIG. 6.8c

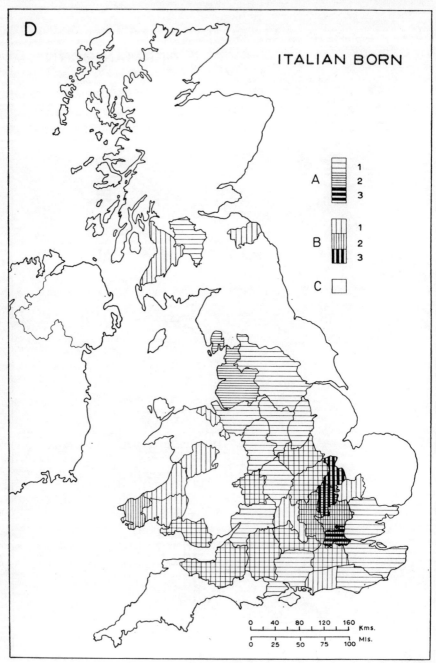

FIG. 6.8d

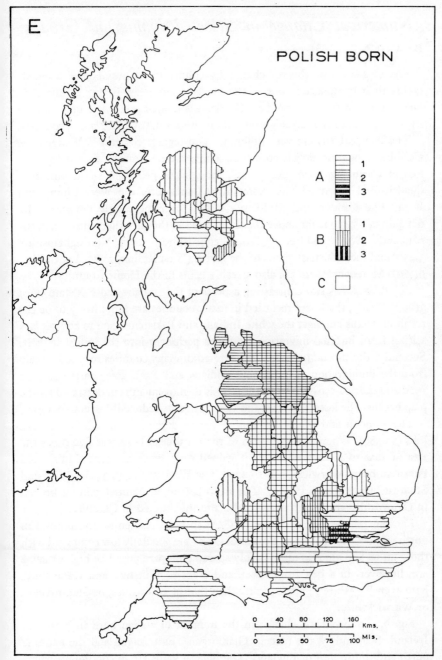

FIG. 6.8e

Numerical Change in Selected Immigrant Groups
BY COUNTY, 1951–61 (fig. 6.9)

Fig. 6.9a–e shows the net change by county in the number of residents giving their birthplace in one of the five selected areas. Empty counties are ones for which there are no data. Scotland is treated as a single unit because the changes are generally slight and there are no statistics for many counties.

The five patterns are very different. The biggest contrast is between the Caribbean (9a) and Polish born (9e). There are no counties recording a net loss of Caribbean-born immigrants, though the gains are slight outside a quadrilateral based on Gloucestershire, Lancashire, the West Riding and Kent. The London and Middlesex unit is overwhelmingly dominant. Its net gain of 85,430 is far above those recorded in the subsidiary clusters in the Midlands (Warwickshire, 17,720; Staffordshire, 7,870; Nottinghamshire, 3,450) and the industrial giants of the North (West Riding, 7,380; Lancashire, 6,460). Moreover, there are also sizeable gains in the Home Counties.

Fig. 6.9b shows two contrasting aspects of the Indian- and Pakistani-born group. Firstly, the losses recorded in many counties are more likely to be the result of deaths amongst the white Indians and Pakistanis than to any net loss arising from internal migration from the periphery into the industrial belt. Secondly, the substantial gains enumerated in many counties resulted largely from the immigration of indigenous Indians and Pakistanis, particularly in 1960 and the pre-census part of 1961. This in-movement is understated on the map because the losses amongst the 1951 residents reduce the overall net gain.

The London and Middlesex unit is not as dominant, though still in the lead (20,580). Whereas its net gain of the Caribbean born was five times the size of that of its nearest rival, it gained only twice as many Indian and Pakistani born (Warwickshire, 10,220). The West Riding (8,340) is third and Staffordshire is fourth (6,590). The main belt of substantial gains is broken in Oxfordshire and Northamptonshire and interrupted in Cheshire.

Fig. 6.9c shows county losses of German-born residents concentrated in north and central Wales and Scotland. Gains are generally low compared with those on 9a and are also more evenly spread (compare 9d). The highest gains are, however, in a belt from Essex and Kent to Wiltshire and Hampshire, here even Berkshire's gain is higher than that in Lancashire, or Staffordshire or Warwickshire.

Fig. 6.9d shows little change in the number of Italian born in Northern Ireland, Scotland, Wales (except Glamorgan), East Anglia and the extreme north and south-west of England. The biggest gains are in contiguous counties stretching north from London and Middlesex (11,200), through Hertfordshire (2,750) to Bedfordshire (4,280). This north to south line is extended by sizeable gains in Huntingdonshire (including Peterborough) and Surrey.

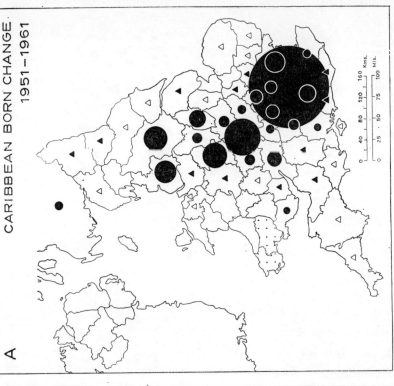

CARIBBEAN BORN CHANGE.
1951–1961

A

FIG. 6.9a

0 40 80 120 160 Kms.
0 25 50 75 100 Mls.

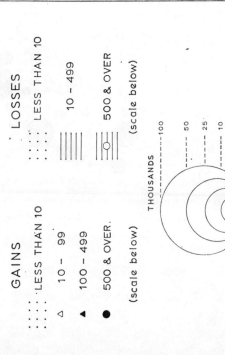

CHANGE IN NUMBER OF UNITED KINGDOM RESIDENTS BORN IN THE CARIBBEAN AREA, INDIA & PAKISTAN, GERMANY, ITALY AND POLAND

GAINS

△ ·LESS THAN 10

△ 10 – 99

▲ 100 – 499

● 500 & OVER.

(scale below)

LOSSES

LESS THAN 10

10 – 499

500 & OVER

(scale below)

THOUSANDS

100
50
25
10
5
2.5
0.5

EMPTY AREAS – DATA NOT AVAILABLE

FIG. 6.9

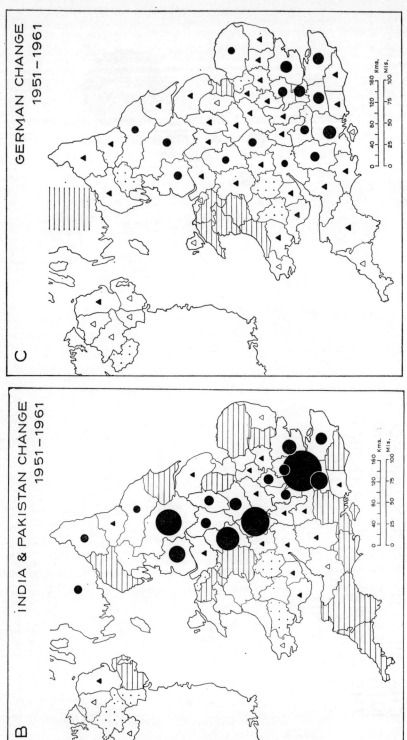

B   INDIA & PAKISTAN CHANGE 1951–1961

FIG. 6.9b

C   GERMAN CHANGE 1951–1961

FIG. 6.9c

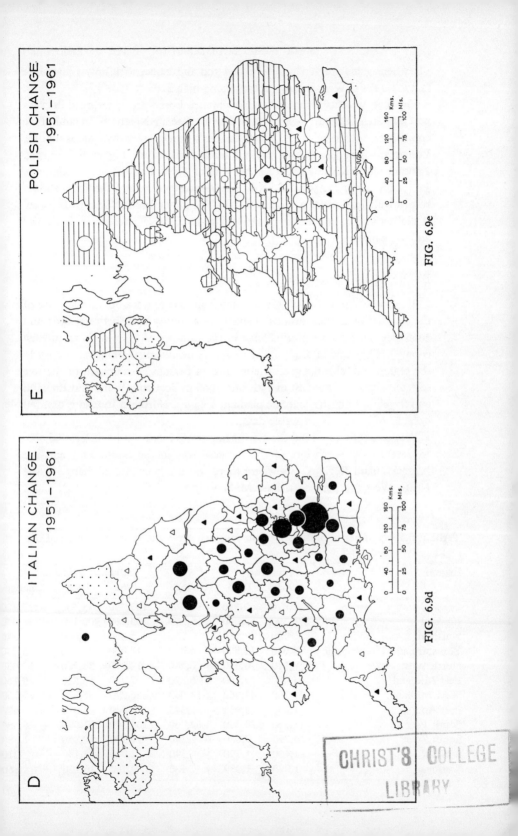

POLISH CHANGE 1951–1961

E

FIG. 6.9e

ITALIAN CHANGE 1951–1961

D

FIG. 6.9d

Elsewhere gains are generally between 500 and 2,000, with only Lancashire (2,370) and the West Riding (2,470) rising higher.

Fig. 6.9e presents a very distinctive pattern. Losses are widespread in every part of Great Britain – there were few to lose in Northern Ireland. Five counties registered gains and Warwickshire's gain of more than 500 is unique. Losses are generally below 500 but often reach much higher figures, e.g. London and Middlesex score a net loss of 8,500 Polish-born immigrants, Lancashire drops 3,330, and Scotland, Gloucestershire and the West Riding respectively lose 2,860, 2,790 and 2,410. The only evidence for a 'drift south' is slight and is to be seen in the small gains in Kent, Hertfordshire, Berkshire and Wiltshire.

BY REGION, 1961–6

The 1966 Sample Census gives insufficient data to work out how the size of the selected immigrant groups changed on a county basis between 1961 and 1966 (see fig. 6.2b for *total* change in the number of overseas born in each county). The scale of study must therefore be switched from the county to the region and table 6.4 gives the number of persons born in each of the five selected areas and resident in 1961 and 1966 in Scotland, Wales and England and the eight English economic planning regions. Northern Ireland is omitted because of its non-comparable data.

Between 1961 and 1966 the Caribbean group increased by at least 96,000. More than three-quarters of the increase was in the South East and the West Midland Regions. Elsewhere there was a higher rate of change in the North West (79 per cent), East Midland (70) and East Anglia (84), and a

TABLE 6.4   Number of persons born in specified areas and resident in each of the regions, 1961 and 1966

Region	Caribbean			India and Pakistan		
	1961	1966	Change	1961	1966	Change
Great Britain	172,870	269,330	+96,460	197,730	315,460	+117,730
England	170,390	266,060	+95,670	185,230	302,190	+116,960
Northern	700	950	+ 250	5,360	6,600	+ 1,240
Yorkshire and Humberside	8,070	12,530	+ 4,460	14,050	29,900	+ 15,850
North West	8,170	14,650	+ 6,480	12,270	24,700	+ 12,430
East Midland	7,480	12,700	+ 5,220	7,720	16,880	+ 9,160
West Midland	28,260	41,900	+13,640	26,270	56,020	+ 29,750
East Anglia	1,590	2,930	+ 1,340	3,600	4,070	+ 470
South East	111,330	174,090	+62,760	104,390	151,070	+ 46,680
South West	4,790	7,080	+ 2,290	11,570	12,950	+ 1,380
Wales	1,400	1,790	+ 390	2,940	3,150	+ 210
Scotland	1,080	1,480	+ 400	9,560	10,120	+ 560

lower rate in the relatively sparsely settled areas of Northern (36), Scotland (37) and Wales (30).

The net increase in the Indian and Pakistani group was nearly 120,000, despite heavy under-enumeration. By 1966 the South East had at least an additional 47,000, the West Midland 30,000, Yorkshire and Humberside 16,000, and the North West 12,500. The percentage change in East Anglia, the South West, Wales and Scotland was less than 14, compared to more than 100 in Yorkshire and Humberside, the North West and the East and West Midlands. Though there was only a 48 per cent increase in the South East, more than half the cumulative total of the group still resided there.

The German-born group increased by a relatively small amount (less than 14,000) and the pattern of change is very different from those of the above groups. Consequently, there is the very unusual sight of bigger absolute gains in the Northern and South Western regions than in Yorkshire and Humberside, and the East and West Midlands. Moreover, Northern had the highest percentage increase and was followed by the South West, Wales and East Anglia. Numerically the South West was by 1966 second to the South East.

The Italians, like the Germans, showed a relatively small net increase (about 15,000). More than half the gain occurred in the South East, the rest being fairly evenly distributed in England. There was a slight net loss in Wales and Scotland.

The Polish-born group was almost 10,000 less by 1966. The South East had most to lose and did in fact shed nearly 5,000. By far the highest proportional loss (23 per cent) was in Wales and the lowest proportional losses were in the East Midlands (2) and East Anglia (under 1). Other regions had fairly consistent losses of between 6 and 9 per cent.

Germany			Italy			Poland		
1961	1966	Change	1961	1966	Change	1961	1966	Change
127,910	141,640	+13,730	87,250	102,380	+15,130	127,240	117,670	−9,570
116,870	129,040	+12,170	76,720	92,080	+15,360	115,930	107,700	−8,230
4,700	6,340	+ 1,640	1,590	1,770	+ 180	2,200	2,060	− 140
8,250	8,970	+ 720	4,660	5,260	+ 600	12,080	11,220	− 860
9,280	10,760	+ 1,480	5,600	7,430	+ 1,830	13,380	12,330	−1,050
6,950	7,740	+ 790	5,540	7,070	+ 1,530	10,370	10,160	− 210
8,320	9,290	+ 970	6,620	7,080	+ 460	12,160	11,410	− 750
4,370	5,210	+ 840	3,310	4,110	+ 800	2,390	2,380	− 10
66,100	69,490	+ 3,390	45,120	54,000	+ 8,880	56,190	51,430	−4,760
8,900	11,240	+ 2,340	4,360	5,360	+ 1,000	7,180	6,710	− 470
4,080	5,010	+ 930	4,610	4,580	− 30	3,570	2,750	− 820
6,960	7,590	+ 630	5,920	5,720	− 200	7,740	7,220	− 520

Many aspects of the spatially uneven distribution of the overseas born and selected immigrant groups have been examined in cartographic form and briefly described in the text. No systematic attempt has, or is, made to explore the patterns from the viewpoints of cause or effect: such studies are rapidly increasing in number and scope. Neither is any attempt made here to project the observed and other observable trends into the future. Rather our concern has been to emphasize the often very pronounced imbalance in the distribution of immigrants. In doing so *all* the overseas born have been treated alike; no special attention has been given to, or distinction conferred upon, the 'coloured' portion. It is with the latter, however, that most writers deal and this emphasis reflects national interest in and concern about colour prejudice and discrimination. Yet, there is no good academic reason why geographers and others should not study the distribution in the United Kingdom of 'white' Poles and Germans, and Canadians and New Zealanders, as well as 'brown' Indians and Pakistanis, and 'black' West Indians and Africans.

With this view in mind this chapter is concluded with fig. 6.10 and a short commentary upon it (see fig. 8.2 for key to general layout and internal division of circles). Fig. 6.10 shows that the ratio of overseas born to total population is generally low in the north and west. No one in the whole of Northern or Northern Ireland lives in a major local authority with a ratio as high as 1 in 50 – it is often very much lower. Moreover, relatively few Scotsmen, Welshmen, North Westerners and Yorkshiremen live in units with ratios above 1 in 50: most of those who do, live in the old cotton towns of the south-east Lancashire conurbation or the wool textile towns of the west Yorkshire conurbation. Even farther south in East Anglia and the East and West Midlands, where important concentrations of overseas born occur, there are administrative counties and county boroughs with less than 1 in 50 of their residents born overseas. This is nowhere the case, however, in the South East or South West. Indeed, more than 8 million south-easterners live in authorities where at least 1 out of every 15 persons is overseas born. Outside the South East only the 560,000 people of Bradford, Derby and West Suffolk live in equivalent areas.

Unlike most of the maps fig. 6.10 looks at one aspect of the distribution at the level of the major local authority units and breaks through the 'county barrier' generally imposed by the data. Studies at ward or enumeration district level would in turn bring out the concentrations of immigrants within the major local authorities.[1]

It is not the purpose of this study to account for the distributional pattern of the overseas born in the United Kingdom. Attention has been focused on describing, mainly at the level of the geographical county, the distributional

---

[1] A good example of a study carried out at this intra-city scale is that of Jones, P. N., 'The segregation of immigrant communities in the City of Birmingham, 1961', *University of Hull, Occasional Papers in Geography No. 7, 1967*

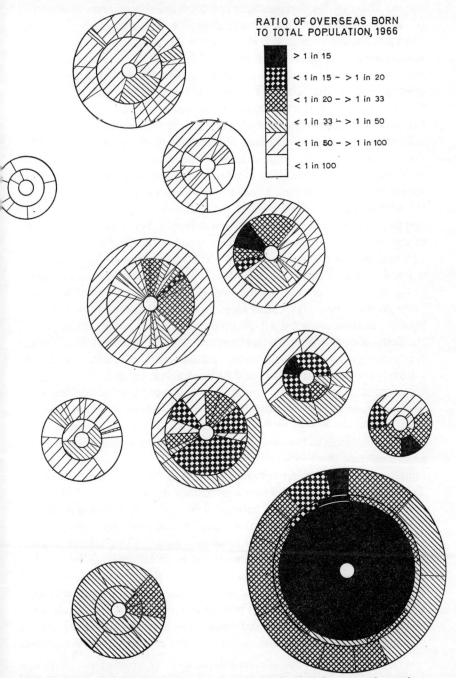

RATIO OF OVERSEAS BORN
TO TOTAL POPULATION, 1966

> 1 in 15

< 1 in 15 − > 1 in 20

< 1 in 20 − > 1 in 33

< 1 in 33 − > 1 in 50

< 1 in 50 − > 1 in 100

< 1 in 100

FIG. 6.10 Ratio of overseas born to total population in 1966, by county borough
and administrative county, arranged by economic planning region. (For key to areas
see fig. 8.2)

pattern of (*a*) all the overseas born and (*b*) selected immigrant groups, and (*c*) the way in which the spatial patterns of (*a*) and (*b*) changed between 1951 and 1966. As noted earlier, it is often not possible to ascertain from published sources what is the spatial arrangement of variations in the size, composition and socio-economic characteristics of the overseas-born population. Consequently, most of the published research has dealt either with England and Wales as a whole or with a particular town or even part of a town. This means that there is as yet insufficient evidence, either in the census or elsewhere, to offer anything other than tentative observations to the question 'why'. With this in mind it is worth while comparing the maps included in this chapter with those in the income and employment chapters. In general, it would appear that there is at least a broad relationship between the changing distribution of the overseas born and the spatial variations in degrees of affluence and employment opportunities in post-war Britain. For instance, the patterns of change in the overseas-born population and in the Caribbean and Indian and Pakistani-born groups are broadly related to regional variations in the demand for labour in the 1950s and 1960s. These, in turn, are reflected in the changing patterns of personal incomes. Those regions with below-average unemployment rates, diversified employment structures and above-average personal incomes attracted a high proportion of the immigrants, especially the South East and West Midland regions, whereas the North Western and Northern regions together with Wales, Scotland and Northern Ireland attracted relatively few immigrants. It should be emphasized, however, that the distribution of immigrants is not simply brought about by economic factors. It is also influenced by, say, the 'pull' of well-established immigrant communities and the rate of movement of the indigenous population from the central urban areas to the suburbs and beyond. The first factor might be the most important of all in some areas. In Bradford, for instance, considerable numbers of immigrants from Pakistan settled in the City during the 1950s.[1] Yet employment opportunities there were limited when compared with those in many other towns of Britain, because of the specialized nature of Bradford's employment structure and the dominance of the relatively stable, labour-shedding textile industry and its associated trades. The Pakistani workers have prospered because of their willingness to do low-prestige jobs and to work long and often irregular hours.[2] The second factor – migration from the inner and often twilight residential areas of the big cities – is probably more important in the more prosperous parts of Britain.[3] A high level of prosperity gives a higher proportion of the indigenous population the chance to move out of the nineteenth-century environments of the city and by so doing there

[1] The development of the immigrant communities of Bradford and other West Yorkshire towns is traced in Butterworth, E. (ed.), *Immigrants in West Yorkshire*, 1967
[2] Cohen, B. and Jenner, P., *op. cit.*
[3] See Peach, G. C. K., 'West Indians as a replacement population in England and Wales', *Social and Economic Studies*, September 1967

would be, especially in the more prosperous areas, a more pronounced 'vacuum' into which immigrants (including the Irish who have not been considered in this study) could move.[1] Such a movement might, in turn, speed up the outward migration and further intensify the spatial contrasts as between different residential areas within a given town, conurbation or region. In Birmingham, for instance, P. N. Jones concludes that 'the un-planned manner' of the movement of immigrants into the 'middle ring' of the city in the 1950s 'has set in motion an accelerating process of decline in both actual living standards and environmental conditions. The true scale of the problem, and its repercussions for city planning and administration, remain largely uncharted.'[2] The way in which this process works locally, in Birmingham and elsewhere, is influenced by the availability of land and housing (at the right price), the efficiency of the transport networks and the policies of the local authorities in such fields as the allocation of council housing, slum clearance, allocation of pupils to particular schools and 'overspill'.[3]

The spatial patterns of the many aspects of the overseas-born population introduced in this chapter prompt several other questions, and topics for more detailed enquiry. Certainly, the differing patterns of the selected immigrant groups show that the constituent elements of the overseas born exhibit both different distributions and trends. Therefore, any attempt to understand the distribution of the overseas-born population would necessarily involve the reconstruction of the factors affecting the decisions made by different waves of immigrants at several critical periods of time.

[1] The movement of coloured immigrants and the Irish into Birmingham in the 1950s is examined by Jones, P. N. (see footnote 1, p. 170). The major reception zone with-in the city has been its 'middle ring . . . a vast expanse of later Victorian and Edwardian housing (neither very good or adapted to present social needs, nor totally inadequate), which has lapsed into a state of neglect which has at its roots the facts of ageing – both of the dwellings and their resident populations'

[2] Jones, P. N., op. cit., 44–45

[3] The Birmingham Corporation Act of 1965 provides a good example of the way in which decisions reached by local politicians and administrators directly influence the distribution of immigrants: see Jones, P. N., op. cit., 26–28

7
Health Services: Medical

The provision of health services in an economically advanced country is a major industry in its own right. The National Health Service of the United Kingdom employs 850,000 people and spends over £1,500 million a year, or rather more than 4 per cent of the gross national product. Each year more than three-quarters of the total population make some use of its facilities.[1] The prime objective of the National Health Service is set out in the Acts of 1946, 1947 and 1948. In simple terms it is to cater for all those people who would otherwise be deprived of adequate care and attention (a) because they tend to prefer, or are obliged to spend their own financial resources on commitments other than health and (b) because they live in localities and regions where facilities for the diagnosis and treatment of illness are inadequate.[2]

The first kind of deprivation is the more easily tackled, at least in theory. It is overcome by widely decentralizing the power to spend money on behalf of the State. 'Every day, every time they (the 40,000 doctors who operate the National Health Service) see a patient, doctors commit the state to expenditure on behalf of their patients. This gives expression to the principles inherent in the National Health Service and the way in which it is financed: that medically qualified people make medical decisions about their patients unhindered by the knowledge that the patient may not be able to afford the treatment they recommend.'[3] In practice the system fails to operate where the needs of patients remain unknown, and such ignorance may result from the second type of deprivation which is essentially a geographical deficiency.

There are, as we shall see, pronounced regional discrepancies in the

---

[1] See T. E. Chester's most useful survey 'How healthy is the National Health Service?' in *District Bank Review*, September 1968, 3–33; Office of Health Economics, *The Cost of Medical Care*, 1964; Abel-Smith, B. and Titmuss, R. M., *The Cost of the National Health Service in England and Wales*, 1956; *Cost of the National Health Service*, Guillebaud Report: H.M.S.O., Cmnd. 9663; and Farndale, J. (ed.), *Trends in the National Health Service*, 1964

[2] The home environment (a) and the facilitative environment (b) reappear as factors in the discussion of education in chapter 10. In so far as the quality of the home environment is markedly influenced by size of income and range of local opportunities for employment, there is clear justification for examining these topics first, as has been done in this book

[3] Quoted from Forsyth, G., *Doctors and State Medicine: a Study of the British Health Service*, 1966, 149

provision of, for instance, teaching hospitals, dentists and general medical practitioners. Such geographical aspects of the National Health Service can be measured. What cannot be so easily ascertained and measured is the spatial pattern of the quality of the service. Obviously a general practitioner with 3,500 patients on his list (some have over 5,000) will have less time to devote to each patient than a colleague with only 1,500, given that the efficiency of the two doctors and the nature of their practices are comparable. But where are the 'best' practitioners, surgeons, anaesthetists and where are the 'best' general and specialist hospitals? Some relevant statistics are collected and published, but for the most part one has to assume, when considering the spatial distributions of most aspects of the National Health Service, that the good, indifferent and bad are evenly spread over the country.

The geographical distribution of manpower and buildings will broadly determine the volume of treatment and the size of what is aptly known as the 'clinical iceberg'. The tip of the iceberg is that part of all 'clinical need' which is receiving treatment, the rest is the submerged volume of morbidity in general practice which goes without investigation and treatment until symptoms become gross, and latent need for medical care becomes translated into overt demand.[1] The size of the 'iceberg' is a matter for conjecture. We are only aware of its tip but its concealed portion is thought to be vast. The size, composition and structure of the 'icebergs' in different parts of the country are also a matter for conjecture. With regard to structure and composition one is dealing here with something far more complex in its elements and valencies than the H_2O frozen into an iceberg.

In 1963 Dr J. M. Last tried to estimate the size of the submerged section of the iceberg for a number of disorders in an 'average' practice of 2,250 patients.[2] If his results apply to England and Wales as a whole then there are very considerable numbers of people in need of, but not receiving, medical treatment.[3] Are all areas of the country equal? According to Dr R. F. L. Logan the clinical iceberg is larger in certain socially vulnerable groups in the average practice.[4] It follows that the icebergs will be larger in *areas* where the socially vulnerable groups, such as the aged, the unskilled and the low income families, are concentrated. As the same areas often have above-average-sized general practitioner lists, it is likely that the greatest latent and unknown need for medical care would be found concentrated particularly in the older industrial areas of the north and west, in parts of

[1] *Ibid.*, 63
[2] Last, J. M., 'The iceberg: "completing the clinical picture" in general practice', *Lancet, ii*, 1963, 28–31
[3] For an estimate of the numbers suffering from given disorders see Forsyth, *op. cit.*, 63–64
[4] Logan, R. F. L., 'Pre-symptomatic detection of vulnerable patients in general practice in the control of chronic disease', *Proceedings of the Royal Society of Medicine*, **56**, 1963, 309–312

Greater London and, despite their favourable G.P./patient ratios, in the less prosperous marginal farming counties characterized by high proportions of the aged and of low income groups.[1]

Data

There is no Atlas of the Health and Welfare Services. The statistics of many aspects of these services are varied in quantity as well as quality. The

FIG. 7.1

framework is often one of very large areas, such as Regional Hospital Board Areas (fig. 7.1). Moreover, the data collected are frequently changed and differ-

[1] In 1968 it was estimated that care of the elderly accounted for 30 per cent of the costs of the N.H.S., although the aged constituted only 12 per cent of the population: *Old Age*, Office of Health Economics, 1968

ent series are collected for different areas. Nor is there an Atlas of Morbidity. Morbidity statistics often show a bunched pattern and reflect not the residential distribution of patients but rather the location of teaching hospitals and other specialized units within the National Health Service. In this sense the data are rather like the employment statistics – both refer to place of 'treatment' rather than place of residence. As a result of these and other disadvantages no attempt is made here to discern the patterns of morbidity. However, it seems reasonable to suppose that such patterns are reflected in the mortality patterns of the population (deaths are normally allocated to usual place of residence of the deceased). Before considering the geography of death we examine the regional distribution of selected aspects of the health and welfare services provided for the living.

HOSPITAL SERVICES

It is widely recognized that there is a regional problem at the heart of the hospital service. The Report of the Ministry of Health for the year 1966 states, 'the number of hospital medical staff has increased by over 60 per cent since 1949, and although more hospital doctors are needed the *main problem is to ensure that all parts of the country have equal facilities.*'[1] To this end the declared aim of *'The hospital building programme: a revision of the hospital plan for England and Wales'* is the achievement of a common satisfactory standard of service *in all parts of the country.*[2]

The chief difficulty in attempting to measure the character and extent of the existing regional variations concerns the choice of indices. On the demand side of the equation are 52 million people, excluding Northern Ireland. The Regional Hospital Boards and Boards of Governors of the teaching hospitals together with the Ministry of Health have the duty to meet their hospital needs.[3] It is beyond the scope of this review to attempt to assess the regional variations in demand or to equate those demands with the provision of services. Much more specialized research is needed to disentangle the relation-

[1] The redistribution of medical manpower in favour of the hospital service is illustrated in the Scottish Home and Health Department's *Scottish Health Statistics, 1965*, H.M.S.O., 1967, 74

Year	Number of doctors in the following services:			
	General Medical	Hospital	Local Authority	All Nat. Health
1948 (est.)	2,600	1,900	250	4,750
1955	2,929	2,649	281	5,859
1960	2,914	2,874	296	6,084
1965	2,806	3,468	308	6,582

[2] H.M.S.O., Cmnd. 3000, 1966

[3] A neat summary of some of the facts the Regional Hospital Boards ought to know can be found in a review of the *Birmingham Regional Hospital Board, 1947-66*, 1966, 176–177. Some of the factors affecting 'demand' are mentioned in the Office of Health Economics pamphlet, *The Costs of Medical Care*, March 1964, 17–22

ship between demand and supply. Research workers generally look at one or the other and rarely tackle both.[1]

In areas where services are known to be inadequate there is little point in the G.P. recording the number of patients requiring particular treatments. Similarly, it is generally found when services are extended, or introduced for the first time, that enough new patients materialize to justify the investment. Because of the interaction of supply and demand it is unlikely that the size of waiting lists for hospital treatment is a good indication of either total demand or the extent of the inadequacy of the hospital service.

Fig. 7.2 illustrates some of the more frequently encountered problems of interpretation. The maps are of intrinsic interest. They show that much more generous provision is made for *male* mental patients in the Liverpool and Welsh areas than in the Oxford and Sheffield areas, and that the three southern areas (South West, Wessex and South East) are much better equipped in terms of places for *female* mental patients than are the Oxford, Sheffield and Newcastle areas. But is it likely that the need for treatment in mental hospitals is distributed in this way? Are there in truth such marked variations between males and females within the North West? Are the females of Wessex so different in their mental health from those of the Oxford region immediately to the north? Without wishing to suggest that there is a significant relationship between successful suicides and the residence rates in mental hospitals it is interesting to compare fig. 7.2 with G. Melvyn Howe's maps showing male and female suicide rates in the period 1954–8.[2] *Male* suicide rates were lower in Liverpool and Birkenhead, the main towns of the Liverpool R.H.A., than in the rest of Lancashire. Rates were also below the national average in South Wales. The outstanding feature of the map of *female* suicide rates is 'the dispersed and geographically isolated character of the areas of high mortality ratios'. Most of Wessex had ratios below, and Lancashire generally had ratios well above, the national average. The reader is left to speculate about the relationship, rational or otherwise.

Five indices have been chosen to illustrate the current variations between the major hospital board regions.

Acute Teaching and Non-teaching Hospitals (table 7.1)

The distribution of acute teaching and non-teaching hospitals and their running costs as measured by the average cost of keeping a patient in hospital

---

[1] For notable exceptions see, Forsyth, G. and Logan R. F. L., *The demand for medical care: a study of the case-load in the Barrow and Furness group of hospitals* (1970) and *Gateway or dividing line? A study of hospital out-patients in the 1960s* (1968)

[2] *National Atlas of Disease Mortality*, 1963, 90–93

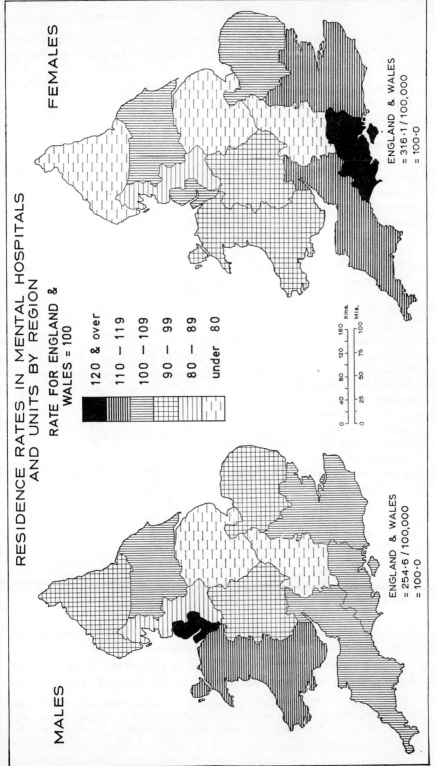

RESIDENCE RATES IN MENTAL HOSPITALS
AND UNITS BY REGION

RATE FOR ENGLAND &
WALES = 100

FEMALES

120 & over
110 — 119
100 — 109
90 — 99
80 — 89
under 80

ENGLAND & WALES
= 316·1 / 100,000
= 100·0

MALES

ENGLAND & WALES
= 254·6 / 100,000
= 100·0

Kms.
0   40   80   120   160
Mls.
0   25   50   75   100

FIG. 7.2

N

per week or for the duration of his stay are two of the most striking features of the hospital service. There are several hundred hospitals classified as

TABLE 7.1   In-Patient Departments (Wards)
Cost Units   (*i*) per in-patient per week   (*ii*) per case

Type 1: Acute Hospitals

Regional Hospital Board areas	(i) £	s.	d.	(ii) £	s.	d.	(iii) Average stay per case
Newcastle	37	10	5	66	2	1	12·3
Leeds	36	6	4	58	14	8	11·3
Sheffield	40	3	2	58	8	10	10·2
East Anglia	40	2	11	59	2	11	10·3
N.W. Metrop.	40	14	9	77	0	1	13·2
N.E. Metrop.	38	0	8	74	9	1	13·7
S.E. Metrop.	40	0	6	69	19	2	12·2
S.W. Metrop.	39	0	8	72	9	4	13·0
Oxford	44	9	1	54	11	4	8·6
South Western	40	18	1	64	15	11	11·1
Welsh	38	15	11	63	9	3	11·5
Manchester	36	16	8	58	7	1	11·1
Liverpool	32	8	1	61	9	2	13·3
Wessex	39	16	3	61	16	2	10·9
Avr. for England and Wales	*38*	*12*	*6*	*64*	*13*	*4*	*11·7*
Birmingham R.H.B. (operating a new costing scheme in 1966)	38	13	5	60	13	8	—
Teaching Hospitals							
London (avr. of 16)	54	7	2	106	2	11	13·7
e.g. St Bartholomew's	53	16	5	128	4	9	16·7
Royal Free	62	15	8	117	13	2	13·0
Lambeth	37	5	8	77	14	9	14·6
Provinces (avr. of 14)	47	3	9	75	14	10	11·2
e.g. Manchester Royal	48	4	0	103	15	4	15·1
Radcliffe (Oxford)	48	2	2	54	1	11	7·9
Royal (Sheffield)	37	17	10	67	14	3	12·5

Source: Ministry of Health: National Health Service, *Hospital Costing Returns Year ended 31st March 1966,* Part I (H.M.S.O. 1966), Section B

Type 1: Acute. But in the whole of England and Wales there are only 30 teaching hospitals and 16 of these are in London.[1]

Table 7.1 shows the average costs per week and per case in the in-patient departments of acute hospitals in each of the Regional Hospital Areas

[1] Attached to the London teaching hospitals are 12 undergraduate medical schools. *The Royal Commission on Medical Education, 1965-68,* H.M.S.O., 1968, recommends that these schools which grew up rather haphazardly, should be merged into six schools

(R.H.A.) and in London and Provincial teaching hospitals. The range is considerable, from £32 8s. 1d. per in-patient per week in Liverpool R.H.A. to £44 8s. 1d. in Oxford R.H.A. and from £47 3s. 9d. in provincial teaching hospitals to £54 7s. 2d. in those in London. Weekly costs in the latter range from £62 15s. 8d. in the now curiously named Royal Free to £37 5s. 8d. in the Lambeth.

Differences in the efficiency of hospital management, and perhaps different views of the role of the hospital within the health and welfare services, are also reflected in the average costs per case. On average, patients are admitted, treated and discharged in the acute hospitals of the Oxford R.H.A. in only 8·6 days compared with 13·3, 13·2 and 13·7 days in the Liverpool, North West and North East Metropolitan R.H.A. areas respectively. Returns for individual teaching hospitals show a bigger range. The Radcliffe at Oxford has the most rapid turnover of patients, each staying on average only 7·9 days, whereas patients at St Bartholomew's stay more than twice as long and at an additional cost of some £74 each and those at Manchester Royal Infirmary stay on average 15·1 days at an overall cost of almost £104 each.

The average duration of stay in acute hospitals has been reduced by over two weeks since 1949. This has enabled a substantially greater demand to be met without the State committing substantial sums of capital on new buildings. The reduction was achieved by a rapid expansion of staff and by advances in treatment, particularly better diagnostic facilities, more successful preventive measures, the development of new drugs, and a general improvement in levels of health. 'Even so, the average length of stay of patients in acute beds, in respect of which clinical decisions represent the main determining factor, remains appreciably higher (in England and Wales) than in many other advanced countries. There are indeed striking variations between different hospital regions. . . . If the length of stay in all regions could be reduced to that of those where it is shortest, this, coupled with a growing ability through rapidly expanding building programmes to provide the necessary additional supporting services, could increase still further the number of in-patients treated per bed and have a significant effect on waiting times before admission to hospital.'[1] But is it simply a matter of 'efficiency'? To what extent can the slower turnover in the Manchester and Liverpool areas and in parts of Metropolitan England be ascribed to the fact that hospitals traditionally act as a kind of 'rest home' for many of their deprived patients because many come from houses known to be unfit to live in, and from areas characterized by heavy pollution, a lack of open spaces and inadequate follow-up facilities?

Turnover is also clearly related to the number of beds available in each region (see below).

[1] Ministry of Health, *Annual Report 1966*, H.M.S.O., July 1967, Cmnd. 3326, 3

Admissions to Teaching and Non-teaching Hospitals
(Fig. 7.3)

An important consequence of the unequal distribution of teaching hospitals is the marked disparity in the proportion of patients admitted to Type 1, Acute Hospitals, who enter teaching hospitals. Just over 15 per cent of

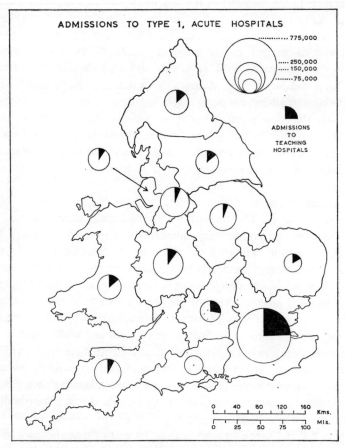

FIG. 7.3

patients admitted to Acute Hospitals in England and Wales entered teaching hospitals in 1966. But the percentage was under 7 in the Sheffield, Manchester and Wessex regions,[1] over 17 in East Anglia, and reached 24 and 28 in the Metropolitan and Oxford regions. These figures, like those on average costs, reflect the gulf – almost two decades after the introduction of a *national* health service – between the Metropolis and Oxford on one side and the Provinces on the other.

[1] There is no teaching hospital in the Wessex region. It is the only region formed since the N.H.S. was founded

Merit Awards to Consultants (table 7.2)

The location of teaching hospitals is also mirrored in the regional incidence of monetary awards made to consultants in the hospital service. At the end of 1968, of the 9,135 consultants in the hospital service in England and Wales, 2,836 (31 per cent) held merit awards ranging in value from £925 per annum for a C award to £4,885 for an A-plus award. However, the 73·1 per cent of

TABLE 7.2   Distribution of distinction awards to consultants by hospital regions at 31 December 1966*

Region	Percentage of award holders in Region	A plus £4,885 (87)	A £3,700 (275)	B £2,175 (825)	C £925 (1649)
	The number of award holders in each region expressed as a percentage of the total number of consultants in each region				
Liverpool	25·4	0·6	2·4	8·3	14·1
Birmingham	25·7	0·6	2·8	7·3	15·0
Manchester	25·9	0·4	2·6	7·3	15·5
Sheffield	26·4	0·3	2·8	7·3	15·9
Leeds	27·1	0·6	3·5	8·4	14·7
Wales	28·2	0·9	3·5	7·7	16·2
Wessex	28·6	0·3	1·9	8·8	17·6
Newcastle	29·9	0·5	2·3	9·1	18·0
South Western	30·3	0·6	2·6	8·2	19·0
East Anglia	30·6	0·7	3·7	9·2	17·0
Oxford	31·5	2·2	2·2	8·8	18·2
All Metrop. Regions	36·8	1·4	3·7	10·7	21·0
England and Wales	*31·04*	*0·95*	*3·01*	*9·03*	*18·05*
Scotland	32·13	0·97	3·00	9·36	18·80

* Rates payable from 1/10/66. Honorary consultants are included. Consultants with appointments in more than one region are included in each

Sources: *Ministry of Health Annual Report, 1966*, Cmnd. 3326, July 1967, 177 and 45; *Health and Welfare Services in Scotland, 1966*, Scottish Home and Health Department, Cmnd. 3337, August 1967, 39

all consultants holding non-teaching hospital posts shared only 49·6 per cent of all merit awards, and two-thirds of their awards were C only. Only 11·5 per cent of the A plus, 21·1 per cent of the A and 37·0 per cent of the B awards were held by the 73·1 per cent of consultants outside the teaching hospitals. Thus the A plus, A, B and C awards are heavily distributed in favour of consultants wholly or partly connected with teaching hospitals. Not surprisingly, metropolitan England leads the field, in relative as well as in absolute terms, in each of the four categories. Under 26 per cent of the consultants in the Liverpool, Birmingham and Manchester regions held merit awards compared with the average for England and Wales of 31, 31·5 per cent in the Oxford region and an average of 36·8 per cent in the four Metropolitan regions.

Additional awards were allocated to Scottish consultants in 1966 in order to bring about proportional parity between Scotland and England and Wales.

Hospital Beds in Use, by Region (table 7.3)

An inquiry into hospital in-patient services in England and Wales in the year 1963 contains a great amount of information on the regional provision of beds for each category of illness. The 1963 rather than the 1966 survey is used here so that comparisons can be made with maps presented in chapter 9. Table 7.3 shows the number of beds in use (in all types of hospital and for all causes of illness) for every million males, females and persons in each region. The index numbers show how the provision of beds in each of the regions compares with the average for England and Wales. There were 3,832 beds for each million males in England and Wales, yet a million men in the Oxford region had only 2,740 beds as compared with the 5,071 beds available in the Liverpool region. Females were more liberally catered for. There were almost 5,000 beds per million females in England and Wales, but those women who happened to live in the area stretching from Barnsley to Leicester and from Derby to Grimsby had only 4,100 beds and would on the face of it have been well advised to move to the South East Metropolitan Area where there were 1,700 additional beds per million females. Beds per million persons were scarcest in the Sheffield and Oxford regions and most plentiful in the Liverpool and North East Metropolitan areas. Despite the Oxford region's very low rating in terms of male beds, the mean waiting time for admission was shorter there than in the South Western, Birmingham, Manchester and Sheffield areas. Similarly, despite the high rating for female beds in the South East Metropolitan area females waited longer for admission there than in eight other regions. All the Metropolitan areas exceeded the national average in their provision of hospital beds.

Reliance upon Overseas-born Doctors (table 7.4)

A survey of hospital doctors in England and Wales in 1967 shows that 31·6 per cent of all hospital doctors were from outside the British Isles.[1] The highest proportions were at the bottom end of the career grades. Only 12·4 per cent of Consultants were born overseas as against 51·1 per cent of

[1] *Ministry of Health Annual Report, 1967*, Cmnd. 3702, July 1968, table 63, 162–3

TABLE 7.3 Hospital beds used per million population, by regional hospital board areas, in 1963

Region	Males		Females		Persons	
	Beds per million	England and Wales = 100·0	Beds per million	England and Wales = 100·0	Beds per million	England and Wales = 100·0
N.E. Metrop.	4,857·2	126·8	5,716·3	115·0	5,307·5	120·1
Liverpool	5,071·2	132·3	5,410·7	108·8	5,248·3	118·8
S.E. Metrop.	4,319·5	112·7	5,877·6	118·2	5,136·0	116·2
Leeds	3,815·5	99·6	5,600·9	112·7	4,733·2	107·1
S.W. Metrop.	3,834·6	100·1	5,491·0	110·4	4,702·6	106·4
N.W. Metrop.	4,030·3	105·2	5,148·3	103·5	4,616·3	104·5
Wales	4,275·0	111·6	4,752·8	95·6	4,519·3	102·3
England and Wales	*3,832·1*	*100·0*	*4,971·9*	*100·0*	*4,418·5*	*100·0*
Manchester	3,876·1	101·1	4,817·0	96·9	4,364·8	98·8
South Western	3,667·0	95·7	4,786·3	96·3	4,240·5	96·0
Birmingham	3,410·7	89·0	4,614·9	92·8	4,018·5	90·9
Newcastle	3,586·6	93·6	4,408·1	88·7	4,004·3	90·6
East Anglia	3,634·8	94·9	4,317·1	86·8	3,980·2	90·1
Wessex	3,202·7	83·6	4,641·7	93·4	3,928·6	88·9
Oxford	2,739·5	71·5	4,793·2	96·4	3,775·6	85·4
Sheffield	3,141·3	82·0	4,090·7	82·3	3,620·7	81·9

Source: Based on Ministry of Health and General Register Office, *Report on Hospital In-Patient Enquiry, 1963, Part I, Tables,* 118

Registrars, 42·6 per cent of Junior House Medical Officers, 63·4 per cent of Senior House Officers, and 41·2 per cent of fully registered House Officers. As no regional data are published with this survey, to gain an impression of

TABLE 7.4   Proportionate contribution made to junior staffing of hospitals by doctors from overseas

Hospital region	Proportion of total staff in junior grades (excluding provisionally registered house officers) represented by doctors not born in Great Britain
	Per cent
England and Wales	*46·1*
Newcastle	57·1
Leeds	57·1
Sheffield	57·1
Manchester	53·8
Birmingham	51·4
East Anglia	48·5
Oxford	47·0
Wales	42·2
Metropolitan (4 regions)	41·9
Liverpool	39·6
South Western	36·3
Wessex	33·5
Scotland	*19·9*
Northern	27·3
South Eastern	25·3
Western	19·1
North Eastern	14·5
Eastern	10·4
Great Britain	*42·8*

Source: based on Table 5 in Ministry of Health, *Report of the Joint Working Party on the Medical Staffing Structure in the Hospital Service*, 88

the regional distribution of overseas-born doctors it is necessary to turn to a Report of the Joint Working Party on the Medical Staffing Structure in the Hospital Service. This gives the proportion of doctors born outside Great Britain holding junior posts in each hospital region.[1] The ratio is above the average in the hospital regions of England (except Liverpool) to the north of

[1] Junior posts here include Registrars, Junior Hospital Medical Officers, Senior House Officers and fully registered House Officers. There were 7,574 doctors holding such posts in Great Britain and 3,242 (42·8 per cent) were overseas born. By 1967 there were 9,030 doctors in such posts and 5,034 (55·7 per cent) were born outside the British Isles (N.B., not Great Britain)

a line joining King's Lynn and Hereford. In Scotland it falls to under one in five (table 7.4).

The proportion of hospital doctors drawn from overseas illustrates two main points. Firstly, the service would be in very dire trouble if overseas-born doctors were to withdraw. In rural and urban areas alike the service would collapse if many of them were to return to their countries of birth. Though we are concerned here with medical staffing it should be noted that overseas-born persons also constitute a high proportion of the nursing and domestic staff in British hospitals, especially in the major urban areas. Secondly, the distribution of overseas-born doctors is a reflection of the relative attractiveness – social as well as economic – of the regions in the eyes of native-born doctors. Many English doctors prefer to work and seek promotion in the south-east and few apply for jobs advertised in the north. As a result many of the junior hospital posts in the northern conurbations can be filled only because Commonwealth doctors come here from abroad.

GENERAL MEDICAL PRACTITIONERS

About 98 per cent of United Kingdom residents are registered as panel patients in the National Health Service. On average they make four visits a year to their G.P.s and they consume each year six of the 300 million prescriptions dispensed by nearly 15,000 chemists in Great Britain at a cost of £160 million. Obviously the health of the community depends largely on the front-line effectiveness of the general medical practitioner service and on the individual and collective skill of its 23,000 doctors. How effectively are these resources distributed regionally?

Table 7.5 shows the average list size of principal general medical practitioners (G.P.s) in the Economic Planning Regions of the United Kingdom in the winter of 1966–7. The least favourably served areas are in England; the East and West Midlands being the worst and the three northern regions of England also having ratios worse then the United Kingdom average.

The county or county borough with the best and worst ratio in each of the major regions is also identified in table 7.5. In Scotland the range is from 2,470 in Lanark to 956 in Sutherland, or from 40·5 to 104·6 principals per 100,000 patients. To the south the widest range occurs in Northern – 32·6 principals per 100,000 patients in Hartlepools C.B. compared with 56·5 in Westmorland. The local authorities with the highest ratios are generally industrial county boroughs such as Barnsley, Burton-upon-Trent, Rochdale and Merthyr Tydfil, whereas the lowest ratios are generally found in sparsely populated, basically non-industrial counties such as Kesteven, East Suffolk, Cornwall, Radnorshire and Sutherland. There are good reasons why the average list size should be much lower in the rural districts. The most important

TABLE 7.5 Average list size of principal general medical practitioners (column i) and number of principals per 100,000 patients (column ii), by country, economic planning region, and extremes within the latter, 1966–7

	(i)	(ii)
United Kingdom	2,396	41·73
England[1]	2,469	40·48
Northern	2,493	40·11
High West Hartlepool, C.B.	3,064	32·63
Low Westmorland	1,770	56·49
Yorkshire and Humberside	2,529	39·54
High Barnsley, C.B.	3,062	32·65
Low East Riding	2,035	49·14
East Midland	2,610	38·31
High Leicester, C.B.	2,811	35·57
Low Kesteven, Lincolnshire	2,185	45·76
East Anglia	2,278	43·89
High Huntingdonshire and Soke of Peterborough	2,631	38·00
Low East Suffolk	2,089	47·86
South East	2,417	41·37
High Bedfordshire and Luton, C.B.	2,863	34·92
Low Bournemouth, C.B.	1,974	50·65
South West	2,188	45·70
High Wiltshire	2,497	40·04
Low Cornwall and Isles of Scilly	1,992	50·20
West Midland	2,669	37·46
High Burton-upon-Trent	3,116	32·09
Low Herefordshire	2,092	47·80
North West	2,570	38·91
High Rochdale, C.B.	2,993	33·41
Low Southport, C.B.	2,269	44·07
Wales[1]	2,219	45·06
High Merthyr Tydfil, C.B.	2,521	39·66
Low Radnorshire	1,434	69·73
Scotland[2]	2,066	48·40
High Lanark	2,470	40·48
Low Sutherland	956	104·60
Northern Ireland[3]	2,019	49·52
High	—	—
Low	—	—

Sources:
1 Ratios as at 1 October 1966. Data derived from *Ministry of Health, Annual Report, 1966*, Cmnd. 3326, July 1967, 84–7. The regions are those constituted for Economic Planning
2 Ratios as at 1 July 1966. Data supplied by the Scottish Home and Health Department
3 Ratios as at 31 March 1967. Data supplied by the Chief Medical Officer to the Government of Northern Ireland

is linked with the question of distance between surgery and patient. Yet there are other factors at work more difficult to quantify, such as the well-known, and well-advertised, advantages of the rural practice which retains the attractions of prestige, cottage hospital involvement and a more immobile population.

The contrasts among county boroughs are less easily justified. They demonstrate the irrational distribution – on social and medical grounds – of G.P.s twenty years after the establishment of the National Health Service. In Lancashire the average list size is 700 less in Southport than in Rochdale, in the West Riding it is 600 less in York than in Barnsley, in Durham 600 less in Gateshead than in West Hartlepool and in Hampshire 650 less in Bournemouth than in Southampton. There is surely a touch of the macabre in the fact that Bournemouth is the best served county borough in the whole of England and Wales.[1]

Fig. 7.4 shows the geographical counties ranked according to the average number of patients on the lists of their principal medical practitioners in 1966–7. County averages range from 948 (Sutherland) to 2,863 (Bedfordshire). The counties are divided into five groups so that each group contains approximately one-fifth of the total number of patients in the United Kingdom.[2]

Group A   Number of patients   = 9,515,000
             Range in average list size = 1 : 2,631–2,863

The composition of Group A is one of the most striking aspects of the overall pattern, in that it contains 'surprises' such as Bedfordshire, Leicestershire and Rutland, Holland (Lincolnshire), Buckinghamshire and Hertfordshire along with counties one is not surprised to find in this category, such as Staffordshire, Nottinghamshire and County Durham.

Group B   Number of patients   = 12,377,000
             Range in average list size = 1 : 2,567–2,583

This group consists of four populous industrial counties, namely Lancashire, Essex, Derby and the West Riding of Yorkshire, together with the north-eastern division of London. The counties in groups A and B form an almost continuous tract across England from Essex in the south-east to the borders of the English Lake District. The only 'outlier' is County Durham and the

---

[1] It is not possible to compare the ratios of all the county boroughs, as some of them are not separated from the geographical counties in which they are located. This arises because the Minister of Health has exercised his power to set up a single executive council covering the area of two or more local health authorities, e.g. Oxford County and City, and Kent and Canterbury

[2] There is of course a difference between the total number of panel patients and the estimated civilian population. In Scotland, for instance, the former exceed the latter by 154,268, or by 2·97 per cent. The citizens of Glasgow seem most adept at spreading their bets and the number of patients exceeds the estimated population by 7·26 per cent

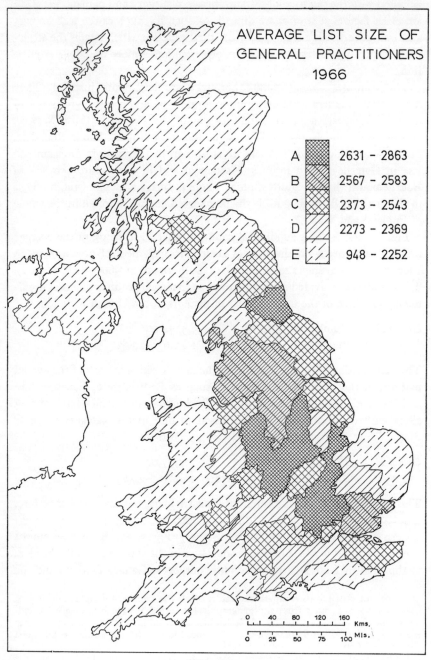

AVERAGE LIST SIZE OF
GENERAL PRACTITIONERS
1966

A	2631 – 2863
B	2567 – 2583
C	2373 – 2543
D	2273 – 2369
E	948 – 2252

FIG. 7.4

main 'interruption' is Northamptonshire which heads the list of counties in Group C.

Group C   Number of patients   = 10,942,000
           Range in average list size = 1 : 2,373–2,543

Counties in this group tend to flank and occasionally bite into the tract formed by those in groups A and B. There are, however, three 'outliers': two of them – Lanarkshire and Monmouthshire – are the only non-English counties with more than 2,369 patients per G.P.

Group D   Number of patients   = 11,248,000
           Range in average list size = 1 : 2,273–2,369

Apart from Renfrew and Glamorgan, counties with ratios between 2,273 and 2,369 are all in England. Almost one-half of the patients living in areas with average lists in this range are in Inner London and south-west London and Surrey. Thus parts of the capital are on a par with well-served counties such as Oxford and Hampshire, and with 'rural' counties such as Cumberland, Shropshire, Cambridge and Isle of Ely and West Suffolk.

Group E   Number of patients   = 11,468,000
           Range in average list size = 1 : 948–2,252

Areas in group E contain about a fifth of the population of the United Kingdom but cover 57 per cent of its area. In this category are Northern Ireland, most of Scotland and Wales, and six peripheral areas in England, namely Westmorland; Norfolk and East Suffolk; Sussex; the Isle of Wight; Hereford, and the four south-western counties of Somerset, Dorset, Devon and Cornwall.

In conclusion, it is apparent that the industrial counties of Scotland and Wales fare better than their counterparts in England; the chief cities of Northern Ireland and Scotland each have a more favourable ratio of G.P.s to patients than the better served parts of London, and that London is a special case with its North East division in group B, South East in C, and South West and Inner in D.

Change

Nationally the trend with regard to average list size has been largely favourable over the last twenty years. The average number of patients per principal general medical practitioner in England and Wales fell from 2,700 in 1949 to 2,300 in 1961. It has since risen steadily to 2,336 in 1963 and 2,472 in 1967.[1] The available manpower has been distributed more rationally and

---

[1] The Royal Commission on Medical Education, 1965-68, H.M.S.O., 1968, predicts a serious shortage of doctors in the 1970s. By 1975 the shortage will be about 11,000 and will steadily worsen unless the present medical school output of 2,500 a year is expanded quickly. The Commission expects 'a disheartening increase in frustration and overwork'. A sizeable increase in average list size seems inevitable

this is one of the main achievements of the National Health Service. By a policy of 'negative direction' of the doctors the proportion of the population of England and Wales living in officially recognized under-doctored areas was reduced from 52 per cent in 1952 to 17 per cent in 1961. By 1961 most of the 7½ million people still in under-doctored areas lived in the coal-field and industrial districts of South Wales, northern England and the Midlands. By autumn 1967, there were 16½ million patients in 'designated' areas as against 4 million in 'restricted' areas: in these categories the respective average list size of principals stood at 2,840 and 1,837.[1] At the end of 1967 Lochgelly in Fife was the only 'designated' area in the whole of Scotland.

Inter- and intra-regional movements of population have affected the pattern too. Though it is not easy to measure the changes in list size regionally, because of changes in the presentation of the data in 1963, what seems to have happened is that 'newcomers' in the areas of in-migration are added piecemeal to existing doctors' lists which thereby become inflated over a number of years. Conversely, whereas the number of principals again tended to remain fairly constant in the areas of out-migration their lists are gradually reduced, in relative if not always in absolute terms, by the losses arising from out-migration and death exceeding, or at the very least forming a significant proportion of, gains from in-migration and local births.

Persuasion is still necessary to attract and keep doctors in the industrial areas of the north and west and to counteract the tendency for doctors to gravitate to the south. A review carried out in the first nine months of 1960 showed that the average number of applications for vacant practices advertised by executive councils was 9 in northern counties and 29 in southern counties. That the regional imbalance in the distribution of G.P.s is not as gross as

TABLE 7.6   Average number of prescriptions per person on National Health Service prescribing list, 1965–7

Region	1965		1966		1967	
Wales	6·69	125·0	7·26	127·8	7·52	128·8
North West	6·02	112·5	6·42	113·0	6·60	113·0
Yorks and Humberside	5·60	104·6	5·99	105·4	6·06	103·8
North	5·63	105·2	5·90	103·8	6·02	103·1
England and Wales	*5·35* = *100·0*		*5·68* = *100·0*		*5·84* = *100·0*	
South West	5·26	98·3	5·60	98·5	5·79	99·1
West Midland	5·03	94·0	5·35	94·1	5·48	93·8
East Anglia	5·00	93·4	5·24	92·2	5·47	93·7
South East	4·99	93·2	5·26	92·6	5·43	93·0
East Midland	4·86	90·8	5·17	91·0	5·25	89·9

Source: *Annual Report of the Ministry of Health, 1967*, Cmnd. 3702, July 1968, table 15, 94

[1] *Annual Report of the Ministry of Health, 1967*, Cmnd. 3702, July 1968, table 6, 82

that of general dental practitioners is due to the work of successive Ministers of Health and members of executive councils who have used their powers to persuade many G.P.s to practise in 'designated' or 'open areas' where average lists are high rather than in 'intermediate' or 'restricted areas' where average lists are low. Yet, this success must be seen in relation to the 'demand', region by region, made upon G.P.s. One measure of this is the number of prescriptions per person per year in each region. This suggests that the demand made upon G.P.s is considerably higher in the north and west than in the Midlands and the south-east (table 7.6). It is not sufficient to aim at an even distribution of G.P.s for the distribution of need for medical care is itself unevenly spread.

THE SCHOOL MEDICAL SERVICE (fig. 7.5)

The range in the number of pupils per school medical officer in the counties of England and Wales in January 1966 is shown on fig. 7.5. The average ratio in England and Wales is just short of 7,000 (6,993). Data for counties and county boroughs are combined where necessary to give the ratio of pupils

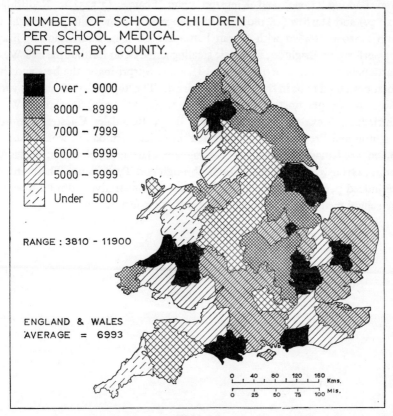

FIG. 7.5

per doctor in the geographical counties. The range is from 3,810 in Cornwall and the Isles of Scilly through 5,710 in Surrey, 5,720 in Lancashire, 5,810 in Greater London and 6,600 in the West Riding to 9,090 in Hertfordshire, 10,050 in Bedfordshire and 11,900 in Rutland. Fig. 7.5 shows a broad belt of counties in England from the West Riding and Lancashire in the north via Hereford and Worcester to Hampshire in the south, in which values are within 10 per cent of the overall average for England and Wales. North and, more particularly, east of this belt values are generally less favourable, whereas to the west they tend to be more favourable. There are notable exceptions. Ratios are conspicuously better than average in Greater London, Surrey and East Sussex and markedly worse in parts of the 'heartland' of Wales and in Pembroke, Flintshire and Dorset.

Despite this fairly simple overall pattern considerable variations at the level of the administrative county and county borough are concealed in the averages used on fig. 7.5. For instance, in England only 10 administrative counties have a ratio of pupils per school doctor better than the average for England and Wales, compared with 8 out of 13 in Wales; the range in Greater London is from Barking (2,090) and Kingston upon Thames (2,525) to Redbridge (12,820) and Harrow (18,180); and the range among the county boroughs is from 2,610 to 16,670 with Wigan better served than Bournemouth, Bury out-performing Brighton, Rochdale stealing a march on Eastbourne and West Hartlepool four times better off than Harrow. Surprisingly, the best and the worst both tend to be in the north of England. The 'top ten', that is those with fewest pupils per doctor, are from 1 to 10 (2,610–5,080) Blackpool, West Hartlepool, Stoke-on-Trent, Swansea, Bury, Rochdale, Chester, Oxford, Brighton and Preston. The 'bottom ten' in order from bad to worse (9,620–16,670) are Kingston upon Hull, Birmingham, Gateshead, Norwich, Wallasey, Luton, Grimsby, Darlington, Middlesbrough and Tynemouth. These orders are indeed perverse and clearly reflect local administrative attitudes towards the school medical service rather than any other factor.

8

Health Services: Dental

The geographical distribution of dentists is a striking demonstration of two important facts: firstly, there are insufficient dentists to go round and, secondly, there is no official policy of 'negative direction' applied to dentists. Dentists, unlike G.P.s, are completely free, apart from *local* planning restrictions on the use of premises, to set up practice wheresoever they wish to live and work. As a result the spatial variations are great and dentists within the National Health Service are not distributed in relation to either potential need or, to a less marked degree, demand. Consequently, the prime objective of the National Health Service – to provide, locally and regionally, facilities for the diagnosis and treatment of illness – is not being met in the dental services. The inequalities in the service are often greatest between one county borough and another, but, even when the analysis is confined to geographical counties, important, if not surprising, differences, can be discerned.

Fig. 8.1 shows the ratio of general dental practitioners providing services under the National Health Service to the civilian population of each geographical county in England and Wales.[1] Where a dental practice takes patients from more than one county it is tabulated under the county containing the largest number of patients. Nationally there was one general dental practitioner to 4,615 persons in 1966 (England 1 : 4,540; Wales 1 : 6,500). The inter-county variations are gross: ratios varying from 1:2,440 in London (City plus former L.C.C. area) to 1 : 8,990 in Brecon. Fig. 8.1 shows that on average a dentist in most parts of the north, the Midlands and Wales had to cope with twice as many potential patients as a colleague working in London, Middlesex and Surrey. In the counties of Brecon, Durham, Lincoln, Nottingham, Merioneth, Monmouth, Stafford and Worcester, each with more than 7,000 persons per dentist, there were two and a half times as many potential patients (three times as many in Brecon) as in the area of the south-east left blank on the map. The regional imbalance would be even greater if school dental officers and 'private' dentists were included in the calculations. Yet, as fig. 8.1 demonstrates, there are considerable differences in the county averages within the regions. In the north, for instance, Westmorland has a better ratio than

---

[1] The civilian population is used rather than number of patients because a person only registers with a dentist for a course of treatment. When it is completed the person is 'unregistered' and the dentist, unlike the G.P., has no 'continuing responsibility' for providing or arranging for the dental care of his 'patients'

Cumberland, Northumberland than Durham, and Cheshire than Lancashire. Similarly, in the well-catered-for south, Hertfordshire is better placed than Essex, Surrey than Kent, and Devon than Cornwall. What is surprising, however, is that the counties of Cambridge, Worcester and, to a lesser extent, Lincoln are so distinctly unattractive to dentists. To even out these inequali-

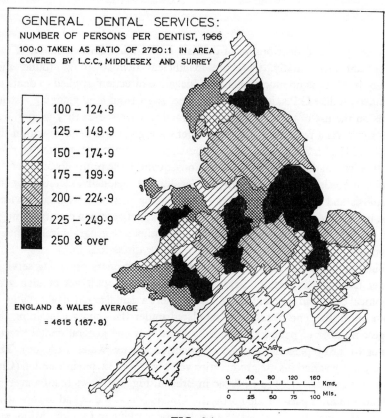

FIG. 8.1

ties and at the same time bring all parts of England and Wales up to the average standard of the south-east would require about 50 per cent or almost 5,000 more general dental practitioners. To bring all parts of England and Wales up to the level of European countries such as Sweden would require more than twice as many dentists.

The actual distribution of dentists from place to place is the most important aspect of the general dental services. The regional imbalance shown on fig. 8.1 would not, however, be a matter of such great concern if the incidence of dental illness was very much lower in 'the North' or if the most efficient dentists were operating in the districts where there were few. Since 1962, when C. A. Moser et al.[1] outlined the available data on dental health and dental services and concluded that little was known about the prevalence and distribution of dental illness in this country, several attempts have been made to explore these distributions. The enquiries carried out by N. D. Richards et al.,[2] R. O. Walker et al.,[3] and P. J. Cook and R. O. Walker[4] are among the most useful in this field of study.

N. D. Richards and his colleagues examine, by way of a random sample drawn from the electoral registers, the dental health practices and attitudes in two English towns: 'Northtown', with more than the average number of persons per dentist, and 'Southtown' with fewer. The team found less hostility and suspicion and correspondingly a greater interest in the survey in Northtown. A preliminary report, published in 1965, presents the respondents' subjective assessments and excludes the results of the clinical examinations. The responses were for the most part similar and few wide variations were noted. This is surprising, for it is often stated that there is a low dental awareness in the north, e.g. Walker et al., 1965. More Southtowners said they had visited a dentist in the previous twelve months (31 as against 25 per cent). In both towns there was a low proportion of private patients and in neither were they drawn largely from social classes I and II. Seventy-five per cent of Southtowners and 72 per cent of Northtowners said they usually received treatment under the National Health Service. Subsequent analysis by the research team showed that 79 and 75 per cent, respectively, had received some dental treatment under the National Health Service. Sixteen per cent of the respondents in Southtown and 15 per cent in Northtown said they had not been to a dentist since the introduction of the National Health Service in 1948.

An excellent survey of many aspects of the geographical distribution of dental care in all parts of the United Kingdom was published in 1967 by P. J. Cook and R. O. Walker: preliminary results were published in 1965 by R. O. Walker et al. The general dental practitioner services of the National Health Service in 1962 (covering about 80 per cent of all dentists) are examined. In the preliminary survey the United Kingdom is divided into ten large regions and in the later study it is divided into 170 executive council districts. The following elements are then described and mapped for the year

[1] Moser, C. A., Gales, K. and Morpurgo, P. W. R., *Dental Health and Dental Services*, Nuffield Provincial Hospitals Trust, 1962
[2] Richards, N. D., Willcocks, A. J., Bulman, J. S. and Slack, G. L., 'A survey of the Dental Health and Attitudes towards Dentistry in Two Communities', *British Dental Journal*, 118, 1965, 199–205. An expanded version of this survey was published in 1968: Bulman, J. S. et al., *Demand and Need for Dental Care*, Nuffield Provincial Hospitals Trust
[3] Walker, R. O., Beagrie, G. S., Jones, M. S., Liptrop, T. H., Taylor, M. N. and Yardley, R. M., 'Dentistry in the United Kingdom: A survey of the present position, and future trends', *British Dental Journal*, 118, 1965, 511–12
[4] Cook, P. J. and Walker, R. O., 'The geographical distribution of dental care in the U.K.', *British Dental Journal*, 122, 1967, 441–7, 494–9 and 551–8

1962 (Scottish figures, 1963) – the number of dentists per 10,000 population, the money spent in a year per head of population, and the average amount of this expenditure received by each dentist. Changes in England and Wales between 1952 and 1962 are examined by region and by executive councils.

The main conclusion reached by Cook and Walker is that there is 'a gross regional imbalance' in the distribution of dentists. The most marked concentration is in the south of England, particularly in the south-east. The lowest average levels of dentists per 10,000 potential patients are found in the Midlands, the north, East Anglia and Wales. Levels in Scotland are intermediate between the south and the north of England. In each of the ten regions the county boroughs have on average a higher proportion of dentists than do the administrative counties. The pattern of distribution of dentists in private practice is seen to be similar to that of dentists in the general dental services and thus the regional discrepancies are reinforced.

Between 1952 and 1962 the proportion of dentists to population fell in more than half the executive council districts of England and Wales. The most serious declines occurred in the north-west, Wales and the administrative counties of the East and West Ridings of Yorkshire. Marked improvements were confined to the south of England, while county boroughs in the Midlands held their position.

To gain some impression of the regional differences in 'dental awareness' the data on the money spent on dental treatment per head of population are analysed for each of the ten selected regions and the executive council districts. The south-east again leads and is followed by the south-west and Scotland. The amount of treatment given in the north, Midlands and Wales is generally low. The level of payments per person is higher in the county boroughs in every region; in East Anglia it is twice as high.

In every region and district of England and Wales more money was spent on dental treatment in 1962 than in 1952, despite the widespread decreases in the proportion of dentists. The increases by region were greatest in the south. Increases by district were generally greatest where most money was already being spent on dental treatment in 1952. They were least in the administrative counties of Wales and parts of the north-west, Midlands and East Anglia.

Payments made to dentists show a rather different pattern. The Midlands and East Anglia lead, despite low dental awareness outside the county boroughs of East Anglia; 'the inference is that the number of dentists is so few that each has to carry out a very large number of treatments to satisfy the limited demands of the public'. In the south, where dental awareness is high and dentists are numerous, the workload is shared and payments are lower, though incomes are undoubtedly boosted by private practice.

Poor conditions persist in Wales and the north-west, despite the fact that these regions showed the greatest increase in payments per dentist between 1952 and 1962. The greater numbers of dentists in the south of England by 1962 absorbed the high increase in money spent on dental treatment, and payments per dentist rose by less than 90 per cent in the south-east and 80 per cent in the south-west. Relatively low increases (less than 80 per cent) were also recorded in the county boroughs of the Midlands, the East and West Ridings and the five most northerly counties of England.

In order to up-date the distributions of dental care shown by Cook and Walker figs. 8.2, 3, 4 and 5 have been constructed from data supplied by the Department of Health and Social Security. The isodemic diagrams illustrate selected aspects of the general dental services in each of the county boroughs and administrative counties of England and Wales in the year 1967–8. The method of graphical presentation bears some resemblance to that used by Cook and Walker. In fact it differs in several ways, mainly in order to accommodate the creation of the Greater London Council in 1964, the introduction of Economic Planning Regions in 1964–5 and the fact that the total population of the county boroughs is greater than that of the administrative counties in both the West Midlands, and Yorkshire and Humberside. If Cook and Walker's technique were followed the inner rings in both these regions would be larger than the outer rings.

On fig. 8.2, 3, 4 and 5 the area within the outer *circle* is proportional to the total population of the Economic Planning Region, whilst the area within the inner *circle*, except in the case of the South East, is proportional to the total population of the county boroughs. The innermost circle is drawn to a constant size simply to avoid cartographic confusion at the centre of each regional diagram. The outer *ring* is thus proportional to the total population of the administrative counties. In the case of the South East Planning Region the inner *ring* is proportional to the population of the Greater London Council area and the middle *ring* is proportional to the total population of the county boroughs in the South East. The rings are then subdivided in proportion to the population of the constituent local authorities, except in the case of the Greater London Council ring where the segments on figs. 8.3, 4 and 5 are proportional to the populations resident in executive council districts which are not straightforward aggregations of the metropolitan boroughs. Within the rings the local authorities are distributed radially in relation to their approximate geographical position vis-à-vis their neighbours (see fig. 8.2 and index to it). This radial allocation is inevitably unsatisfactory because of the great variations in size and the degree of clustering of authorities encountered within the regions, particularly in the case of the county boroughs in the North West. In several instances local authorities shown separately on the diagrams are in fact not independent executive council districts, e.g. Nottingham and Nottinghamshire, Oxford and Oxfordshire, and south-east London,

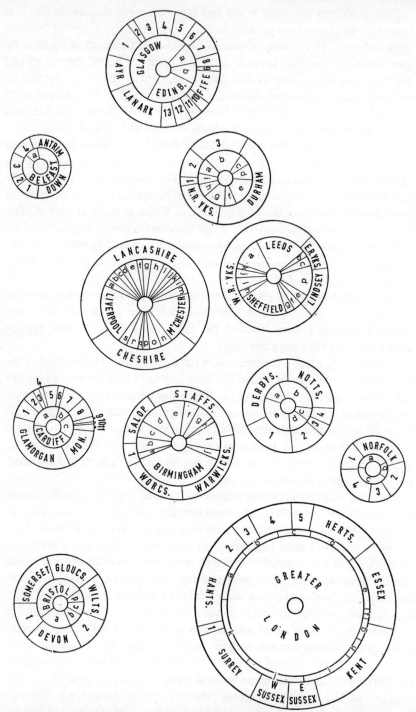

FIG. 8.2   Isodemic chart of county boroughs and administrative counties, arranged by economic planning region in England and Wales, 1966

Index to unnamed Counties (numbered) and County Boroughs (lettered) on fig. 8.2

SOUTH EAST

Counties:
1 Isle of Wight
2 Berkshire
3 Oxford
4 Buckingham
5 Bedford

County Boroughs:
a Bournemouth
b Reading
c Oxford
d Luton
e Southend on Sea
f Canterbury
g Hastings
h Eastbourne
i Brighton
j Portsmouth
k Southampton

SOUTH WEST

Counties:
1 Cornwall
2 Dorset

County Boroughs:
a Plymouth
b Exeter
c Bath
d Gloucester

EAST ANGLIA

Counties:
1 Huntingdon and Soke of Peterborough
2 East Suffolk
3 West Suffolk
4 Cambridge and Isle of Ely

County Boroughs:
a Norwich
b Great Yarmouth
c Ipswich

EAST MIDLANDS

Counties:
1 Leicester and Rutland
2 Northampton
3 Holland, Lincs.
4 Kesteven, Lincs.

County Boroughs:
a Derby
b Nottingham
c Lincoln
d Northampton
e Leicester

WEST MIDLANDS

Counties:
1 Hereford

County Boroughs:
a Worcester
b Warley
c Dudley
d Wolverhampton
e Stoke on Trent
f West Bromwich
g Walsall
h Burton upon Trent
i Coventry
j Solihull

WALES

Counties:
1 Carmarthen
2 Pembroke
3 Cardigan
4 Merioneth
5 Caernarvon
6 Anglesey
7 Denbigh
8 Flint
9 Montgomery
10 Radnor
11 Brecon

County Boroughs:
a Swansea
b Merthyr Tydfil
c Newport

YORKSHIRE & HUMBERSIDE
Counties:

County Boroughs:
a Bradford
b Wakefield
c York
d Kingston upon Hull
e Grimsby
f Doncaster
g Rotherham
h Barnsley
i Huddersfield
j Halifax
k Dewsbury

NORTH WEST
Counties:

County Boroughs:
a Bootle
b St. Helens
c Southport
d Wigan
e Blackpool
f Barrow in Furness
g Preston
h Bolton
i Blackburn
j Burnley
k Bury
l Rochdale
m Oldham
n Stockport
o Salford
p Warrington
q Chester
r Birkenhead
s Wallasey

NORTH
Counties:
1 Westmorland
2 Cumberland
3 Northumberland

County Boroughs:
a Gateshead
b Newcastle upon Tyne
c Tynemouth
d South Shields
e Sunderland
f Hartlepool
g Middlesbrough
h Darlington
i Carlisle

SCOTLAND
Counties:
1 Renfrew
2 Argyll and Bute
3 Dunbarton
4 Stirling
5 Orkney, Sutherland, Caithness, Inverness,
   Ross & Cromarty, Zetland
6 Perth
7 Aberdeen, Banff, Moray & Nairn
8 Angus & Kincardine
9 Clackmannan & Kinross
10 West Lothian
11 Midlothian
12 Berwick, East Lothian, Peebles,
    Roxburgh, Selkirk
13 Dumfries, Wigtown & Kirkcudbright

County Boroughs:
a Aberdeen
b Dundee

NORTHERN IRELAND
Counties:
1 Armagh
2 Fermanagh
3 Tyrone
4 Londonderry

County Boroughs:
a Londonderry

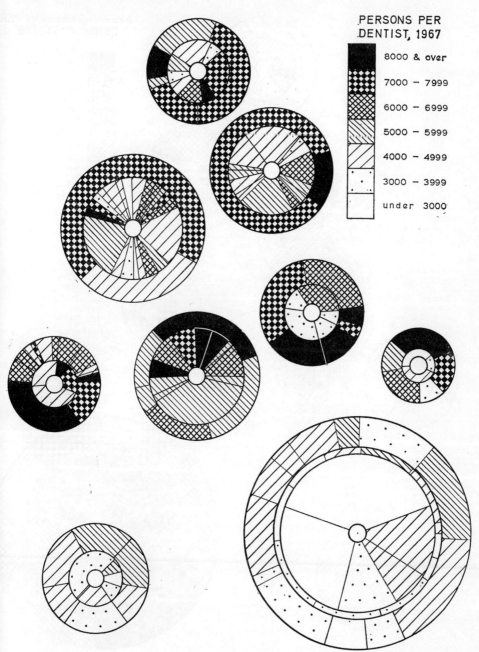

PERSONS PER
DENTIST, 1967

8000 & over

7000 – 7999

6000 – 6999

5000 – 5999

4000 – 4999

3000 – 3999

under 3000

FIG. 8.3 Average number of persons per dentist, by executive council area, 1967

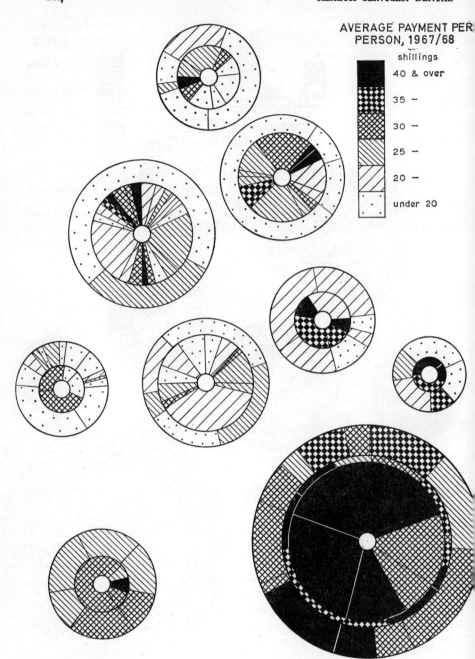

FIG. 8.4 Average payment per person for dental treatment, by executive council area, 1967–8

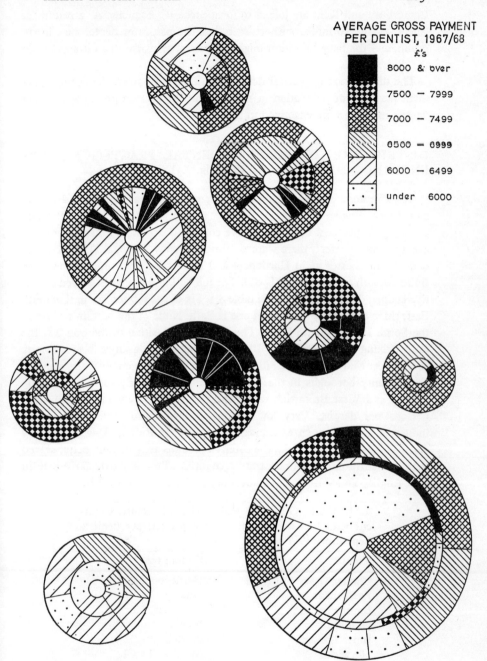

AVERAGE GROSS PAYMENT
PER DENTIST, 1967/68
£'s

8000 & over

7500 — 7999

7000 — 7499

6500 — 6999

6000 — 6499

under   6000

FIG. 8.5   Average gross payment per dentist, by executive council area, 1967–8

Canterbury and Kent are joined to form executive councils. As a result, the 'shadings' of the linked authorities reflect the nature of dental care in the group, and the 'local' position might be better, or worse, than it appears on the diagrams.

The distribution of general dental practitioners in 1967, the average payment per head of population in 1967–8, and the average gross payment per dentist in 1967–8 are examined in turn.

DISTRIBUTION OF GENERAL DENTAL PRACTITIONERS IN ENGLAND AND WALES IN 1967 (fig. 8.3)

At 30 September 1967 there was one dentist per 4,600 persons in England and Wales (England 1 : 4,524; Wales 1 : 6,415). They were not distributed evenly: 58·6 per cent of the executive councils fared worse than the overall average and, in effect, there were six times as many National Health Service dentists in Chester as in Hartlepool and more than four times as many in Bournemouth as in Merthyr Tydfil. The ten best and ten worst served executive council districts are listed in table 8.1. Six of the top ten are in the South East, three are county towns and one is Bath. None of the bottom ten are in the South East or South West. The favourable position of the South is the most striking feature of fig. 8.3. In contrast there is not a single local authority in the West Midlands with a ratio better than the England and Wales average. Even county boroughs in the West Midlands are poorly served, especially Dudley and West Bromwich where there are respectively 11,100 and 9,100 persons per dentist. Very low manpower levels also occur in populous industrial counties such as Lancashire, the West Riding, Durham, Derby and Glamorgan. As in 1962, the county boroughs are generally better served than the surrounding administrative counties. This is particularly true in East Anglia, Yorkshire and Humberside, and the East Midlands.

TABLE 8.1   General Dental Services : Executive Councils with best and worst ratios of persons per dentist, September 1967

Top ten	Bottom ten
Chester (1,880 : 1)	Hartlepool (12,350 : 1)
Eastbourne	Dudley
Bournemouth	Kesteven, Lincs.
Hastings	Bootle
Inner London	Norfolk
Norwich	Merthyr Tydfil
Bath	West Bromwich
Preston	Breconshire
Middlesex	Lindsey, Lincs.
West Sussex (2,910 : 1)	Glamorgan (8,750 : 1)

The Distribution of Dental Care, 1967-8 (fig. 8.4)

The most useful index of dental care is 'average payment per person'. This is arrived at by dividing the sum of payments made to dentists for courses of treatment carried out by the total resident population of the area (fig. 8.4). In England and Wales the average payment per person in 1967-8 was £1 9s. 4d. Seventy-four of the 133 executive council districts are below the national average: in Brecon and Norfolk the average payment is less than half the national average. At the other extreme payments in Chester are more than double the national average. The top and bottom ten executive councils are listed in table 8.2. More than half of the top ten are county towns and their rating might well be so high because dentists are also treating people from inadequately served surrounding disticts. Seven of the bottom ten are relatively sparsely populated and/or remote rural counties. The worst county boroughs are Merthyr Tydfil and Hartlepool.

Fig. 8.4 is broadly a reversed image of fig. 8.3 and demonstrates the overriding importance of the distribution of manpower. The South East leads and is followed by the South West. Elsewhere the standard of dental care is often very low indeed: West Suffolk is the only administrative county where the average payment exceeds the national average. The county boroughs are generally better served and some, as table 8.2 shows, are in the top ten. Conditions in the populous industrial counties of Wales, the Midlands and the North are generally abysmal.

The Distribution of Average Gross Payments per Dentist, 1967-8 (fig. 8.5)

The considerable variations in the work-load of general dental practitioners, resulting in large measure from the unequal distribution of both manpower and the demand for dental care, is reflected in fig. 8.5. In England and Wales the average gross payment per dentist in 1967/8 was £6,700: 51 of the 133 executive councils fell below this average. The top and bottom ten districts are listed in table 8.3. All the top ten are county boroughs and most are creations of nineteenth-century industrialization. Their manpower position is poor but there is a sufficient demand for dental care to boost gross earnings to very high levels. In contrast, the bottom ten are a mixture of both attractive and unattractive county boroughs and counties and reflect both high levels of manpower (e.g. Inner London) and high (e.g. Southend) and low levels of demand (e.g. Anglesey). In general, incomes are very high in the West and East Midlands, and in industrial counties such as Glamorgan, Lancashire, the West Riding and Durham. Gross incomes fall below the national average in many of the big county boroughs, e.g. Birmingham, Liverpool, Manchester, Sheffield, Leeds and Bradford, and in much of the South East. Clearly, it is not simply the economic return from general dental services that is attracting dentists to London, south-east coast towns, the south-west, and northern counties such as Cheshire and Northumberland. Unfortunately there is no

TABLE 8.2   General Dental Services : Executive Councils with the highest and lowest payments per person, 1967–8

Top ten	Bottom ten
Chester (£3 1s. 5d.)	Breconshire (13s. 6d.)
Norwich	Norfolk
Reading	Anglesey
Bournemouth	Cumberland
Preston	Lindsey, Lincs.
Wakefield	Merthyr Tydfil
Eastbourne	Kesteven, Lincs.
Lincoln	East Riding, Yorks.
Inner London	Glamorgan
Brighton (£2 5s. 6d.)	Hartlepool (17s. 10d.)

TABLE 8.3   General Dental Services : Executive Councils with highest and lowest gross payments per dentist, 1967–8

Top ten	Bottom ten
Hartlepool (£10,910)	Hastings (£4,660)
Dudley	Montgomeryshire
Bootle	Caernarvonshire
Walsall	Eastbourne
Burton upon Trent	Anglesey
Burnley	Isle of Wight
Wigan	Wallasey
Coventry	Inner London
Barnsley	Salford
Southend on Sea (£8,910)	Bolton (£5,720)

information on the average gross returns in these areas from private practice. One therefore does not know to what extent dentists are willing to accept a lower income in order to derive other, mainly social, benefits from practising in such well-manned (or should we say well-mannered) areas of the country.

Why are certain parts of the country so attractive to dentists? The question is obviously one which cannot be satisfactorily tackled here. Several fields of inquiry are, however, clearly important. The following three aspects might be of particular relevance.

Social-class Structure of the Population

Cook and Walker show that whereas there is no association between the staffing of the general dental services of an executive council area and the total population of the area,[1] there is clear evidence in England and Wales,

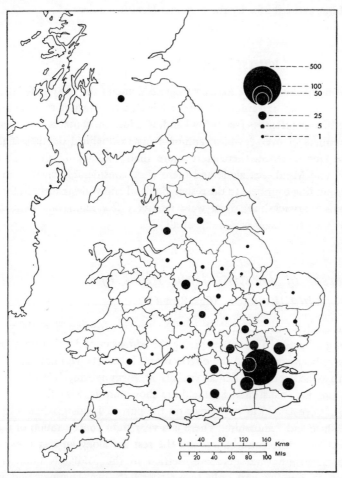

FIG. 8.6   Distribution of immigrant dentists, 1966

[1] There is, however, a link between size and change through time. Between 1952 and 1962 the executive council areas with populations of under 100,000 fared worst, with a median decline in the ratio of dentists to population of 15 per cent. In contrast councils with populations of over 500,000 had the same median value in both years. Overall the pattern of movement between 1952 and 1962 was largely regional, with a drift towards London and the South East: Cook and Walker, *op. cit.*, 6 June 1967, 494

though not in Scotland, of an association with the social class structure of the population. This conclusion holds good for the 1967–8 data examined above. Thus, the higher the proportion of persons in socio-economic group I (employers, managers and professional workers) the higher the proportion of dentists, and the higher the proportion of persons in socio-economic group III (mainly unskilled and semi-skilled manual workers) the lower the proportion of dentists. Notable exceptions to the first generalization are the counties of Warwick and Worcester. There is a similar association between the social class structure of an executive council area and the volume of treatment carried out and paid for by the National Health Service.

Immigrant Dentists (fig. 8.6)

Scrutiny of the *Dentists Register* suggests some of the reasons for the good conditions in southern England. The area is clearly attractive to fairly recently qualified British dentists (see below) and, in addition, contains very considerable numbers of overseas-born and/or overseas-qualified dentists (fig. 8.6). In 1966, for instance, there were more than 500 'immigrant dentists' in London and Middlesex alone and there were considerable clusters in all of the surrounding counties. In the rest of England and Wales, except in Staffordshire and Warwickshire, there were relatively few immigrant dentists and in many counties there were none at all.

Dispersal of Dentists from Place of Qualification (figs. 8.7a–f)

For each dentist resident in Britain the *Dentists Register* gives the year and place of graduation. The entries giving the addresses of dentists on 1 January 1966 have been sorted and the distribution of dentists who graduated in the years 1956–60 from the dental schools at Birmingham, Bristol, Durham, Leeds, London (R.C.S.) and Sheffield are shown on fig. 8.7a–f.

Map A reveals a clear preference on the part of Leeds graduates to settle in Yorkshire and Lancashire. There is a very tight concentration of them in the West Yorkshire conurbation and the rest are along an east-to-west axis through Leeds. Several graduates settled in the Midlands but only five ventured to London and only two reached the well-manned and much-favoured south coast.

Map B is a curiously stretched-out inland distribution, though one Sheffield graduate reached the Scillies. The majority settled within a few miles of the route being taken by the M1 from London to Leeds. Many stayed in Sheffield.

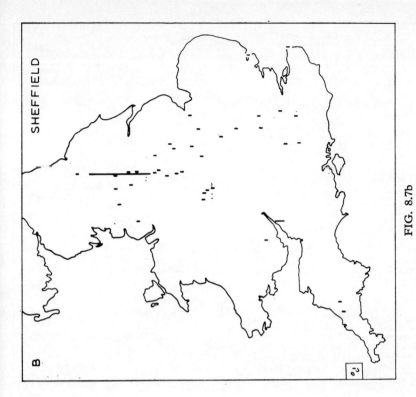

LEEDS

25
20
15
10
5
0

A

FIG. 8.7a

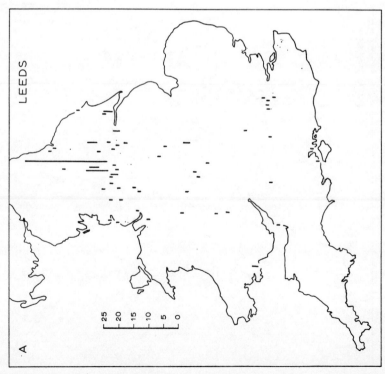

SHEFFIELD

B

FIG. 8.7b

P

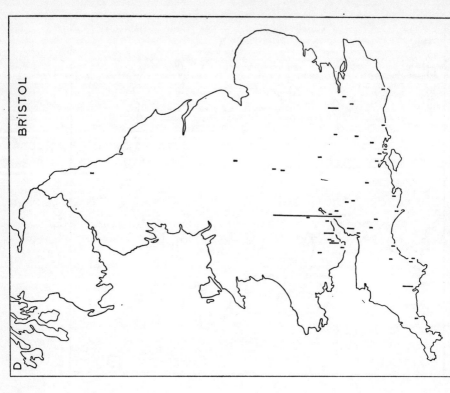

BRISTOL

FIG. 8.7d

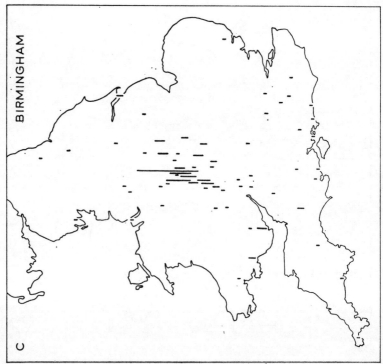

BIRMINGHAM

FIG. 8.7c

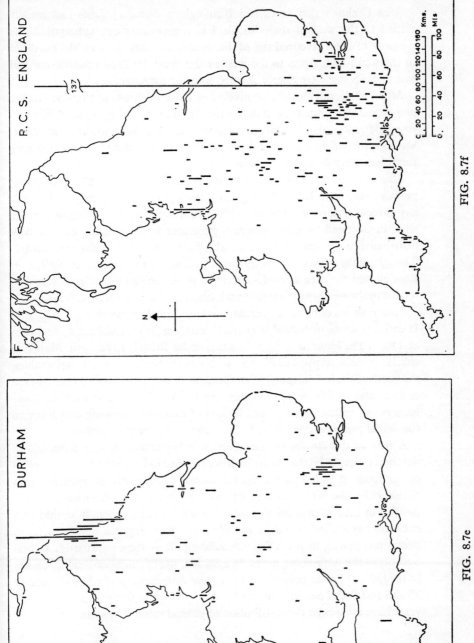

FIG. 8.7e

FIG. 8.7f

Map C shows that successful Birmingham dental students had usually settled to the west of their Sheffield contemporaries and colleagues. The majority of them favoured the Midlands and as many went to 'the north' as to the south-east. Areas to the west of the West Midland conurbation and east of Leicester were clearly deemed to be unattractive.

Map D indicates that the relatively few Bristol dentists of 1956–60 vintage had clustered within a few miles of the Bristol Channel by 1966. A few had streamed eastwards to London and more funnelled down to the south coast, leaving some of their number en route. Only four ventured beyond the northern boundary of Gloucestershire!

Map E shows that Durham's output was very considerable. These 'Durham' graduates are from King's College, Newcastle, which now forms the University of Newcastle upon Tyne. Map E does not show that four Durham dentists were in Scotland by 1966. Durham graduates were obviously more widely distributed than were those of Leeds, Sheffield, Birmingham and Bristol. Though many stayed in north-east England, more than thirty settled in London and the area immediately north of it. On the other hand very few settled in the south-west, on the south coast, in Wales or on Merseyside.

Map F shows only those dentists whose sole qualification is R.C.S. England. It excludes those with double qualifications, e.g. Bristol and R.C.S., or Leeds and R.C.S. The latter have been classified under Bristol, Leeds, etc. Map F is similar in some respects to Map E. It differs in the degree of clustering along the south coast, in Liverpool, in all the areas in and around London and in the almost total avoidance of the Northern Region. If the movement of Durhamers to London were matched by that of Londoners to north-east England the dental manpower situation in the latter would be transformed.

A part of the answer to the question 'what makes an area attractive to dentists' seems to be that many dentists practise in or within fifty miles or so of the town in which they lived for several years as dental students. This should cheer the Welsh for they can look forward to retaining a sizeable proportion of graduates from the new Cardiff Dental School. It should also encourage those interested in reducing the gross regional discrepancies in dental manpower, to press for the building of, or the extension of, Dental Schools in the unfavoured areas. In addition, the products of Dental Schools in the favoured areas could be more evenly distributed if the Department of Health and Social Security adopted policies similar to those which for twenty years have influenced the distribution of general medical practitioners.

The School Dental Services (fig. 8.8)

It is not unusual to find the writers of official reports on the School Dental Service adopting a tone of reluctant but inevitable resignation and, more

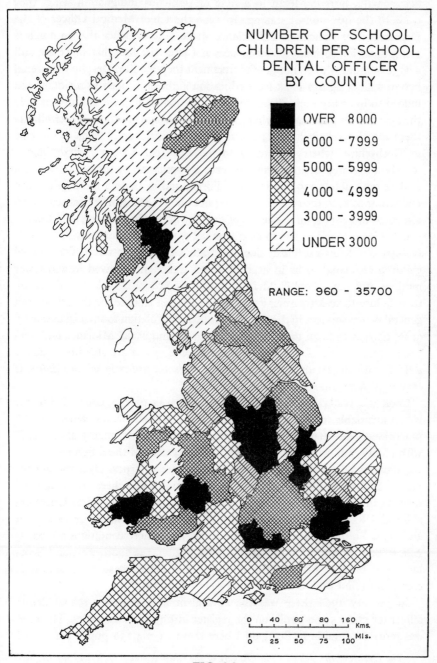

NUMBER OF SCHOOL
CHILDREN PER SCHOOL
DENTAL OFFICER
BY COUNTY

OVER 8000
6000 - 7999
5000 - 5999
4000 - 4999
3000 - 3999
UNDER 3000

RANGE: 960 - 35700

FIG. 8.8

occasionally, bursting forth in a tone of righteous indignation when they come to the question of staffing. In 1966 the Chief Medical Officer of the Department of Education and Science wrote: 'the evidence that so much is being done for so many children does not alter the fact that there are still a large number who do not get the treatment they require. Despite the overall better staffing figures most local education authorities need to maintain and indeed to intensify their efforts to recruit dental staff . . . it is unfortunately the case that in those areas where there is a shortage of school dental officers there are also relatively few general dental practitioners.'[1] Such is the case in Derbyshire, where, according to the Principal School Dental Officer, 'barely a hundred dentists exist to serve a population of three-quarters of a million with about 120,000 school children, and of these a mere half-dozen endeavour to keep the school dental service alive'.[2] Some of the consequences are noted in a report on the health of the City of Sheffield where, as in Derbyshire, there is 'good reason to be concerned with the difficulties which cannot be separated from a seriously depleted staff, less than one-tenth of the school children estimated to be in need of dental treatment received it, and fewer mothers and pre-school children attended the school dental clinics' and by their failure to seek treatment they are storing up trouble for the school and general dental services in the future. It is little consolation to such an authority or its citizens to learn that 'parts of Wales, the industrial Midlands and northern areas and parts of the eastern areas of England are still inadequately staffed' with the result that '*the standard of dental fitness in school children is very much lower than should be tolerated*'.[3]

Cook and Walker, writing about the situation in 1962–3, concluded that it is 'not invariably true that (local) authorities with relatively few general dental practitioners also have few school dental officers, or that plenty always goes with plenty, but there is a clear regional segregation of the different possible combinations especially of these two more extreme types. Over the greater part of Yorkshire, East Anglia, the Midlands and Wales there are far too few dentists in either branch of the service. Glamorgan, Derbyshire, Leicestershire and Rutland, Nottingham City and County, Staffordshire, Kesteven and West Bromwich stand out as the authorities where conditions are particularly bad. However, in the metropolitan region, the south-west and Scotland, and even in parts of the Northern and North-western regions it is common to find both branches relatively well staffed.'[4]

In January 1966 there was the equivalent of a full-time school dental officer for every 5,460 pupils on the register in England and Wales. The ratio was more favourable in Scotland where there were 4,250 pupils per school

[1] *The Health of the School Child. Report of the Chief Medical Officer of the Department of Education and Science for the years 1964 and 1965*, H.M.S.O., 1966, 99
[2] *Ibid.*, 99
[3] *Annual Report on the Health of the City of Sheffield 1964*, 1965, 30
[4] Cook and Walker, *op. cit.*, 446

dental officer on 31 July 1965.[1] These averages conceal a staggering range in the staffing position from one authority to another. In Scotland, for instance, 17 counties have ratios of one dentist to fewer than 3,000 pupils, yet the ratio is 1 : 10,530 in Glasgow, 1 : 9,700 in the City of Aberdeen, 1 : 6,460 in Lanark, 1 : 6,100 in Renfrew and 1 : 6,080 in Ayr – a revealing commentary on the problem of attracting dental practitioners to the more heavily populated cities and industrial areas. Yet the staffing situation is very much worse in many English areas. For instance, in the administrative county of Derbyshire there are 24,400 pupils per dentist and in that of Leicestershire there is an even more astronomical 35,700 pupils per dentist. Furthermore, the ratio is on the wrong side of 10,000 in the administrative counties of Berkshire,

TABLE 8.4   Number of Schoolchildren per School Dentist, by Geographical County

Average ratio	England*	Wales	Scotland†	Great Britain
Under 3,000	1	2	17	20
3,000–3,999	4	2	7	13
4,000–4,999	14	5	4	23
5,000–5,999	8	0	0	8
6,000–7,999	10	3	3	16
8,000 and above	8	1	2	11
	—	—	—	—
	45	13	33	91

* Including the Ridings of Yorkshire, the three parts of Lincolnshire, and two parts of Suffolk and Sussex. The Isle of Ely is linked with Cambridgeshire and the Isle of Wight with Hampshire
† Including the four city counties of Aberdeen, Dundee, Edinburgh and Glasgow

Holland (Lincolnshire) and Nottingham.[2] County boroughs with more than 10,000 pupils per school dentist are Bootle (11,000), Hull (11,500), Luton (12,350), Middlesbrough (14,930), Oxford (14,930), Preston (12,820), Salford (10,100), Sheffield (14,700) and Southend-on-Sea (18,870). In contrast there are about the same number of boroughs with ratios of under 3,500 and these too form a mixed bag of northern and southern towns, such as Dewsbury and Eastbourne, Rotherham and Exeter, Sunderland and Kingston upon Thames, as well as places like Smethwick and West Bromwich (one of the worst in 1962) in the West Midlands.

Data on the staffing of the school dental service in the administrative counties and county boroughs have been aggregated where necessary to

[1] Scottish Home and Health Department, *Scottish Health Statistics 1965*, H.M.S.O., 1967, 112; Ministry of Health, *Annual Report 1966*, 1967
[2] Yet the administrative counties are obviously more successful in attracting dental than medical officers into the school service: 25 have ratios for school dentists more favourable than the average for England and Wales compared with only 10 in the case of school medical officers

obtain average figures for the geographical counties of Great Britain. The results are shown on fig. 8.8 and summarized by country in table 8.4.

Fig. 8.8 depicts a complex pattern with no readily apparent zoning, though four points do emerge relatively clearly. Firstly, areas with favourable ratios are most extensive in Scotland, East Anglia, along the south coast of England and in central and northern Wales. Secondly, the most extensive area with generally unfavourable ratios is that between the Thames and the northern boundaries of Lincolnshire, Nottinghamshire and Derbyshire. Thirdly, South Wales, the North Riding of Yorkshire and a group of English counties flanking the Welsh border also have more than 6,000 pupils per school dentist. Fourthly, changes from county to county in the same general area are often abrupt, e.g. Radnor and Hereford; West and East Suffolk, and Denbigh and Merioneth. The poor performance of counties on the northern flank of Greater London might reflect a population explosion in the schools and be associated with New Towns and the fairly general influx of migrants from other parts of the Home Counties, from the rest of Britain and from overseas.

It should not be inferred that the standard of dental treatment for children of school age is directly related to the pattern indicated on fig. 8.8. In the first place the school population is taken as being that in maintained schools only. Secondly, a valid assessment of the adequacy of the dental services provided for children cannot be made by a consideration of the school dental services alone.[1] It is also necessary, in each area, to take into account the dental care for children which is being contributed in some instances by hospital dental officers or by private dental surgeons working in the National Health Service under contract to the Local Executive Councils (compare figs. 8.1, 3 and 8). In recent years the latter have provided an increasing service for children. Yet, despite the improvement overall, there are still too many children who do not benefit. The fact that these children *are unevenly distributed is due to the considerable variations in the staffing position from authority to authority.* This in turn gives rise to a 'benign spiral'. The more staff an authority acquires the more attractive it becomes because of the higher standard of dental care it is able to offer, with wider clinical opportunities and fewer frustrations. There is the corollary that an inadequately staffed service is less likely to attract new staff.

Many of the aspects of the dental service for school children noted above can be illustrated with reference to detailed information published by the Scottish Home and Health Department in 1967 on the School Dental Services in Scotland in the year 1965.[2] From these data it is possible to calculate the

---

[1] The statements in the rest of this paragraph are based on *The Health of the School Child. Report of the Chief Medical Officer of the Department of Education and Science for the years 1964 and 1965*, H.M.S.O., 1966

[2] Scottish Home and Health Department, *Scottish Health Statistics 1965*, Section VIII, 112

TABLE 8.5   School Dental Service in Scotland

Education Authority Areas	No. of children on registers per School Dental Officer	Percentage of total school populations seen at routine inspections	No. of children treated by school dental officers as a percentage of no. of children on registers	No. of children who would have been treated given the same intensity of care as in the control areas (average of 6)
	1	2	3	4
Scotland	4,250	43·3	17·3	251,660
Cities				
Aberdeen	9,700	64·2	10·8	11,110
Dundee	3,500	92·4	22·8	7,170
Edinburgh	3,520	46·5	17·2	17,980
Glasgow	10,530	20·0	10·8	60,320
Counties				
Aberdeen	4,620	59·3	14·1	7,400
Angus	2,960	66·5	22·9	3,360
Argyll	2,860	88·0	36·8	750
Ayr	6,080	14·9	11·0	21,000
Banff	4,070	99·0	40·1	Control
Berwick	1,800	49·7	38·2	260
Bute	4,870	99·2	24·7	410
Caithness	2,430	54·8	46·1	Control
Clackmannan	2,390	88·1	35·9	690
Dumfries	2,980	85·5	23·5	3,280
Dunbarton	3,780	21·6	21·8	8,060
East Lothian	4,590	56·8	11·1	3,160
Fife	3,500	46·5	19·2	15,040
Inverness	1,980	50·5	28·4	2,540
Kincardine	3,210	52·7	9·3	1,630
Kirkcudbright	2,340	74·2	18·3	1,270
Lanark	6,460	31·3	7·6	42,200
Midlothian and Peebles	1,940	39·8	28·9	3,870
Moray and Nairn	3,500	74·9	14·6	3,250
Orkney	2,980	40·0	43·0	Control
Perth and Kinross	2,610	56·0	17·3	5,700
Renfrew	6,100	33·0	19·5	15,850
Ross and Cromarty	2,140	66·1	32·2	1,430
Roxburgh and Selkirk	2,410	62·2	25·7	1,920
Stirling	3,230	65·0	24·6	7,090
Sutherland	2,300	63·2	46·8	Control
West Lothian	2,460	69·8	30·5	2,770
Wigtown	2,640	39·5	45·7	Control
Zetland	960	64·5	61·1	Control

Source: Based on tables in Scottish Home and Health Department: *Scottish Health Statistics 1965* (1967), Section VIII, 112

ratio of school dental officers to pupils on the register, the number of children treated by school dental officers as a proportion of the school population, and the number of children who would have been treated by school dental officers if the intensity of care found in the top six authorities[1] was equalled elsewhere. These items, together with the percentage of the total school population seen at routine inspections, are shown in table 8.5 for each of the education authority areas.

One can sense in these figures 'the benign spiral' at work. Even after making allowance for variations in the efficiency of the school dental service from authority to authority, the contrasts in columns 2 and 3 of table 8.5 are in general terms the direct result of the numerical adequacy of school dentists in the given authorities. Thus in Glasgow there are fewer than one-twelfth of the school dental officers in Scotland to serve almost one-fifth of Scotland's school population. As a result there are more pupils per dentist than in any other authority and not surprisingly fewer than one-quarter of the pupils are seen at routine inspections and only one-tenth are treated by school dental officers. The general standard of children's teeth must be very bad indeed, and the situation can hardly be much better in counties such as Lanark, East Lothian and Dunbarton. It may be even worse in Ayr. In contrast there are areas where the staffing situation is good and where as a result a very high proportion of children are seen regularly by their school dental officers and in many cases treated by them.

The corollary of such wide variations in the 'adequacy' of the school dental service is that the general dental services are faced by an equally uneven demand. As already noted, general dental surgeons and school dental officers are often either thinly or thickly distributed on the ground in the same areas. This should be borne in mind when examining column 4 of table 8.5. It is reasonable to assume that a high proportion of the schoolchildren in places such as Glasgow, Renfrew, Lanark and Ayr who were not treated by their school dental service would not be treated outside it. In these four local education authorities alone as many as 139,370 children would have been treated if there had been the same intensity of care and need as in the six Scottish local education authorities with the highest proportions of schoolchildren treated by their school dental services.

The considerable regional inequalities in the general and school dental services in England and Wales are reflected in figures showing the proportion of the resident population of the hospital regions seen as patients in a given year. Table 8.6 shows that whereas on average more than one-fifth of the total population of England and Wales was seen by the school dental and

[1] The six education authorities are Banff, Caithness, Orkney, Sutherland, Wigtown and Zetland. In these areas in 1965 not less than 40 per cent of the children on school registers were treated by school dental officers. On average 45·5 per cent of children at school were treated in these six areas compared with the Scottish average of 17·3 per cent

general dental services,[1] the best levels of dental care were in the four London, the Oxford and the South West regions. All of the southerly regions, except Wessex, topped the national average and Wessex was the best of the regions below it. At the extreme more than two and one-half times as many people were seen in the South West Metropolitan region than in the Birmingham region and twice as many in the South West compared with the Newcastle, Sheffield and Leeds regions.[2]

TABLE 8.6   Combined General and School Dental Service demand rate

Hospital region	Percentage of population	Index number
S.W. Metropolitan	37·5	171
South West	32·1	146
N.W. Metropolitan	29·5	134
S.E. Metropolitan	29·3	133
Oxford	27·1	123
N.E. Metropolitan	25·8	117
Average for England and Wales	*22·0*	*100*
Wessex	21·4	97
Liverpool	20·3	92
Manchester	18·7	85
Wales	18·5	84
East Anglia	17·2	78
Newcastle	16·4	74·5
Sheffield	16·4	74·5
Leeds	15·6	71
Birmingham	14·7	67

Twenty years after the inauguration of the National Health Service – established to give adequate care and attention to each individual, irrespective of his means and place of residence – the Minister of Health laid before Parliament a Green Paper entitled 'Administrative structure of the medical and related services in England and Wales' (H.M.S.O., 1968). In it, attention is focused on the ill-effects resulting from the multiplicity of authorities concerned in the present health service. There are 15 Regional Hospital Boards, 330 Hospital Management Committees, 36 Boards of Governors (26 of which are in London), 134 executive councils and 175 local health authorities. All told, there are nearly 700 separate authorities in the present administrative structure. No wonder the geographical discrepancies, some of which have

---

[1] *On the State of the Public Health*, H.M.S.O., 1966, 140
[2] Table 8.6 does not include the number of patients treated by the hospital and specialist orthodontic service, 'the development of which varies considerably from region to region and for which separate regional figures are not available. The overall figures might, therefore, show a *slightly* different picture' – *On the State of the Public Health, 1965*, 1966, 139

been spotlighted in this and the previous chapter, are so gross. It is inevitable that 'the published development plans of (175) local authorities (should) show wide variations between different areas in standards of service, both actual *and planned*' (*Green Paper*); that the evidence should show similar wide areal variations in the hospital service, when the staffing, equipping and running of the *national* hospital service is in the hands of 350 authorities in England and Wales alone; that there should be such gross regional inequalities in the general dental service, when there are 134 executive councils sharing responsibility for providing an adequate service throughout the country. The Green Paper proposes the establishment of about 40 or 50 Area Boards, with an average population of about 1¼ million, and each would be responsible for providing a *comprehensive* health service. Such a reorganization, if it goes through, would be sure to receive a great welcome from all those research workers who, for the first time, could look forward to analysing different sets of data on the health service relating to the same geographical base. A *comprehensive* 'Geography of Health' could then be written. In the meantime, we have to be content with the analysis of *selected* aspects of the health service, using data variously presented by regional hospital board, or executive council, or local authority areas, and, as a result, each series being more often than not non-comparable with other series. Yet, using the current framework of up to 700 units (the 700 separate 'health' authorities referred to above) and the infinite number of ways in which these might be arranged, the irrationality of the geographical distribution of medical and dental manpower and facilities has been discerned. Regional discrepancies are indeed marked. Some of the consequences of this situation, and of the geographical inequalities in the health service over the past few decades, are demonstrated in the following chapter.

9

Mortality

Some of the regional variations in the geography of the medical and dental services examined in chapters 7 and 8 demonstrate the limited usefulness of thinking of the United Kingdom, or even of its constituent countries and regions, as an area, or areas, with a population of uniform characteristics. The well-being of the population and the medical facilities available to people are partly determined by where they happened to live in the past and where they happen to live now. That these factors are of great importance is most clearly shown by an examination of mortality rates in different parts of the realm. Fortunately, this is one field of inquiry in which the data are generally adequate and amenable to geographical analysis. Indeed, the United Kingdom is at present the 'best laboratory for those interested in the bio-statistical approach to medical geography',[1] for recording the mortality and cause of death is much more accurate than in most parts of the world and the information is generally available for administrative units as low in the hierarchy as urban and rural districts. In consequence maps of mortality variations in the United Kingdom are fairly reliable.

The geography of death has been the subject of intense, indeed lively, interest in the last decade. Geographers such as Howe,[2] Murray,[3] and Stamp[4] and research workers in medicine and allied fields, such as Ashley, Court Brown *et al.*, Crofton, Doll, Hewitt, and Morris *et al.*,[5] have directed attention

[1] Murray, Malcolm A., 'The geography of death in the United States and the United Kingdom', *Annals, Association of American Geographers*, **57**, 1967, 303
[2] Howe, G. Melvyn, 'The geographical distribution of cancer mortality in Wales, 1947–53', *Transactions and Papers, Institute of British Geographers*, **28**, 1960, 199–214; 'The geographical variations of disease mortality in England and Wales in the mid-twentieth century', *Advancement of Science*, **17**, No. 69, 1961, 415–25; 'Geographical distribution of disease with special reference to cancer of the lung and stomach in Wales', *British Journal of Preventive and Social Medicine*, **13**, 1959, 204–10; *National Atlas of Disease Mortality in the United Kingdom*, 1963
[3] Murray, Malcolm A., 'The geography of death in England and Wales', *Annals, Association of American Geographers*, **52**, 1962, 130–49; see also footnote 1 above
[4] Stamp, L. Dudley, *Some Aspects of Medical Geography*, 1964; *The Geography of Life and Death*, 1964, 160 pp.
[5] For instance, Ashley, D. J. B., 'The distribution of lung cancer and bronchitis in England and Wales', *The British Journal of Cancer*, **21**, No. 2, 1967, 243–59; Court Brown, W. B. *et al.*, 'Geographical distribution of primary tumours of bone in England and Wales', *British Journal of Preventive and Social Medicine*, **15**, 1961, 167–70; Morris, J. N. *et al.*, 'Hardness of local water supplies and mortality from cardiovascular disease in the county boroughs of England and Wales', *The Lancet*, **1**, No. 7182, 1961,

to the spatial variations in the incidence of mortality from specific diseases and from all causes. Their findings demonstrate the existence and nature of wide regional variations in mortality rates in the United Kingdom.

From a geographical point of view G. Melvyn Howe has worked on the frontiers of this research activity in the United Kingdom. As a professional geographer his main concern has been with the mapping of the incidence of mortality rather than with the explanations of the patterns so described. For instance, in papers published in 1959 and 1960 he explored the pattern of cancer mortality in Wales in the period 1947–53. On the basis of his mapping of the areal incidence of mortality rates from cancers of selected organs of the human body Howe concludes that an examination of the irregularities and apparent anomalies in these geographical distributions might suggest profitable lines of medical and geographical research. He finds, for example, that the distribution in Wales of mortality from lung-bronchus cancer offers sufficient correlation with the pattern of selected indices of atmospheric pollution to imply an association with atmospheric carcinogens. Similarly, Howe postulates that there would appear to be a parallelism worthy of further study between the incidence of stomach cancers and the daily use in the Welsh countryside of untreated acidic water supplies and in particular with the consumption of water containing toxic chemicals derived from run-off from the abandoned lead, zinc and copper mines so common in Cardiganshire and counties farther north.

By far the most important contribution to date in the field of medical geography appeared in 1963 in the form of the *National Atlas of Disease Mortality in the United Kingdom*. Prepared by Howe on behalf of the Royal Geographical Society it is probably the most detailed analysis of its kind in the world. In the foreword to the atlas the late Lord Nathan wrote, 'a glance at these maps shows how often clear patterns of geographical variation are discernible. Such variations suggest possible relationships between disease of different kinds and environmental factors ... soil, geology, relief, climate, water, communications, settlement patterns, indeed geographical factors of every kind, have all at one time or another been shown to have influenced patterns of disease distribution.' To this list we might add, as Howe reminds us, that 'regional variations in the distribution of diseases may reflect the habits, the tempo, the mental tensions and the anxieties of our twentieth century existence, our diet, or the increasingly sedentary nature of our work'.

The atlas employs a uniform method of portraying the distribution of all, or of specific, causes of death throughout the United Kingdom in the period

---

860; Hewitt, D., 'Geographical variations in in the mortality attributed to spina bifida and other congenital malformations', *British Journal of Preventive and Social Medicine*, **17**, 1963, 13–22

1954-8, mapping the standardized mortality ratios[1] for males and females separately. The only exception is the age classification analysis of infant mortality where no distinction is made between males and females and where crude death rates are employed rather than standardized mortality ratios. The results are most significant, for the maps must surely assist research workers in many fields of study in the formulation of hypotheses as to what, if any, are the correlations between the various distributions of mortality experience and those of various environmental factors, be they organic, inorganic, social or cultural. If such causal factors can be isolated it might in time be possible to introduce preventive measures to counteract the recognized tendencies and anomalies.

Spatial Variations in Mortality Rates

Where are the areas in which people stand a better than even chance of 'dying before their time'? It is clear that the mortality rate from all causes and from selected diseases is often well above the national average in the markedly urbanized areas of South Wales, Lancashire, West Yorkshire, Central Scotland, and in certain instances, Greater London. In contrast, it is well below the national average in the less intensively urbanized areas, especially those of eastern and southern England. Howe contends that the maps showing the distribution of male and female deaths from all causes[2] are probably the most meaningful; all mortality hazards are taken into account and they may be considered to reflect the human responses to the total complex of environmental factors and the ways of life which exist in, and vary from district to district over, the United Kingdom. If this is the case then it should be noted that the counties and county boroughs with the highest standardized *male* mortality ratios are all, with the exception of three London boroughs, in the north and west of the country and those with the lowest are all in the south and east of the country. The average risk of death in the county borough with the worst s.m.r. (Salford) is 46 per cent greater than in the county borough with the best s.m.r. (Canterbury). Towns with the worst ratios include Belfast, Bradford, Glasgow, Liverpool, Merthyr Tydfil, Middlesbrough, Rochdale and Stoke-on-Trent. Towns with the most favourable

[1] For a detailed explanation see *Registrar-General's Statistical Review of England and Wales, 1954, Part 3, Commentary*, 1957, 30, 32 and 57; Howe, G. M., *National Atlas of Disease Mortality in the United Kingdom*, 1963, 2-6. The S.M.R. is used in order to take local age-sex structures into account. The United Kingdom ratios of mean annual deaths to the population of each sex and age-group during the period being investigated are multiplied by the corresponding figures for a given local population (county borough, urban district, etc.) and the resulting products aggregated to give 'expected' local annual deaths. The annual mean of actual death is then expressed as a percentage of the 'expected' annual deaths to give the S.M.R.
[2] *National Atlas of Disease Mortality*, 22-5

male mortality experience include Bath, Canterbury, Ipswich, Norwich, Oxford and Reading. For the administrative counties ratios in the urban areas of some of the worst counties (e.g. Carmarthenshire) are at least 40 per cent higher than for some of the better counties (e.g. Berkshire or Oxfordshire). The map of standardized *female* mortality ratios tells a similar story. With the exception of four London boroughs and the small towns in Kesteven and Rutland, the area south and east of a line from the Humber to the Severn has mortality ratios not much above, and often below, the national average, while that to the north and west of the line (except for the rural areas of Westmorland) have ratios in excess of the national average. The average risk of dying in the county borough with the worst s.m.r. (Burnley) is 60 per cent greater than in the county borough with the best s.m.r. (Oxford). 'Black spots' include Clydebank, Glasgow and the urban districts of Argyll, Fife, Kinross and Renfrew in Scotland; Middlesbrough in north-east England; Burnley, Oldham, Salford, St Helens and Rochdale in north-west England, and Merthyr Tydfil in Wales (all with an s.m.r. of 130 or over). The towns with the most favourable overall female mortality experience are Bath, Bournemouth, Canterbury, Gloucester, Oxford and Southampton (each with an s.m.r. between 86 and 93). For the administrative counties, the differences between those with high ratios (e.g. Dunbarton and Carmarthen) and those with low ratios (e.g. West Sussex and Oxford) are of the same order.

Are such variations important? Howe's comment deserves very careful consideration. 'It is remarkable that disparities of such magnitude occur for both male and female mortality ratios within the small compass of the United Kingdom, and this must constitute a major challenge to the authorities concerned with the health of the people in the less favoured areas and also to the public itself in those areas.' But, as shown in many parts of this book, the black areas are those which tend to have specialized and restricted employment opportunities, below average incomes and below average provision of public services, including those of the National Health Service. Not surprisingly an American geographer looking at the situation as an interested but detached observer finds mortality maps of England and Wales 'almost embarrassing in the degree to which they strongly support our intuitive preconceptions as to what the areal mortality differences should be . . . the association between total death rate variations and other distributions, both cultural and physical, is readily apparent to those familiar with the geography of this region'. The commentator, Malcolm A. Murray, mapped, for England and Wales, the male mortality patterns in the period 1950-3 attributed to the seven largest 'cause of death' categories, e.g. bronchitis, pneumonia, tuberculosis of the respiratory system and vascular lesions affecting the central nervous system; the death rate variations from all causes, 1948-57, and infant mortality (males *and* females – period not given). With one exception (mortality from all causes) Murray took data for administrative counties and county boroughs and the results are not therefore so refined as those in Howe's atlas. In a more recent paper, published in 1967, Murray studied the patterns of overall mortality from all causes and infant mortality in England and Wales during the period 1958–62. These maps are, therefore, more up to date than those in the *National Atlas of Disease Mortality*, but Scotland and Northern Ireland are excluded. Murray reached the same conclusion in both of his studies. 'With some exceptions, the [mortality] rates tend to be distinctly higher in the industrialized, exploitive, and densely populated areas; for example, the Lancashire-Yorkshire manufacturing area, the Birmingham and Black Country district, southern Wales, Durham, and Tyneside, and more isolated examples such as Stoke-on-Trent. The London area is about average. The more prosperous agricultural counties of the south and east generally experience lower rates than the farming and grazing counties of the north and west. On a broad basis, northern England, the Pennine area, and most of Wales experience higher rates than southern and eastern England.'

Murray's use of adjectives in describing the overall mortality pattern could be misleading in that it might suggest to some readers that the reasons for the spatial variations in mortality are known and that they are clearly linked to, say, prosperity of farming, density of population and extent of manufacturing industry. In fact, as pointed out above, the reasons, where known, are varied; mortality patterns reflect the past conditions of life as well as the present. For instance, the high S.M.R.s of places such as Merthyr Tydfil, Middlesbrough, Glasgow and Liverpool are part of the price being paid for the 'Hungry Thirties'. They reflect the composition of the population in terms of social class, educational standards, income and job security. High S.M.R.s there, and elsewhere, also symbolize the inadequacy of medical care, now and in the past.

The rates of infant mortality, and mortality from tuberculosis of the respiratory system and bronchitis, are often taken to be indicative of the socio-economic level of living in an area. For this reason geographical variations in the under-one age-group and in the two specified categories are examined in the following sections.

Infant Mortality

Infant mortality refers to deaths of children under one year of age. As an age category rather than a classification of cause of death the rate consists of deaths from all causes, medical and otherwise; the aggregate infant mortality rate of a given community results from a multiplicity of medical characteristics and the interaction of physical and social factors. Owing to its close association with certain socio-economic phenomena the rate is generally thought to be a good index of living standards.

The areal variations in infant mortality rates in the United Kingdom in the years 1954–8 and, for England and Wales only, in the period 1958–62 have been mapped by Howe and Murray,[1] respectively.

1954–8

In this period an average of 22,689 babies died each year, and the average annual infant mortality rate for the United Kingdom was 27·5 per 1,000 live births. The rate was as low as 23·8 in England and Wales and as high as 29·4 in Scotland and 30·2 in Northern Ireland. Howe found that the rate was particularly high in the *rural* districts of Carmarthenshire, Cumberland, the West Riding of Yorkshire, Stirlingshire, Ayrshire and the four western counties of Northern Ireland. High rates were recorded in the *urban* districts of the South Wales coalfield, Staffordshire, south Lancashire (particularly St Helens and Warrington), the North Riding of Yorkshire and Durham (especially Middlesbrough and West Hartlepool), Lanarkshire, Glasgow itself and the Ulster counties of Armagh, Down and Tyrone.

Infant mortality rates were particularly low (under 20) in three widely separated Scottish counties (Sutherland, Aberdeen and Peebles) and several eastern and south-eastern counties in England, e.g. Kesteven, Hertford, Middlesex, Berkshire and East Sussex.

1958-62: England and Wales only

Murray found the areal pattern of infant mortality at this time corresponded fairly closely with the pattern of overall mortality variations from all causes. As Murray plots the data for the rural districts, rather than the aggregated figures for the administrative counties, his map is more complex. Because the rates for the rural districts often vary widely within a county it is more difficult and certainly more dangerous to make broad generalizations. Moreover, the number of deaths in many sparsely populated rural areas will be very low and the annual average rate of infant mortality should not be taken as being as statistically reliable as in the urban areas with many more deaths and births. It is apparent, however, that the pattern is very much the same as that of the preceding five-year period. Most of the black spots, with more than 28 deaths per 1,000 live births, are north and west of a line from the Humber to the Exe. Within this area they are particularly common in Wales, Lancashire and the north-east.

---

[1] Howe, G. M., 1963, *op. cit.*, 76, 80 and 81; Murray, M. A., 1967, *op. cit.*, 304

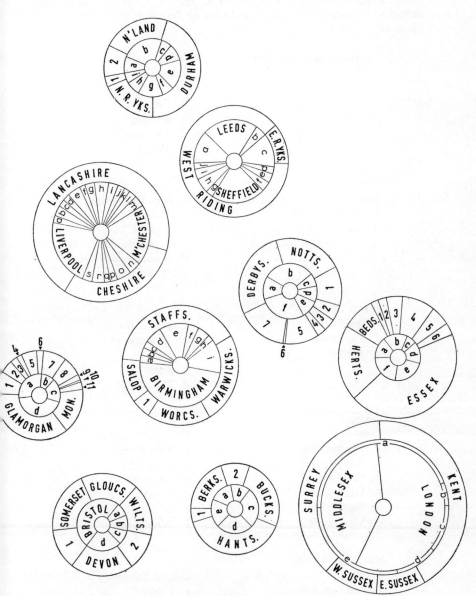

FIG. 9.1 Isodemic chart of county boroughs and administrative counties, arranged by the standard region, 1961 (index to unnamed units on pp. 230-2)

1961: STANDARD REGIONS – ISODEMIC CHART   Index to
unnamed Counties (numbered) and County Boroughs (lettered) on
fig. 9.1

LONDON AND SOUTH EASTERN
Counties:

County Boroughs:
a   Croydon
b   Canterbury
c   Hastings
d   Eastbourne
e   Brighton

SOUTHERN
Counties:
1   Isle of Wight
2   Oxford

County Boroughs:
a   Reading
b   Oxford
c   Portsmouth
d   Southampton
e   Bournemouth

SOUTH WESTERN
Counties:
1   Cornwall
2   Dorset

County Boroughs:
a   Gloucester
b   Bath
c   Exeter
d   Plymouth

EASTERN
Counties:
1   Huntingdon
2   Isle of Ely
3   Cambridge
4   Norfolk
5   East Suffolk
6   West Suffolk

County Boroughs:
a   East Ham
b   Norwich
c   Great Yarmouth
d   Ipswich
e   Southend on Sea
f   West Ham

NORTH MIDLANDS
Counties:
1   Lindsey, Lincs.
2   Kesteven, Lincs.
3   Holland, Lincs.
4   Soke of Peterborough
5   Northampton
6   Rutland
7   Leicester

County Boroughs:
a   Derby
b   Nottingham
c   Lincoln
d   Grimsby
e   Northampton
f   Leicester

(WEST) MIDLAND

Counties:	County Boroughs:
1 Hereford	a Worcester
	b Smethwick
	c Dudley
	d Wolverhampton
	e Stoke on Trent
	f West Bromwich
	g Walsall
	h Burton upon Trent
	i Coventry

WALES

Counties:	County Boroughs:
1 Carmarthen	a Swansea
2 Pembroke	b Merthyr Tydfil
3 Cardigan	c Newport
4 Merioneth	d Cardiff
5 Caernarvon	
6 Anglesey	
7 Denbigh	
8 Flint	
9 Montgomery	
10 Radnor	
11 Brecon	

EAST AND WEST RIDINGS,
YORKSHIRE

County Boroughs:
a Bradford
b York
c Kingston upon Hull
d Wakefield
e Doncaster
f Rotherham
g Barnsley
h Huddersfield
i Halifax
j Dewsbury

NORTH WESTERN

Counties:	County Boroughs:
	a Bootle
	b St Helens
	c Southport
	d Wigan
	e Blackpool
	f Barrow in Furness
	g Preston

NORTH WESTERN—*cont.*

Counties:

County Boroughs:
h Bolton
i Blackburn
j Burnley
k Bury
l Rochdale
m Oldham
n Stockport
o Salford
p Warrington
q Crewe
r Birkenhead
s Wallasey

NORTHERN
Counties:
1 Westmorland
2 Cumberland

County Boroughs:
a Gateshead
b Newcastle upon Tyne
c Tynemouth
d South Shields
e Sunderland
f West Hartlepool
g Middlesbrough
h Darlington
i Carlisle

1959–63: Isodemic Chart of Infant Mortality in England and Wales (fig. 9.2)

Both Howe and Murray use conventional base-maps in their mapping of infant mortality. By appropriately shading the geographical areas occupied by the administrative units being studied, their maps reflect the areal extent rather than the population size of the units. The great variations in size of population and thus the significance of the shadings in terms of the relative volumes of deaths are obscured, except in so far as the map-reader is accustomed to equating a multiplicity of small administrative units in a given area with urbanized districts. Fig. 9.1 has therefore been constructed to allow mortality variations from place to place to be shown in relation to size of population rather than area. This is achieved by using a base-map on which the administrative units, in this case administrative counties and county boroughs arranged according to *standard regions*, are shown in proportion to the size of their total population in 1961. As a result, Radnor, which normally occupies a much greater area than Birmingham, is here very much smaller. Similarly, East Sussex is very much smaller than Middlesex.

The data for fig. 9.2 cover the five years 1959–63 and are drawn from the latest *Decennial Supplement* of the Registrar-General for England and Wales.

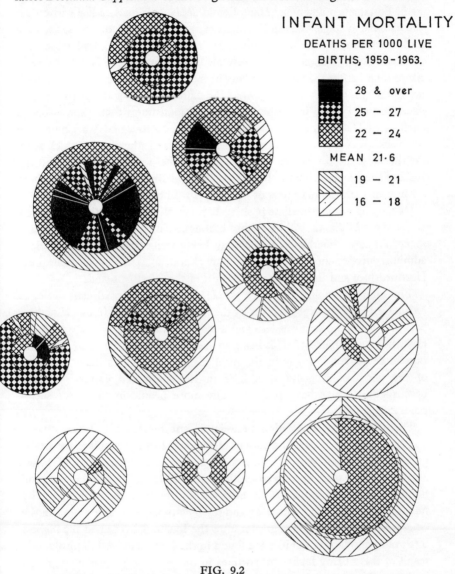

INFANT MORTALITY

DEATHS PER 1000 LIVE
BIRTHS, 1959-1963.

28 & over
25 — 27
22 — 24

MEAN 21·6

19 — 21
16 — 18

FIG. 9.2

On average, 17,474 infants died each year, giving a death rate of 21·64 per 1,000 live births.

The bulk of the populations of the South Eastern, Eastern, Southern, South Western and North Midland standard regions live in major administrative units with an infant mortality rate more favourable than that for England and Wales as a whole. The rest, in the counties of Isle of Ely,

234 MORTALITY

Lindsey and London (a huge area in terms of population) and the county boroughs of Bournemouth, Derby, Gloucester, Grimsby, Leicester, Nottingham, Portsmouth and West Ham, live in areas with rates rather worse than the national average. Only in Nottingham is the rate markedly worse than the national mean. At the other end of the scale are the standard regions of East and West Ridings, Northern, Wales, and worst of all, North Western. More than half of the urban dwellers in the North West Region live in black areas, the rest are in areas worse than the national mean, with the paradoxical exception of Barrow-in-Furness. Fig. 9.2 demonstrates that whereas places such as St Helens, Preston, Burnley, Oldham, Salford and Warrington are jet-black areas it is the blackness of Liverpool and Manchester which is by far the most important fact in terms of both the number of deaths and the scale of the problem. Similarly, the blackness of Bradford is very much more significant than the blackness of Merthyr Tydfil or Newport.

Occupying an intermediate position between the good and the bad regions is the West Midlands. All its county boroughs have rates above the national mean, Dudley, Smethwick and Walsall being well above, but the populous administrative county of Warwick is more akin to areas like Buckinghamshire, Hertfordshire and Surrey than to the rest of the West Midlands.

The infant mortality rate rises as one descends the social class scale, as recognized for statistical purposes by the Registrar-General. In the immediate post-war years the rate was two and a half times higher in the lowest social class than in the highest.[1] This being so one would expect the infant mortality rate to be higher in many of the rural districts and older industrial areas of the north of England than it is in the south and east of England because the former have proportionally more people in the lower socio-economic groups.

The fairly close association between infant mortality and the general standard of living is due to a variety of reasons. In the first place the risk is greater for infants born to mothers on a poor diet, to mothers of below average stature, to mothers who continue at work longer before delivery, and to unmarried mothers. In 1964 in Scotland, for instance, the infant mortality rate for legitimate children was 23 and for illegitimate children 37 (43 in the cities). Secondly, the risk is greater after the fourth delivery and the highest birth rates and largest families are found in the north and west. Thirdly, as a result of there being higher proportions in the lower socio-economic groups in the north and west it is likely that the overall level of ante- and post-natal care and assistance will be of a lower order than it is in the south and east.[2]

[1] Registrar-General, *Statistical Review of England and Wales, 1951, Text Volume*, 1954, 207
[2] Naturally there are similar differences within a Regional Hospital Board area (see Chart 23 in the *Quinquennial Report of the work of the Sheffield R.H.B., 1957–62*, which, for the year 1962, shows the proportion of hospital deliveries in the sub-units within the Board's area – from Leicester to Barnsley and Derby to Skegness). J. S. G.

Fourthly, the unsatisfactory nature of much of the housing and general physical environment in the north and west leads to a lower standard of household facilities, the more rapid spread of disease in overcrowded households and the many problems associated with overcrowding.[1]

During the post-war period the infant mortality rate has continued to fall dramatically and all parts of the United Kingdom now have much lower rates than twenty years ago. In England and Wales the rate has fallen from 30 deaths per 1,000 live births in 1950 to 25 in 1954 and 20 in 1964. In Scotland it has fallen from 56·2 deaths per 1,000 live births in 1945 to 38·6 in 1950, 30·4 in 1955 and 23·1 in 1965. For comparison, infant mortality rates per 1,000 live births in 1964 were 68 in Portugal, 47 in Poland, 40 in Hungary, 27 in Eire, 25 in West Germany, 24 in the U.S.A., 23 in France, 19 in Switzerland, 17 in Finland and 15 in the Netherlands.

Tuberculosis of Respiratory System

Fig. 9.3 shows the areal variations in male deaths certified as due to tuberculosis of the respiratory system, for which 11,325 male deaths were recorded in the five-year period 1959–63. The average S.M.R. in the recognized conurbations (115) is high compared with urban areas with populations under 50,000 (95) and rural districts (71).

Judged by population rather than areal extent the black areas are most extensive in the North West, followed by Wales and the West Midlands. In these regions ratios rise in the county boroughs to 284 in Bootle, 238 in Stoke-on-Trent, 235 in Dudley, 226 in West Bromwich, 224 in Salford and 206 in Liverpool. In Wales the highest ratios are in the administrative

---

Burnett's study of 'The provision of hospital accommodation and its effective use in relation to perinatal mortality rates in the North-West', *Monthly Bulletin of the Ministry of Health and the Public Health Laboratory Service*, **26**, March 1967, 48–50, illustrates one of the possible results of such sub-regional variations in care. Burnett notes that in 1965 the perinatal mortality rate in the 17 Lancashire county boroughs plus Stockport varied from 27·75 in Southport to 43·7 in Rochdale. He found that with two exceptions the towns with the highest hospital delivery rates have the best perinatal rates and that the range for hospital delivery (89·3/53·9) is very great and suggests a sad disparity in hospital bed provision between one town and another. The data suggest that where hospital delivery rates are low perinatal mortality rates are poor and that with better hospitalization the mortality rates improve. It seems odd, writes Burnett, that in the late 1960s there are industrial towns still unable to provide hospital confinement for much more than half their expectant mothers. Bolton is cited as a good example of a town that is making the best use of a plentiful supply of beds with very satisfactory results. Liverpool, with its long-standing record of poverty, unemployment and bad housing, is doing likewise with similar results. Conversely, other south Lancashire towns are apparently unable to provide the same degree of hospitalization and are not utilizing what they have to the best advantage

[1] See Humphrys, G., 'A map of overcrowding in the British Isles', in *Population Maps of the British Isles, 1961* (Ed. A. J. Hunt), published by *Institute of British Geographers*, April 1968

counties of Caernarvon (241), Merioneth (246) and Glamorgan (194). Ratios in
Eastern, North Midland, South Western, and Southern are particularly low.

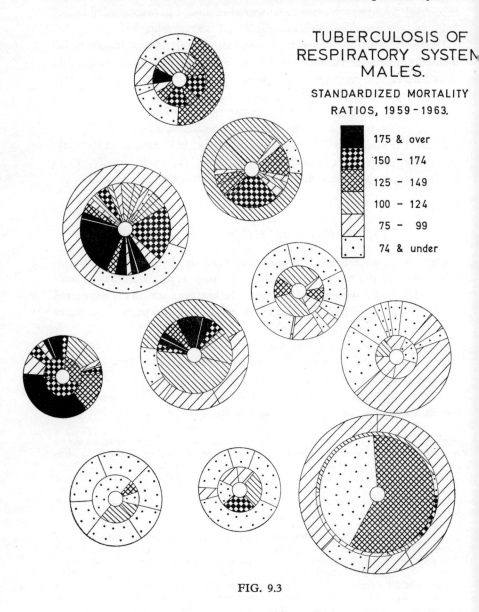

TUBERCULOSIS OF
RESPIRATORY SYSTEM
MALES.
STANDARDIZED MORTALITY
RATIOS, 1959 - 1963.

175 & over
150 - 174
125 - 149
100 - 124
75 - 99
74 & under

FIG. 9.3

The huge population of London has a ratio almost twice as high as Middlesex
and together with Hastings has the worst ratio in the South East region.
Hastings finds itself in peculiar company, being in the same category as
Sheffield, Sunderland, Swansea and Southampton.

Bronchitis

The regional incidence of deaths certified as due to bronchitis has been mapped by Howe and Murray. Murray mapped standardized mortality ratios of male deaths in the years 1950–3 in the major local authority areas of England and Wales while Howe constructed separate maps of male and female deaths in the major administrative districts of the United Kingdom in the years 1954–8.[1] These maps suggest a clear relationship between the areas of above average mortality experience and the regions of dense industrial populations. The patterns of male and female mortality are very similar though it should be noted that between two and three times as many male deaths are attributed to bronchitis. 'The urbanization gradient of male deaths from bronchitis is particularly steep, the death rate in the conurbations being nearly three times as great as in the selected rural districts.'[2]

Howe summarizes the male mortality pattern as follows: 'The conurbations of south-east Lancashire and Merseyside together constitute the worst area, (and are) closely followed by Greater London, the West Riding of Yorkshire, the west Midlands, south Wales, Tyneside and central Clydeside. Apart from such large towns as Stoke-on-Trent, Hull, Doncaster, Barnsley and Nottingham, the remainder of the country generally has a relatively favourable mortality experience from this disease. . . . The dichotomy between high mortality ratios and big towns on the one hand, and low mortality rates and smaller towns and rural districts on the other, is most marked in England and Wales.' In Scotland and Northern Ireland the rate is generally well below the national average, except for Glasgow and Belfast.

Figs. 9.4 and 9.5 show respectively the standardized mortality ratios for male and female deaths due to bronchitis in each of the major administrative units of England and Wales in the five-year period from 1959–63. Both 'maps' are plotted on a base where the size of the units is proportional to their population in 1961 (fig. 9.1). There were 109,576 male deaths in the period and only 45,948 female deaths. In the four southern standard regions only Gloucester, Portsmouth, East and West Ham and London have a *male* mortality experience above the national mean. Populations with mortality rates at least 50 per cent above the mean are concentrated in the county boroughs of the North West. There ratios reach 203 in Manchester and 239 in Salford, and these towns are placed in the same unenviable league table as the metropolitan boroughs of Bethnal Green (206), Stepney (216) and Shoreditch (251). In contrast the ratio is 72 in Bath, 67 in Barrow-in-Furness, 62 in Bournemouth, 58 in Eastbourne and 57 in Ipswich. Ratios are usually lower in the administrative counties, ranging from under 50 in Cornwall,

[1] Murray, M., 1962, *op. cit.*, figure 3; Howe, G. M., 1963, *op. cit.*, 58–61
[2] Registrar-General, *Statistical Review of England and Wales, 1953, Text Volume*, 1956, 175

Norfolk, East Suffolk, Montgomeryshire and Radnor to between 120 and 140 in London, Staffordshire, Glamorgan and Monmouthshire.

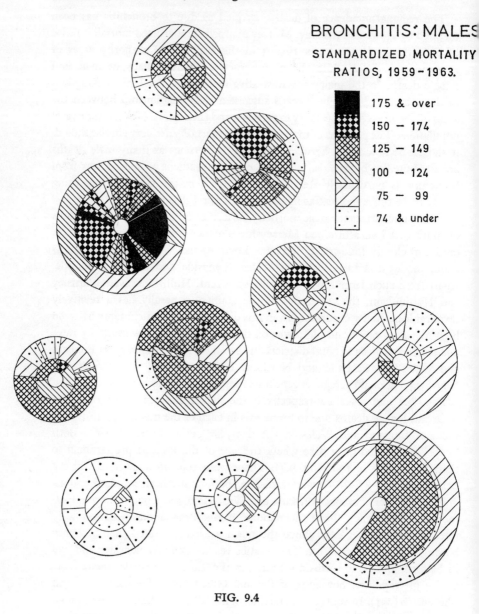

BRONCHITIS: MALES
STANDARDIZED MORTALITY
RATIOS, 1959-1963.

175 & over
150 — 174
125 — 149
100 — 124
75 — 99
74 & under

FIG. 9.4

Fig. 9.5 shows the distribution of *female* deaths from bronchitis. The pattern is broadly the same as that for males, though Wales and Northern are now on the right side of the mean and the West Midlands is much nearer to it. The only region which is markedly worse is the North West. There most of the Lancashire county boroughs and Lancashire itself slip a grade, so that all but three (Dewsbury, Barnsley and West Bromwich) of the blackest units are in the North West. In Bootle, Manchester and Oldham the ratio

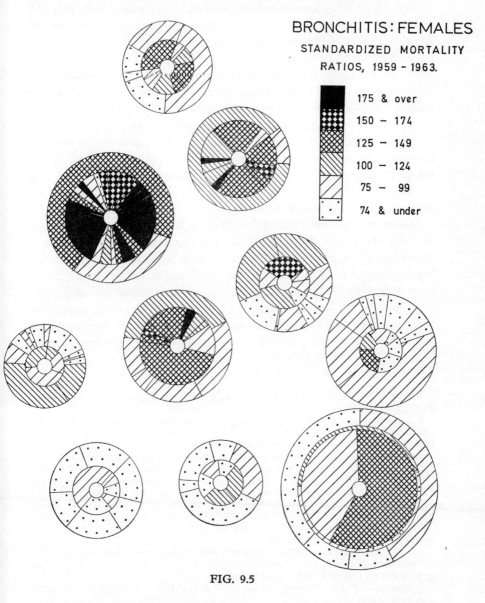

BRONCHITIS: FEMALES

STANDARDIZED MORTALITY

RATIOS, 1959 - 1963.

175 & over

150 — 174

125 — 149

100 — 124

75 — 99

74 & under

FIG. 9.5

is more than twice the national mean and in Salford it is two and one half times the mean. Women in such towns should give priority to computing the odds with their sisters in Barrow (S.M.R. 58), Bath (66), Bournemouth (47), Eastbourne (38) and Oxford (58).

Once again the lower socio-economic groups tend to suffer most from bronchitis, especially the males. It is they who work in the most exposed jobs, who more frequently stand in bus-queues in rain, fog and polluted air in order to return to homes inadequately heated, and often damp, and with their water-closets at the bottom of the garden or yard. Many of them still live cheek by jowl with their places of work in densely crowded urban areas polluted by the factories and dwellings in which they spend almost all their lives. In the 1950s the Registrar-General reported that 'mortality from bronchitis in men and single women was almost six times as high among the unskilled manual workers . . . as among farmers . . . and professional people. . . . It is evident though from the similar tendencies displayed by married women (classified by husband's occupation), that these large differences in mortality owe little to direct occupational effects, and must be attributed to the more general socio-economic or environmental factors.'[1] As Murray remarks, the more unfavourable combinations of these factors occur in the industrial north, the Midlands, South Wales and in the London area.

One of the most important of the operative factors is undoubtedly that of air pollution. It has long been recognized that persistent air pollution in densely populated areas has an adverse effect on respiratory ailments, including bronchitis.[2] In the short term the results can be most dramatic: deaths from bronchitis increased eight times in one week in the famous London smog incident in 1952.[3] In the long term the effects of air pollution and other socio-economic and environmental factors can best be illustrated by comparing those places with very high male mortality rates from bronchitis, such as Salford, Shoreditch and Oldham, with those places with very low rates, for instance, Eastbourne, Bath, Bournemouth, and Canterbury.[4] The most sur-

[1] Quoted by Murray, M., 1962, from Registrar-General's *Decennial Supplement, England and Wales, 1951, Occupational Mortality, Commentary*, I, Part 2, 1957, 53

[2] A table in the Scottish Home and Health Department's *Health and Welfare Services in Scotland, 1964*, Cmnd. 2700, September 1965, illustrates the prevalence of bronchitis deaths in Britain as compared with other countries. The figures refer to *crude* mortality rates per 100,000 population for males (first figure) and females (second figure): Scotland, 71·9 and 27·0; England and Wales, 99·4 and 38·5; Northern Ireland, 67·1 and 32·0; Eire, 63·7 and 30·7; Sweden, 4·7 and 3·9; Denmark, 10·3 and 5·4; France, 4·9 and 3·0; U.S.A., 3·2 and 1·3; Canada, 7·0 and 2·2; and Switzerland, 6·8 and 3·3. The same Department's report for 1965 (Cmnd. 2984, May 1966) asserts that 'control (of lung cancer and bronchitis) is a matter of prevention rather than cure. . . . No apology is offered for repeating in this Report that the benefits to the health of the community which will be derived from an effective reduction in atmospheric pollution and tobacco smoking would be at least as great as any other operation in preventive medicine. The primary difficulty is that the public have, so far, resisted any significant change in their social habits'

[3] Logan, W. P. D., 'Mortality in the London Fog Incident, 1952', *The Lancet*, I, No. 6755, 1953, 338

[4] Respiratory disease in schoolchildren appears to be more prevalent in some parts of the country than in others: of every 1,000 children examined in periodic medical examinations in 1965 the number with lung disease was 7 in Bournemouth, 33 in Plymouth, 24 in Sheffield, 53 in West Bromwich and 52 in St Helens: *The Health of the School Child, 1964 and 1965*, 1966, 9

prising feature of Howe's distribution maps of mortality from bronchitis is the relatively favourable mortality experience in the industrial areas of Scotland, apart from Glasgow itself. For these areas have on average the worst housing conditions in Britain, relatively low personal incomes, an above average proportion of their population in the lower socio-economic groups and by no means the most favourable climates. The importance of climate is illustrated by the fact that the significant fall in the number of deaths from bronchitis in the first quarter of 1964 was attributed to the mild winter.[1]

Conclusions

Two main conclusions may be drawn from this brief review of the geography of life and death. The first is that mortality experience in the United Kingdom is obviously not equal in all parts of the realm, even when allowance is made for the differing age compositions of the populations. Indeed, the regional variations are very considerable and at least in some instances correspond closely to a number of environmental differences.[2] Within a society of relatively high living standards many millions of people are living and dying in unsatisfactory environmental conditions. The second point follows from the first. Arising from the unequal opportunities in the United Kingdom to lead a healthy life and undergo a 'normal' death, it is all the more important that the National Health Service should distribute its resources with the regional problem in the foreground of its decision-making. Ideally the policy should be to raise the worst and in-between areas to the level of the best, rather than to even out the discrepancies by averaging out somewhere in the middle. But if either of these choices is made it will be necessary as a matter of deliberate policy to counteract the market forces which in post-war Britain have worked to the detriment of most areas outside eastern and southern England apart, that is, from much of inner London. The distribution of general practitioners, if not hospital doctors, in the National Health Service shows what can be done; the distribution of dental practitioners and the patterns of mortality show what needs to be done. It is not necessary to await the recognition and analysis of all the causal factors involved. Sufficient is already known to encourage central and regional decision-makers to meet the situation in a more determined manner than has been the case hitherto.

[1] *Annual Report of the Registrar-General for Scotland, 1964,* 110, 1966, 31
[2] Such differences are associated with the physical as well as the socio-economic environment. Water hardness is one aspect which has been studied in the past decade. A survey published in 1968 showed that in the 61 county boroughs of England and Wales with populations of more than 80,000 in 1961, there is 'a strong negative' correlation between the death rate in middle and early old age, and water hardness': Crawford, M. D. *et al., The Lancet,* 1968, 828–31. See also Morris, J. N. *et al.,* 'Hardness of local water supplies and mortality from cardiovascular disease in the county boroughs of England and Wales', *The Lancet,* 1961, 860–2

It will be recalled that the National Health Service was designed to cater for all the people. Twenty years after its inauguration the unequal geographical distribution of resources means that many people are (a) leading more limited lives than is necessary, (b) submerged in the 'clinical iceberg', and (c) dying because of the failure to allocate resources to counteract regional imbalance in housing, pollution, dereliction, education and health and welfare services. In reality some regions are allowed to be 'more equal than others'. As a result of our past social and economic history the need for medical care and facilities is unevenly spread not only within our towns, conurbations and countryside but also between our towns, conurbations and rural districts. At both the local and the regional levels the inequality of opportunity in life and in death is an important aspect of the social and economic environment of Britain.

IO

Aspects of the Geography of Education

From the Industrial Revolution to the beginning of the twentieth century Britain was well favoured by geography and history. The country had long been politically united; insularity had fostered a maritime, mercantile tradition, and an empire overseas was being created. Coal was plentiful near the sea, and many other minerals were quite adequate at first as foundations for industrial development. The people were enterprising and skilful, and were becoming increasingly better educated.

Britain seized her opportunities and pre-empted for herself the headway of an early start. This advantage diminished through time until now it no longer exists. Nor can insularity, home-produced coal and other minerals, political unity, and the Commonwealth be deemed specially advantageous to Britain today. Her remaining major resource is the high standard of education, skill and enterprise of her people. It is therefore all the more necessary now to make the utmost use of their talents by developing educational systems that will quickly minimize wastage. This need relates, however, not only to Britain's continuing ability to compete as an economic unit in a commercial world, but also to the social well-being of her people, each one of whom should have the opportunity to be equipped according to his or her inherent talents for a satisfying life both at work and at leisure.

Education aims to be constructive, creative and positive, and no doubt the educational systems of the United Kingdom are functioning fairly satisfactorily in all these respects. But are they succeeding equally well and to a high standard throughout the country? Are the provisions made and the standards attained in, for example, County Durham, Merthyr Tydfil and Kent comparable to those in Carmarthenshire, Sunderland and Surrey? The object of this chapter is to reconnoitre certain spatial aspects of education in England and Wales,[1] and thus to go part way towards answering these questions.

Given that children differ in their genetic and, therefore, mental potential at birth, the degree to which most of them are able to develop and so use

[1] The United Kingdom cannot be viewed as a single unit for education. Separate analyses would be needed for Scotland and Northern Ireland whose educational systems differ from that of England and Wales

their inherent talents depends mainly upon two factors: their home environment and their facilitative environment. The first is largely concerned with parental attitudes to education but would include also the attitudes of other adults and children in the immediate neighbourhood. The second includes the educational facilities available outside the home, the quality of schools and the provisions made for education by local authorities and other bodies.

Vigorous parental encouragement can compensate for both a lower level of innate ability and a mediocre facilitative environment. Moreover, wealthy parents can if they wish give more help than poor ones. Thus parental encouragement can achieve its most positive effect in helping a child to develop his potential if income is high. It will not for instance be necessary financially for the child to leave school at fifteen to earn a living. He may well be encouraged to stay on to have the fullest possible chance of development.[1] His parents may even decide to pay for him to attend a school outside the state system. This decision may or may not be in the child's best interest, but it is certainly not a choice open to poorer parents who have to make do with the local school, whether it be good or indifferent. Home environment is undoubtedly the dominant factor governing the realization of innate ability. It has its most positive effect, however, where financial support reinforces a constructive parental attitude to education.

The facilitative environment, in contrast, is the dominant positive factor where parents are comparatively poor and have themselves little regard for the worth of formal education in the upbringing of their children. The latter will make more of their talents, therefore, in areas where the local education authority operates a school system affording the greatest possible scope for encouragement and development of the child and a generous scheme of awards for further education.

Since both the home and facilitative environments vary from neighbourhood to neighbourhood and among local authorities, spatial analysis of both environments would seem desirable. Neither, however, can be assessed directly, or independently, but certain statistical data about education are available on a local authority basis,[2] and it is through examination of these that it is hoped not only to shed some light on the varied spatial functioning of both factors but also to hazard an opinion about the degree to which

[1] The 'late-developer' undoubtedly has a better chance if his parents have a reasonably high income
[2] (i) *Statistics of Education 1967*, H.M.S.O., 1968, *1* and *5*
   (ii) *Local Education Authorities, List 69*, H.M.S.O., annually to 1967
   (iii) *Selected Statistics Relating to Local Education Authorities in England and Wales, List 71*, H.M.S.O., annually
Other relevant data are published in:
   (iv) *List of Independent Schools in England and Wales, List 70*, H.M.S.O., annually
   (v) *List of Direct Grant Grammar Schools in England and Wales, List 73*, H.M.S.O., annually

innate ability is being effectively fostered by the local education authorities of England and Wales.

The Geography of 'Opting Out'

There are three ways of opting out of the state system of education: by attending (a) an independent or a direct-grant school as a boarder, (b) an independent school as a day scholar, or (c) a direct-grant school as a day scholar.

BOARDING SCHOOLS

By choosing to send their children to boarding school, parents indicate not only their ability and willingness to pay but also their wish to place their children wholly in a formal education environment for about three-quarters of each year. Influences of the home and its neighbourhood are thereby reduced for these children. No doubt if one were to ascertain the home-addresses of boarders a marked bias towards the wealthier south would appear in the distribution, but this would be of limited interest in our present discussion since neither home nor local authority plays the major role in nurturing the innate ability of these children once they have entered a boarding school.

Many such schools are known as Public Schools, and it is a significant feature of the social geography of Britain that these are mainly to be found in southern England. Their distribution (fig. 10.1) does not closely reflect the pattern of population. It corresponds more to the pattern of wealth and perhaps also to the pattern of influence (fig. 11.2).

DAY SCHOLARS IN THE INDEPENDENT SECTOR

To opt out by going to a recognized[1] independent school as a day scholar is also a feature largely restricted to southern England. In 1964 the number of children attending such schools was equivalent to only 2·7 per cent of the total attending maintained and direct grant schools (excluding boarders), but all counties south of a line from Suffolk to Gloucester, except Essex, Wiltshire, Somerset and Cornwall are shown to exceed this proportion on fig. 10.2. West Suffolk, Hertfordshire, Buckinghamshire, Berkshire and West Sussex have at least twice the national figure, while Surrey has the highest proportion (14 per cent) representing over 31,000 children.[2] Away from the

[1] Recognized as efficient by the Department of Education and Science
[2] Data used here refer to the county framework before the setting up of the Greater London Council

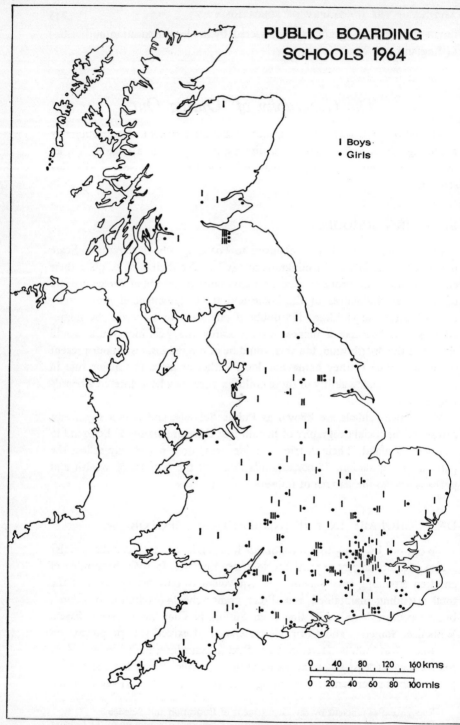

PUBLIC BOARDING
SCHOOLS 1964

I Boys
• Girls

0   40   80   120   160 kms
0   20   40   60   80 100 mls

FIG. 10.1   Sources: (i) Headmasters' Conference (Boarding) Schools list;
(ii) Principal Girls' (Boarding) Schools, *Whitaker's Almanac*

south only Cheshire and Northumberland are above the mean. Fig. 10.3 shows the absolute distribution by counties of day scholars at independent schools and together with fig. 10.2 establishes the existence of a firm southerly trend, biased in absolute terms towards the London area. There must without

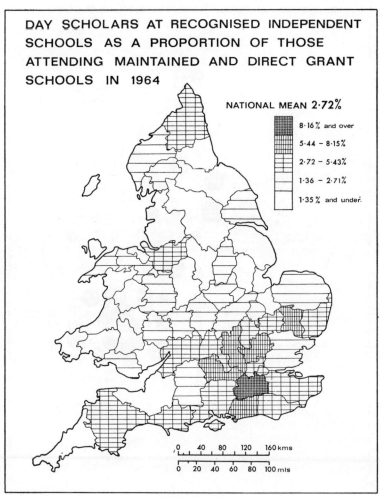

DAY SCHOLARS AT RECOGNISED INDEPENDENT SCHOOLS AS A PROPORTION OF THOSE ATTENDING MAINTAINED AND DIRECT GRANT SCHOOLS IN 1964

NATIONAL MEAN 2·72%

8·16% and over

5·44 – 8·15%

2·72 – 5·43%

1·36 – 2·71%

1·35% and under.

0   40   80   120   160 kms

0   20   40   60   80   100 mls

FIG. 10.2

much doubt be a close correlation with high incomes. Unfortunately the data for incomes are not presented on a residential basis and the distribution of numbers of high incomes cannot therefore be compared very precisely with the distribution of children attending independent schools. Nevertheless 45 per cent of day scholars at such schools in England and Wales were in

the metropolitan area (London, Middlesex, Essex, Hertfordshire, Buckinghamshire, Surrey and Kent[1]), which had about 40 per cent of the incomes
over £3,000 in England and Wales in 1964–5, excluding those of civil servants.

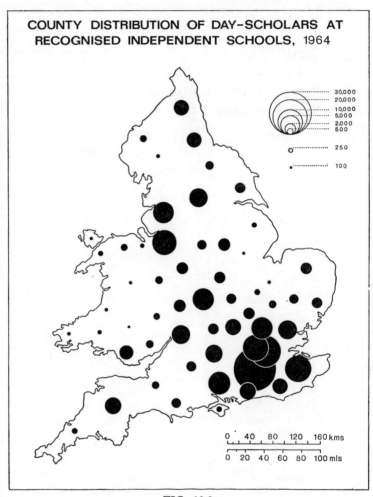

FIG. 10.3

The northern populous region (Lancashire and the West Riding together
with Cheshire) records, in contrast, only 12 per cent of day scholars attending
recognized independent schools and only 15·75 per cent of incomes over
£3,000. There is also considerable similarity between the distribution of

[1] This area was used in chapter 3 (see pp. 45–9) for the analysis of employment,
during the discussion of the two major concentrations of population and employment
in Britain

Socio-Economic Groups 1, 2, 3 and 4 (fig. 10.4) and the pattern shown on fig. 10.2.[1]

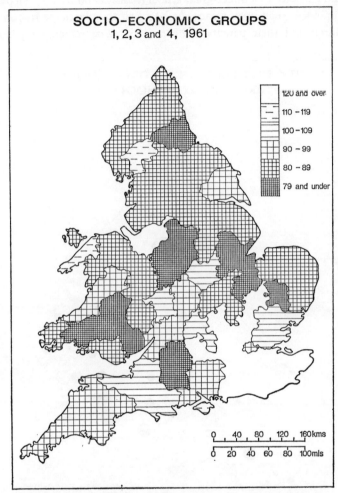

FIG. 10.4   Distribution of Socio-Economic Groups 1, 2, 3 and 4 (managerial and professional), 1961, expressed as a proportion of the economically active male resident population. The mean proportion for England and Wales, 13·3 per cent, has been converted to the index number 100, and county proportions have been recalculated accordingly. Primary analysis by courtesy of Dr Mary Waugh

[1] Data for fig. 10.4 have been calculated by Dr Mary Waugh. The Socio-Economic Groups referred to are, respectively
  1 Employers and managers (large establishments)
  2 Employers and managers (small establishments)
  3 Professional workers (self-employed)
  4 Professional workers (employees)
Waugh, Mary, 'The changing distribution of professional and managerial manpower in England and Wales between 1961 and 1966', *Regional Studies*, **3**, *2*, 1969, 157–69

DIRECT-GRANT SCHOOLS

To gain entrance to a direct-grant school (D.G.S.) is rather more dependent upon attainment than upon means. At least half the places are free so far as the children and their parents are concerned. The remaining places are

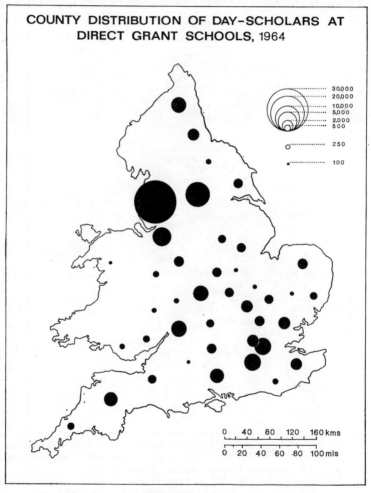

FIG. 10.5

allocated by the school governing bodies to fee-payers, with power to remit fees where appropriate. In so far, therefore, as it is possible for wealthier parents to opt out of the fully maintained sector of education by sending their children to D.G.S.s the opportunity is largely restricted to entrance to their primary departments which are unsupported by government grants. Thus the pattern of places available at D.G.S.s does not reflect the pattern of income.

TABLE 10.1 Day scholars at Direct Grant and Recognized Independent Schools in 1964

County	Direct Grant Total in attendance	Direct Grant R.C. Foundations	Recognized Independent Total in attendance	Recognized Independent R.C. Foundations	Total Direct Grant and Recognized Independent
Lancashire	31,320	17,940	7,228	3,514	38,548
Cheshire	5,473	1,645	10,236	4,301	15,709
West Riding	9,981	4,034	5,393	795	15,374
Total: Northern Group	46,774	23,619	22,857	8,610	69,631
Nottinghamshire	878	—	2,269	691	3,147
Derbyshire	—	—	1,316	449	1,316
Staffordshire	1,452	1,452	1,983	722	3,435
Worcestershire	382	—	2,266	897	2,648
Warwickshire	3,637	—	7,502	1,298	11,139
Leicestershire	1,276	—	1,781	1,057	3,057
Northamptonshire	1,199	459	1,477	528	2,676
Total: Midland Group	8,824	1,911	18,594	5,642	27,418
County of London	4,607	—	15,857	2,215	20,464
Middlesex	2,191	—	10,898	4,275	13,089
Essex	2,428	1,218	5,643	1,681	8,071
Hertfordshire	1,549	—	7,645	2,864	9,194
Buckinghamshire	—	—	4,300	1,637	4,300
Surrey	4,651	374	31,418	7,525	36,069
Kent	1,952	384	11,164	3,819	13,116
Total: South-eastern Group	17,378	1,976	86,925	24,016	104,303

Fig. 10.5 shows how many places were taken up by day scholars in each county in 1964, and contrasts markedly with fig. 10.3. Direct-grant schools are clearly a northern phenomenon, for almost half their pupils in England and Wales are to be found in Lancashire, the West Riding and Cheshire. The explanation of this northerly emphasis is social and historical rather than economic. Many of the D.G.S. places in the three counties are in Roman Catholic schools. Lancashire alone provides 18,000 out of the total of 34,000 attending Roman Catholic D.G.S.s in the whole of England and Wales. Table 10.1 sets out some comparable figures for counties in the north, the Midlands, and the south-east.

As well as emphasizing the tendencies towards independent schooling in the south-east and attendance at D.G.S.s in Lancashire and the West Riding, table 10.1 shows how comparatively badly off the Midlands are for places in schools outside the local authority sector of education. Other areas where 'opting out' is particularly difficult for want of places, are Cumberland, Westmorland, Durham and the North Riding in northern England; Lindsey, Holland and Ely in eastern England, and the whole of Wales. Devon, in contrast, stands out among south-western counties as having a high proportion of places in independent schools and D.G.S.s combined.

It must be stressed, however, since the catchment areas of these schools are not restricted by local authority boundaries, that a shortage of places in one county may to some extent be compensated for by places being available in schools located a short distance away in an adjacent county. This situation exists on Tyneside, for example, where all the direct-grant schools in the conurbation are in Newcastle upon Tyne.

The Geography of Maintained Secondary Education and Awards for Further Education

If all parents were equally desirous of furthering their children's education; if all homes had the same income, spending habits, reading habits and books, took the same newspapers, and watched television with the same degree of enthusiasm; if all local authorities were equally efficient and standardized in their provision of schools and educational finance, and if there were no schools at all outside the maintained sector, analysis would reveal spatial patterns varying only in relation to the innate ability of the children. We should be mapping intelligence. Such ideal laboratory conditions cannot, however, be found. Analysis has, therefore, to be undertaken in a multivariate system in which most of the factors cannot be separately measured. Nevertheless, an attempt is made in this chapter to discern where local facilities, home background and perhaps even innate ability have marked effects. The analysis is restricted to two aspects. These are the extent to which children (a) stay on at school after sixteen, and (b) follow courses in further education beyond the age of eighteen.

SIXTH-FORM PLACES

The numbers of pupils aged sixteen and seventeen in maintained schools are published annually for every local education authority (L.E.A.) in England and Wales, and each of these age-groups is expressed respectively as a percentage of pupils aged thirteen, three and four years earlier. Boys and girls are listed separately.[1]

Maintained schools serve the great majority of the populace. These data reflect therefore, on the one hand, the opportunities available to the majority of children to make the most of their talents, and on the other hand, the degree to which L.E.A.s are succeeding in their attempts to foster these talents efficiently. There is, however, one potentially important defect in the statistics which cannot be resolved satisfactorily. Children who leave school at fifteen or later to enter establishments for further education (F.E.E.) not classified as schools are excluded from the data, though many of these children are taking courses and examinations very similar to those available in school. This defect in the statistics would be unimportant for spatial analysis if it were evenly spread among L.E.A.s. Since, however, some authorities may rely more heavily than others upon F.E.E.s to provide places for children wishing to continue their full-time education beyond the minimum age for leaving school, maps prepared from the statistics may under-represent the overall performance of certain L.E.A.s.

Although the real 'loss' to the school sector cannot be gauged from the published statistics for L.E.A.s, an approximate *regional* assessment can be made for pupils aged fifteen to seventeen inclusive, in the maintained sector.[2] The regions are ranked in the following descending order according to the reliance that they place upon F.E.E.s rather than schools to provide *full-time* education for the age-group: East Anglia; North; North West; South West; East Midlands; Wales; West Midlands; Yorkshire and Humberside; South East. In East Anglia, out of about 15,500 fifteen- to seventeen-year-olds attending either school or F.E.E.s full-time, the latter provided almost 25 per cent of places during 1967. The proportion in the South East was only 11·5 per cent.

Despite this limitation, the patterns discussed below are far from uninteresting and the spatial variations that they display surely call for the publication

---

[1] See p. 242, footnote 2, (i) and (ii)

[2] *Statistics of Education 1967*, *1*, table 7, pp. 25 to 27, and *3*, table 4, p. 6. The assessment is approximate mainly because the data refer to different months in the same calendar year

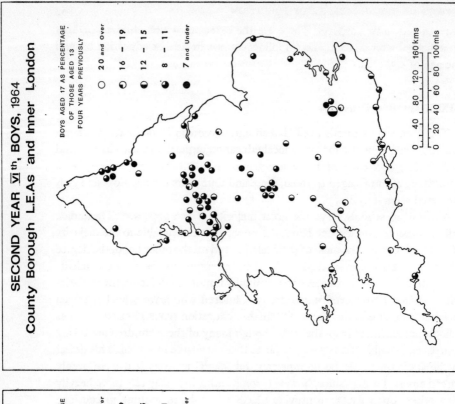

SECOND YEAR VIth BOYS, 1964
County Borough L.E.As and Inner London

BOYS AGED 17 AS PERCENTAGE
OF THOSE AGED 13
FOUR YEARS PREVIOUSLY

○ 20 and Over
◔ 16 – 19
◑ 12 – 15
◕ 8 – 11
● 7 and Under

0   40   80   120   160 kms
0   20   40   60   80   100 mls

FIG. 10.6b

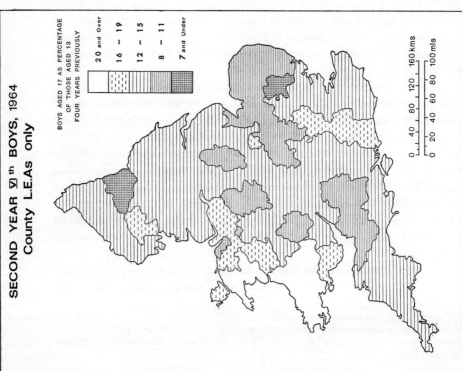

SECOND YEAR VIth BOYS, 1964
County L.E.As only

BOYS AGED 17 AS PERCENTAGE
OF THOSE AGED 13
FOUR YEARS PREVIOUSLY

20 and Over
16 – 15
12 – 15
8 – 11
7 and Under

0   40   80   120   160 kms
0   20   40   60   80   100 mls

FIG. 10.6a

of data in forms amenable to more precise geographical measurement.[1] The analysis relates to pupils aged seventeen who, for the most part, made up the school population of upper sixth forms in 1964 and 1967.

THE UPPER SIXTH IN 1964

Fig. 10.6a shows for each county L.E.A. the number of school places held in 1964 by seventeen-year-old boys, expressed as a proportion of the number aged thirteen attending secondary schools four years earlier.[2] The national mean for England and Wales stood at 12·9 per cent. The darker the shading on fig. 10.6a, the lower is the take-up of places. Durham and West Suffolk are particularly low, and Somerset, Wiltshire, Herefordshire, Staffordshire, Flintshire, Nottinghamshire, and the block of counties comprising East Suffolk, Norfolk, Holland, Huntingdon, Bedford, Ely and Northampton are poor. The largest area well above the mean comprises most of Wales plus Cheshire. Apart from Flintshire, the counties of Monmouth and Radnor are the only ones in Wales with less than 16 per cent in their upper sixth forms. Both of them have over 14 per cent however, and thus are above the national mean. Hertford, Middlesex, Surrey and West Sussex make up another block of counties recording more than 16 per cent. Moreover, they are flanked to the east and west by areas which, though classified in the middle grade (12 to 15 per cent) on fig. 10.6a, are all above the national mean.[3] Other counties in the middle grade but above the mean are Cornwall, Devon, Gloucester, Kesteven, Lindsey, the Soke of Peterborough, the East Riding and Warwick. Among these the most surprising figure is the high proportion (15.5 per cent) returned by the East Riding authority.

The take-up of upper sixth-form places, in the county boroughs and what is now Inner London, is shown on fig. 10.6b by the same grades as are used for the counties on fig. 10.6a. No county borough has more than 20 per cent. The best are Exeter, Bath, Croydon, Oxford, Wallasey, Southport, Blackpool, Lincoln and Halifax. The presence of Halifax in this category is unexpected,

[1] From 1919 until nationalization in 1948 comparative data in minute detail about the performance of local electricity authorities were published annually by the Electricity Commissioners. Perhaps independent Commissioners should be appointed to do the same for education which is surely as important as electricity to the national community and of far greater concern to the electorate in a democratic society. The organization and local monopolistic tendency of education is closely comparable in form to electricity before nationalization. Except for the public school sector, however, education has nothing to compare with the grid system of electricity transmission whereby deficits in one area may be made good almost automatically from surpluses available elsewhere

[2] For cartographic convenience the counties have been shaded in their entirety on fig. 10.6a and on similar figures throughout this chapter. It should be borne in mind that county councils are not responsible for education within the territorial enclaves served by the county boroughs

[3] Essex, London, Kent, East Sussex, Buckingham, Berkshire, Hampshire and Isle of Wight

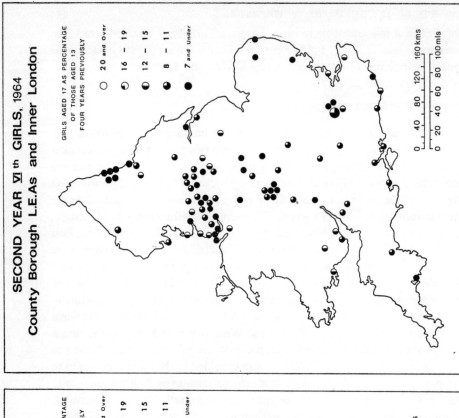

SECOND YEAR VIth GIRLS, 1964
County Borough L.E.As and Inner London

GIRLS AGED 17 AS PERCENTAGE
OF THOSE AGED 13
FOUR YEARS PREVIOUSLY

○ 20 and Over
◔ 16 – 19
◑ 12 – 15
◕ 8 – 11
● 7 and Under

0 20 40 60 80 100 mls
0 40 80 120 160 kms

FIG. 107b

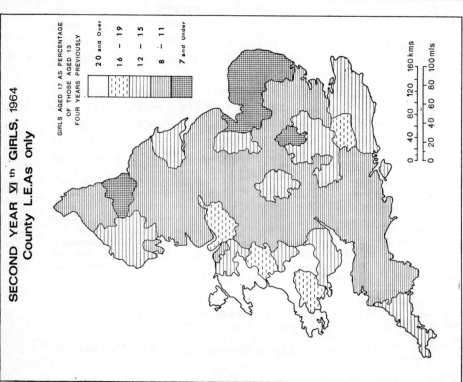

SECOND YEAR VIth GIRLS, 1964
County L.E.As only

GIRLS AGED 17 AS PERCENTAGE
OF THOSE AGED 13
FOUR YEARS PREVIOUSLY

20 and Over
16 – 19
12 – 15
8 – 11
7 and Under

0 20 40 60 80 100 mls
0 40 80 120 160 kms

FIG. 107a

for an initial hypothesis based on geographical experience would postulate poor performance in old industrial towns. All the county boroughs of South Wales, even including Merthyr Tydfil, are in the middle grade and thus contrast sharply with those of north-east England. There is indeed a preponderance of middle-grade authorities in the south of the country while low grades are dominant in the Midlands and the North. It is intriguing to find, however, that Blackburn, Bolton and Stockport are better than Burnley, Bury and Chester, for example, and one wonders why Darlington should register a higher percentage than Derby. It would, however, be inadvisable to proceed with these conjectures on the basis of the performance for one year and before examining the corresponding data for girls in 1964.

Fig. 10.7a shows for girls what fig. 10.6a shows for boys, and it is at once apparent that generally over the country the latter surpass the former. The national mean for girls in the upper sixth was only 10·6 per cent in 1964, and a far larger amount of the country falls below 12 per cent on fig. 10.7a than on fig. 10.6a. The whole of Wales except Flintshire is above 12 per cent,[1] likewise a sizeable area of south-east England. The East Riding once more is surprisingly high, whereas Durham, Bedfordshire and much of East Anglia are low.

Fig. 10.7b shows the pattern for girls in the county boroughs and Inner London in 1964, and should be compared with fig. 10.6b. Not one borough rises above the middle grade of 12 to 15 per cent, and in many instances there is a drop in grade for the girls when compared with the boys. Eastbourne, Canterbury, Chester, Rotherham and Middlesborough are exceptional in rising one grade against this general trend. Falls of more than two grades are apparent in Exeter, Hastings, Bath, Oxford, Birkenhead and Halifax. Finally it should be noted that the county boroughs of South Wales, except for Cardiff, are in the same grade on both maps, thus going regionally against the national trend. Perhaps the education of girls is more highly valued by the Welsh than by the English.

THE UPPER SIXTH IN 1967

By 1967 the national mean for boys had risen to 15·8 per cent. Boundary changes associated with the creation of the Greater London Council made it impossible for the Department of Education and Science to produce statistics for much of south-east England, and it is necessary, therefore, to use data for the South East Economic Planning Region to supplement the information shown on the maps for 1967 (figs. 10.8a and b).

Wales and the South East clearly maintain their ascendancy of 1964 into 1967. As regions, each has 18·7 per cent of boys (aged 13 four years previously)

[1] All but four counties (Flint, Glamorgan, Monmouth and Radnor) in Wales are above 15 per cent, and six counties exceed 20 per cent

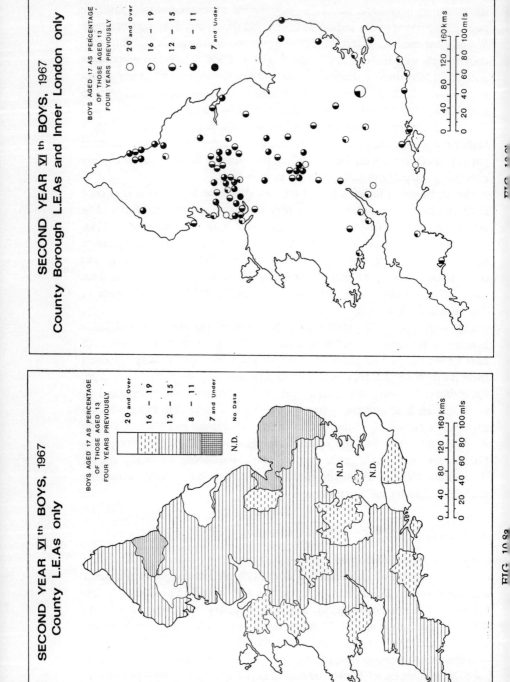

SECOND YEAR VIᵗʰ BOYS, 1967
County Borough L.E.As and Inner London only

BOYS AGED 17 AS PERCENTAGE
OF THOSE AGED 13
FOUR YEARS PREVIOUSLY

○ 2 0 and Over
◖ 16 – 19
◕ 12 – 15
● 8 – 11
● 7 and Under

0   40   80   120   160 kms
0   20   40   60   80   100 mls

SECOND YEAR VIᵗʰ BOYS, 1967
County L.E.As only

BOYS AGED 17 AS PERCENTAGE
OF THOSE AGED 13
FOUR YEARS PREVIOUSLY

2 0 and Over
16 – 19
12 – 15
8 – 11
7 and Under

N.D.   No Data

0   40   80   120   160 kms
0   20   40   60   80   100 mls

FIG. 10.8₂

FIG. 10.8₁

in its upper sixth forms. Merioneth, Caernarvonshire, Cardiganshire, Carmarthenshire and Pembroke all record over 25 per cent (fig. 10.8a). Cheshire shows an improvement from 18·4 to 22·4 per cent between 1964 and 1967; the East Riding rises from 15·5 to 20·4; Westmorland from 16·1 to 22·1; Berkshire from 15·5 to 20·1, and Durham improves its lowly quota from 6·1 to 9·3 per cent to share with Herefordshire the distinction of being the only counties with less than 10 per cent in the upper sixth. These two authorities and three in East Anglia remain the lowest in the country. It is noteworthy too that north-east England and South Wales, similar in many other respects, look to have very different attitudes to sixth-form education. Other counties that remain rather low, but which are not picked out by the grades of shading used, are Bedford 12·2 per cent; Northampton 12·6; Nottingham 13·0; Shropshire 12·8;[1] Stafford 12·4, and West Suffolk 12·0 per cent. For the most part, therefore, the analysis of data for 1967 seems to correspond fairly closely, given a general increase in places, with that for 1964. One need not, therefore, be very anxious that statistics for only one year may grossly misrepresent performance over a period of years; the less so with large than with small authorities, but it will not have escaped notice that the small county authorities in Wales, and those of Isle of Wight and Westmorland are consistently high at both dates.

The percentage for boys in the county boroughs and Inner London are shown on fig. 10.8b. Beginning in the south, the following authorities appear in the top two grades: Exeter, Bournemouth, Eastbourne, Hastings, Bath, Bristol, Swansea, Cardiff, Newport, Oxford, Reading, Inner London, Southend, Solihull, Wallasey, Stockport, Doncaster, Southport, Bolton, Blackpool and Darlington. Halifax and Lincoln, star performers in 1964, have fallen from grace. The following authorities are to be found in the bottom two grades, again working northwards over fig. 10.8b: Canterbury, Ipswich, Yarmouth, Norwich, Coventry, Birmingham, Warley (Smethwick), Dudley, West Bromwich, Stoke, Derby, Nottingham, Grimsby, Bootle, St Helens, Warrington, Salford, Manchester, Bury, Rochdale, Preston, Burnley, Barnsley, Dewsbury, Wakefield, York, Middlesbrough, West Hartlepool, Gateshead, Sunderland, Tynemouth and Carlisle. There are some good gradings in the Midlands and the north, but the outstanding fact is the absence of bad gradings, except for Canterbury, in the south. If data were available, two or three of the Outer London boroughs would probably be seen also to have low gradings but the majority would doubtless be very high. Only two authorities, Halifax and Lincoln, deteriorated into the next lower grade between 1964 and 1967, but eight boroughs (Blackburn, Burton, Ipswich, Preston, Rochdale, Wakefield, Walsall and Warrington) deteriorated without changing grade. In contrast, Bournemouth and Eastbourne both rose by two grades (from 13·7 to 20·1 and 8·9 to 16·7 per cent respectively).

[1] Shropshire stood at 12·8 per cent also in 1964

The national mean for girls rose proportionally rather more than that for boys between 1964 and 1967, when it had reached 13·9 per cent. An even higher proportional increase was recorded for girls in the *lower* sixth between the two dates so that by 1967 the sexes had come close to parity (boys 28·6 and girls 27·3 per cent).

Like fig. 10.8a, fig. 10.9a is affected by the boundary changes in and around Greater London. Nevertheless, one can be reasonably sure that the South East and Wales are the major areas with a high proportion of girls in the upper sixth. But whereas their regional percentages for boys are identical at 18·7, Wales with 18·1 per cent leads easily for girls over the South East Economic Planning Region which has only 16·1 per cent. It is doubtful if there is a simple explanation why Wales, with such a low proportion of women in employment, should succeed in keeping more of its girls in the sixth form not only than the South East where the female activity rate is much higher, but also than the South West where the activity rate is only a little higher.

In detail, fig. 10.9a shows a persistence of low percentages in Durham and East Anglia (cf. fig. 10.7a), the maintenance of high percentages in the East Riding, Kesteven and Cheshire, and the emergence of a high proportion in Westmorland. Nearly all counties show improvement, but the most notable feature on fig. 10.9a is the low percentage range of several midland counties (Nottingham, Leicester, Northampton, Stafford and Worcester). Thus much of the Midlands is, perhaps unexpectedly, bad.

The take-up of places in upper sixth forms by girls in the county boroughs in 1967 is shown on fig. 10.9b. Considerable improvement is seen to have occurred in many towns since 1964 (fig. 10.8b). The leading county boroughs in 1967 are: Southampton, Eastbourne, Canterbury,[1] Swansea, Newport, Bath, Southend, Oxford, Solihull, Chester, Stockport and Southport. The following authorities are to be found in the bottom two grades: Plymouth, Hastings,[2] Gloucester, Luton, Ipswich, Yarmouth, Norwich, Birmingham, Dudley, Warley, Walsall, West Bromwich, Wolverhampton, Burton, Stoke, Derby, Nottingham, Lincoln, Grimsby, Hull, Bootle, Liverpool, Birkenhead, St Helens, Warrington, Wigan, Salford, Manchester, Oldham, Bury, Preston, Burnley, Bradford, Dewsbury, Wakefield, York, Barrow, and every county borough in the Northern Economic Planning Region except West Hartlepool. This list is much longer for girls than for boys and, in the Midlands and North, is relieved by the presence of only four county boroughs in the top two grades.

[1] The consistently high performance by girls in Canterbury and low performance by boys is very odd. It cannot be explained by the local authority availing itself of places for girls but not for boys in direct grant or independent schools

[2] Hastings maintains its disparity between boys (fig. 10.8b) and girls (cf. figs. 10.6b and 10.7b)

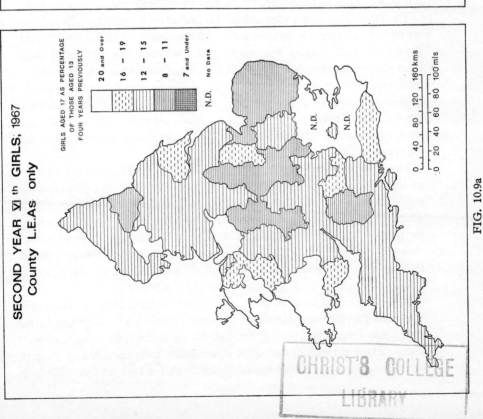

SECOND YEAR VIth GIRLS. 1967.
County Borough L.E.As and Inner London only

GIRLS AGED 17 AS PERCENTAGE
OF THOSE AGED 13
FOUR YEARS PREVIOUSLY

○ 20 and Over
◔ 16 — 19
◑ 12 — 15
◕ 8 — 11
● 7 and Under

0   40   80   120   160 kms
0   20   40   60   80   100 mls

FIG. 10.9b

SECOND YEAR VIth GIRLS; 1967
County L.E.As only

GIRLS AGED 17 AS PERCENTAGE
OF THOSE AGED 13
FOUR YEARS PREVIOUSLY

20 and Over
16 — 19
12 — 15
8 — 11
7 and Under

N.D.   No Data

N.D.
N.D.   N.D.

0   40   80   120   160 kms
0   20   40   60   80   100 mls

FIG. 10.9a

Thus, for places in the upper sixth, there was considerable improvement between 1964 and 1967 over most of the country, the more so for girls than for boys. Certain areas, however, seem throughout to have been better than others. Notwithstanding relatively lower incomes and comparatively poor opportunities for employment, especially for girls, Wales stands out for the most part as an area of high opportunity for education at school beyond the compulsory school-leaving age. Parental attitudes in Wales are no doubt exceptionally constructive, and local authorities even in very poor areas such as Merioneth and Anglesey are highly successful in providing sixth-form places. It must be remembered, however, that places in further education establishments as alternatives to sixth forms are scarce in Wales, especially in the sparsely peopled counties.

With the notable exception of Darlington and Westmorland, in which county the lack of a sufficient population to support colleges of further education may affect the number of sixth-form places, as also in Merioneth for example, the authorities in the Northern Region fail abysmally to match up to those in Wales, where both counties and county boroughs are good. But the Northern Region, among all regions in the country, has the next to highest proportion of full-time places within the fifteen- to seventeen-year-old age-group in F.E.E.S. Substantial waste of talent seems likely in the north but judgment must be deferred until further evidence has been examined.

The South East seems very satisfactory, as indeed it should be, for incomes are high, employment is diverse, and the proportion of leading socio-economic groups is greater than in any other region. Whether the number of sixth-form places even then is high enough to satisfy the demand cannot, however, be assessed, save perhaps to observe that parents and L.E.A.s are doing less for girls in the South East than in Wales, and that children of poorer parents in the South East may not stand as good a chance of making the most of their talents as similar children in Merthyr Tydfil, Swansea and Carmarthenshire, for example.

East Anglia on the whole is evidently a bad area for sixth-form education, an impression arising not only from this series of maps but also from the regional statistics of the Department of Education. Like the Northern Region which is almost as bad, it has, however, a high proportion of places available for fifteen- to seventeen-year-olds in F.E.E.S. South-west England should probably be classified an intermediate area for education in the upper sixth. It is close to the national mean for each of the sexes and also for places in F.E.E.S.

The complicated areas to interpret are the Midland Regions, the North West and Yorkshire and Humberside, which contain a wide disparity among their many county and county borough L.E.A.s in the take-up of sixth-form places. Those authorities that serve a population comprising a large proportion of people in the higher income brackets have a high take-up. Cheshire,

Wallasey, Southport and Solihull are cases in point. Warrington, Barnsley, Salford, Stoke, Smethwick–Warley, and West Bromwich one might expect to have a low take-up largely for the opposite reason. But it is hard to understand why, for example, Derby, Nottingham, Coventry, and York are so low, while Blackburn, Bolton, Stockport, Halifax, Rotherham, Doncaster and Lincoln are appreciably higher. Both Bolton and Blackburn make great use of places arising from the plentiful supply of direct-grant schools available to them. Stockport was operating a great variety of different types of school in 1967, as well as sending children to direct-grant and independent schools. Rotherham had adopted the comprehensive system but had retained 16 per cent of grammar school places (including a small proportion in D.G.S.s). Doncaster had more than the national mean of grammar school places plus nearly 20 per cent in schools classified as 'other secondary', which probably means 'bilateral'.[1] Derby, however, had no D.G.S.s near at hand to relieve its shortage of grammar-school places, and it lacked comprehensive or other schools with sixth forms. Nottingham too was short of grammar-school places, although it had three times as many children in the 'other secondary' classification,[2] again meaning bilateral. York was still operating secondary modern schools preponderantly. Coventry had very few grammar-school places and about 50 per cent in secondary modern schools. There is, therefore, no clear school-type syndrome that might help to explain the differences noted for 1967, except that all the 'high' boroughs, excluding Rotherham, were using a far larger proportion of grammar-school places than the national average, while among the 'low' boroughs Derby, Nottingham and Coventry were appreciably below and York was only slightly above the mean.

Generally speaking the impression created is that of the county and county borough authorities in Lancashire, Yorkshire and Cheshire being on average better than those in the Midlands. This impression is confirmed when a points scale is applied to the grades shown on the maps and by the regional statistics published by the Department of Education. Perhaps parents in the Midlands are less interested in education than parents farther north in Lancashire, Yorkshire, Cheshire and parts of Lincolnshire. Perhaps the Midland L.E.A.s are weak. Whatever the cause, there is clearly more scope for improvement in the Midland Regions than one would expect to find in comparison with the North West, and Yorkshire and Humberside, especially when one recollects that much of the Midlands is more affluent. There is, however, great scope for improvement in all three regions.

As an individual authority, that of the East Riding may well be one of the

[1] Bilateral schools contain both academic and non-academic streams, but are generally associated with a selection system which aims to cream off the brightest children into grammar schools
[2] The Statistics of the Department of Education and Science classify secondary schools as: modern (non-academic), technical, comprehensive, other secondary, and grammar

TABLE 10.2 Sixth-form Places and Types of School, 1967

Authority	Second year VIth. Pupils aged 17 as a percentage of those aged 13, four years previously	First year VIth. Pupils aged 16 as a percentage of those aged 13, three years previously	Percentage of thirteen-year-olds in schools of the following types				
			Modern	Technical	Comprehensive	Other Secondary	Grammar (inc. D.G. and Ind.)*
England and Wales	14·9	27·9	56·1	2·0	14·1	7·0	20·7
East Riding	18·9	34·7	1·8	0	13·6	67·6	17·0
North Riding	13·6	22·2	71·3	0	0·2	7·0	20·6
West Riding	14·7	25·5	61·8	0·4	15·1	1·1	21·6
Lancashire	14·9	26·8	68·9	0·8	6·5	0·2	23·6
Cheshire	21·5	35·0	64·9	0·2	0	0	34·8
Warwickshire	15·4	29·7	68·8	0·1	5·3	5·4	20·4
Norfolk	10·2	19·7	77·9	0·3	0	0	21·9
Devonshire	14·7	27·8	64·8	1·1	13·4	0	20·8
Carmarthenshire	24·9	36·7	56·8	0	3·8	0	39·2
Cambridgeshire and Ely	13·1	26·4	71·7	0	0	4·4	24·0
Merioneth	31·1	52·0	0·2	0	97·5	1·8	0·4
Anglesey	23·9	37·1	0	0	100·0	0	0
Leeds	13·4	24·7	62·0	1·6	16·3	0	20·1
Hull	11·2	20·8	62·0	15·5	10·3	0	12·3
Manchester	11·1	22·2	61·0	14·5	5·2	0	19·3
Nottingham	10·4	21·7	24·4	0	9·2	50·2	16·3
Sheffield	13·3	26·4	45·1	6·8	30·3	0	17·8
Stockport	16·9	26·8	58·9	4·6	10·1	0	26·4
Solihull	24·3	40·8	61·2	0·2	0·2	0	38·5
Oxford	18·8	29·9	66·1	6·3	0·2	0	27·5
Bath	19·4	34·3	65·1	8·4	0	0	26·5

* Direct grant and independent school places paid for by the local authority.

most interesting and effective in the country so far as sixth-form opportunities are concerned. Table 10.2 compares a selection of county and county borough authorities for the year 1967. One would not expect the East Riding to produce a greater proportion of sixth-formers than Cheshire, Solihull or Bath, which are residentially wealthier places, well above the national norm in their quota of the top socio-economic groups. Conversely, one would not expect Warwickshire (comprising within it the wealthier fringes of the Birmingham conurbation), Norfolk (an agricultural county like the East Riding), and Cambridgeshire and Ely (similarly agricultural but containing also the University of Cambridge) to be considerably worse than the East Riding.

The explanation of the latter's success seems to be ascribable to the type of school it is for the most part operating. The county has virtually no secondary modern schools left, for nearly 70 per cent of its children are in bilateral schools, the system adopted also by Surrey[1] but in a setting far different for wealth and social class from that of the East Riding. The remaining 30 per cent are in grammar or comprehensive schools. Systems effective in some places are not necessarily successful in others, however, as the entries for Nottingham in table 10.2 seem to indicate. The table also shows that the availability of a high percentage of grammar-school places (Carmarthenshire, Cheshire and Solihull) and the adoption of a totally comprehensive system (Anglesey and Merioneth) tend to be equally effective in swelling numbers who stay at school into the sixth form.

Higher Education

Higher education is provided by universities, colleges of education, polytechnics, and other establishments for further education. Many of these are not controlled by L.E.A.s, and in most instances draw students from beyond their local areas. Thus the only way, without extensive research, of ascertaining the origins of students and thereby to a large extent relating higher education to the spatial distribution of sixth-form places is to analyse L.E.A. statistics of awards to students.[2]

The main purpose at present of a place in the sixth form is to prepare the student for higher education. If one local authority is providing too many such places in relation to the abilities of the holders, the number who go on to higher education from that authority may be expected to show a fall

[1] Statistics for Surrey in 1967 are not available and cannot, therefore, be included in table 10.2
[2] List 69 and Statistics of Education 1967, 5, table 28. These sources tabulate the following data: new awards taken up in any one year comprising (i) full and lesser value awards at university, (ii) full value awards at further education establishments, (iii) lesser value awards at further education establishments, (iv) colleges of education, students (other than postgraduate) entering courses of initial teacher training

greater than that experienced by another authority that is more accurately and less extravagantly assessing the potential of its pupils. For example, many of the Welsh authorities have a very high proportion of pupils continuing into sixth forms. Is this apparent generosity justified? Is the barrel of academic intelligence being so thoroughly scraped in Wales that the wood is coming off in large slices? Perhaps this analysis will show. Whether it does or not, the patterns of origin of students in certain categories of higher education is worth knowing. Two of these categories are examined here, namely, university students and those at colleges of education.

UNIVERSITY AWARDS

Fig. 10.10a shows proportionately how many awards each county education authority made annually on average in 1965, 1966 and 1967 to students proceeding to university, in relation to the national mean of 57 per 1,000.[1] The highest ratios are found in Cardiganshire (103 per thousand, equal to an index number of 180), Surrey (96 per thousand), Cheshire (88) and Carmarthenshire (83). The lowest ratios occur in Holland (36 per thousand, index number 62·5), Durham and West Suffolk (both 39 per thousand). The whole of Wales, except for Flint, Denbigh and Monmouth, is above the national mean, as is much of southern and south-eastern England. Essex and Kent are, however, well below the counties to the west of them. Among midland counties only Warwick and Worcester exceed the national mean, while the rest fare worse than all the northern counties except Cumberland and Durham, thus confirming the lowly status of the latter two and of the Midlands, observed in the analysis of sixth-form places. The East Riding grants the number of university awards that its high sixth-form status leads one to expect. Lancashire, in contrast, does rather better than the numbers in its maintained sixth forms seem to warrant, but its large supply of direct-grant schools is probably the explanation. Indeed the scarcity of such schools in much of the Midlands may go far to explain the very low performance of, for example, Nottinghamshire and Derbyshire, and the failure of Warwickshire to rise higher above the national mean for university awards than it does.[2]

Some of the small Welsh counties may be 'scraping the barrel' very clean, but it is likely that in much of England there is a large untapped reserve of university ability. If Carmarthenshire, hardly a well-to-do county, can com-

[1] Table 10.3 can usefully be consulted as fig. 10: 10a to 10.12b are discussed. On it a more detailed placing of all L.E.A.s in England and Wales is presented

On fig. 10.10a the national mean of 57 per 1,000 of the appropriate, resident age-group has been converted into the index number, 100. The ratios for each county (and county borough on fig. 10b) have been converted similarly. This exercise has been undertaken to make figs. 10.10 (universities) and 10.11 (training colleges) readily comparable

[2] Figs. 10.4 and 10.10a show interesting similarities and differences

pete in the same league as wealthy Surrey, and if Anglesey, one of the poorest counties in England and Wales, the East Riding, Gloucestershire and Dorset

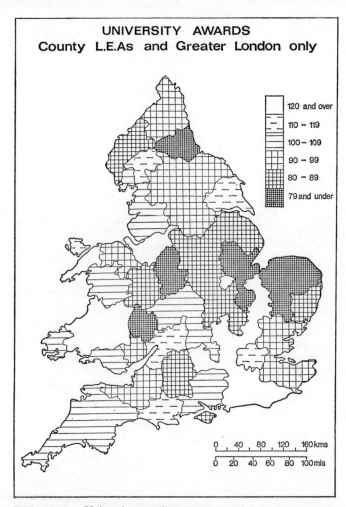

FIG. 10.10a University awards, 1965, 1966 and 1967. Annual mean for England and Wales (57 per 1,000 of the appropriate age-group) has been converted to index number, 100. County means have been converted accordingly

can achieve good results, there must surely be large reserves of ability awaiting discovery, encouragement and opportunity in many other counties.

Fig. 10.10b shows the same information for the county boroughs, Inner London, and the outer metropolitan boroughs. The highest proportions of awards for university places occur in Barnet (120 per thousand, index number 211), Solihull (116 per thousand) and Richmond (112), that is to say, in two outer suburbs of London and a well-to-do part of the Birmingham conurbation.[1] Among 'free-standing' towns the best rates are recorded by Southport, Oxford, Bournemouth, Exeter, Eastbourne, Bath and Cardiff. The most remarkable of these is Cardiff, and even more remarkable is

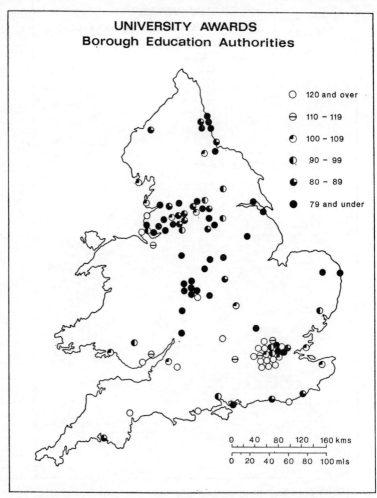

FIG. 10.10b   University awards, 1965, 1966 and 1967. Annual mean for England and Wales (57 per 1,000 of the appropriate age-group) has been converted to index number, 100. Borough means have been converted accordingly

the bracketing of Newport (Monmouth) with Chester and Reading in the next lower grade. Other non-London boroughs above the national mean are Blackpool, Bolton, Darlington, Huddersfield, Northampton, Swansea, Southend, Barrow, Canterbury and Bristol, a strange assortment

[1] Many other outer London boroughs return high proportions, as also does Wallasey

notable especially for the inclusion of Bristol, the only large provincial city to record a proportion greater than the national mean.

The lowest proportions are found at New Ham (19 per thousand, index number 34), Barking (20 per thousand), Gateshead (26) and Salford (27). These four are in effect poor districts within large urban agglomerations. Like the wealthy suburbs that top the list, the poor ones at the bottom simply provide a glimpse of the variations that would be found to exist within most large towns if the module of measurement were small and regular.[1] Disparity of ability and parental attitude rather than ineffectual local management of education are probably revealed by the feeble academic performance of such places as New Ham and Salford.

A better, but still imprecise, indication of local authority effectiveness can perhaps be discerned among the towns that achieve less than three-quarters of the national mean of university awards. Among these are Barnsley, Burton, Coventry, Derby, Gloucester, Great Yarmouth, Grimsby, Hull, Nottingham, Portsmouth, Stoke, Warrington and Wigan. Some at least of these are surely unnecessarily low; perhaps all of them are.

The regional distribution shown on fig. 10.10b is fairly straightforward and conforms quite well with the pattern of fig. 10.10a, as far as the uneven distribution of county boroughs will allow. The south of the country, including South Wales, has a clear preponderance of ratios above the national mean whereas, apart from Darlington, the boroughs of the Northern Economic Planning Region are all below average. In the North West, and Yorkshire and Humberside Regions there is a mixture of high, medium and low values, but the Midlands are predominantly well below average. The view expressed earlier that in the Midlands sixth-formers and sixth-form places are scarce and that this is a cause for concern is confirmed to a large extent by this analysis of both county and county borough awards to university students. Much, therefore, remains to be done by many local authorities, especially those in the Midland and Northern Regions, before the barrel of ability is fully tapped.

ENTRANTS TO COLLEGES OF EDUCATION

Teacher training courses are clearly not in favour among county pupils in south-east England where, as fig. 10.11a shows,[2] only in Hertfordshire does the number of entrants rise more than 10 per cent above the national mean (45 per thousand). Throughout Wales and in most northern counties, however, there is a high proportion of entrants. Outstandingly high ratios are found in Cardigan, Anglesey, Carmarthen and Merioneth, each with over 82 per thousand, while the highest in England are those of Lancashire, the

---

[1] See chapter 11, pp. 291–3
[2] Cf. table 10.3

East Riding, Cheshire, Durham and Northumberland, each with over 58 per thousand.

The lowest proportions are to be found in West Suffolk, Oxfordshire,

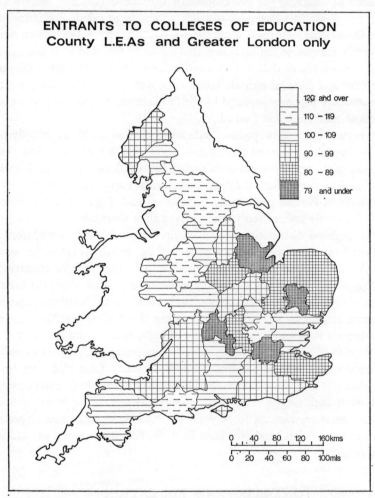

ENTRANTS TO COLLEGES OF EDUCATION
County L.E.As and Greater London only

120 and over
110 – 119
100 – 109
90 – 99
80 – 89
79 and under

0   40   80   120   160kms
0   20   40   60   80   100mls

FIG. 10.11a   Entrants to colleges of education, 1965, 1966 and 1967. Annual mean for England and Wales (45 per 1,000 of the appropriate age-group) has been converted to index number, 100. County means have been converted accordingly

Greater London and Holland (less than 35 per thousand), but East Anglia and much of the East Midlands and lower Severnside, as well as the South East, also fall below the national mean. Comparison of figs. 10.10a and 10.11a yields a major regional contrast, in that while most northern counties, notably Northumberland, Durham, the West and North Ridings and Lindsey, compensate strongly for their poor showing in the granting of university awards by sending large proportions of sixth-formers to colleges of education, many midland counties compensate weakly or not at all. Here is further evidence, therefore, of the mediocre attainment of the latter region in higher

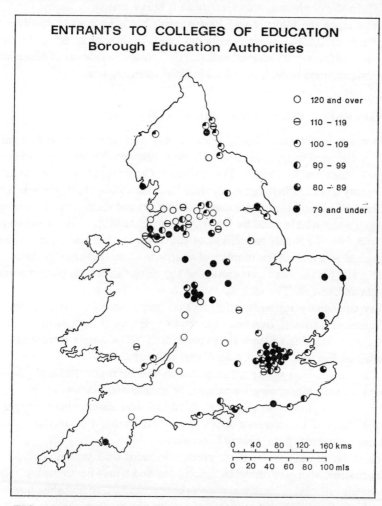

FIG. 10.11b   Entrants to colleges of education, 1965, 1966 and 1967.
Annual mean for England and Wales (45 per 1,000 of the appropriate age-group) has been converted to index number, 100. Borough means have been converted accordingly

education. Somerset, Wiltshire, Kent and Cumberland also make a poor showing on both maps.

Data for county boroughs (fig. 10.11b) conform largely to the county pattern. Most outer London boroughs are low, except for Richmond and Kingston. Exeter, Bath, Gloucester and Oxford are high, but the remaining southern boroughs are either near average or clearly below. All those in

South Wales are above the national mean. In Lancashire, the West Riding and Cheshire only eleven out of thirty county boroughs are below average but include the four largest cities (Leeds, Liverpool, Manchester and Sheffield). In the north-east, only Gateshead is below average.

Once more the Midland and East Anglian boroughs register consistently poor returns. Indeed, there is little difference in these two regions between figs. 10.10b (university awards) and 10.11b (entrants to colleges of education). No compensation occurs, as it does in some other regions.

UNIVERSITY VERSUS TRAINING COLLEGE

Distinct preferences clearly exist as between university and training college entrance in some localities. Especially remarkable are the extreme inverse tendencies in County Durham and Cambridgeshire. Few went to university from Durham but many went from Cambridgeshire. Many entered colleges of education from Durham but few entered them from Cambridgeshire. To test whether and by how much similar tendencies occur elsewhere, the number of entrants to colleges of education in 1966 and 1967 has been expressed as a ratio of the number of awards to undergraduates sponsored by each L.E.A. for the same two years, and the results have been plotted on figs. 10.12a and 10.12b. The national ratio was 80·7 per cent.

For the county authorities (fig. 10.12a) very convincing evidence for the existence of a smooth trend-surface appears. It clearly inclines upwards for entrance to training colleges in north-westerly and westerly directions from south-east England. The only significant interruptions of the trend are found in Cheshire, which unlike other populous northern and midland counties shows a preference among its parents, or greater aptitude among its pupils, for university education, and in Bedfordshire and Essex where colleges of education receive preference above the national ratio. Fig. 10.12b shows a similar trend among the county boroughs.

In so far as universities make greater demands than training colleges on the academic ability of students, figs. 10.12a and b may be deemed to reflect the broad variation in intelligence over the country.[1] More probably, however, it is the regional and local attitudes of parents and teachers that are reflected. Support for this opinion may be inferred, for example, from the extreme polarity of preference, as between university and training college, that is recorded for County Durham, where entrance to training college may be considered such an advance up the ladder of ambition and such a gain in prospective security that admission to the less vocational training available at university tends to be discouraged.

---

[1] Whether this observation is valid or not there can be no doubt that continuance of the trend will result in primary schools throughout the country being increasingly staffed by northern recruits to the teaching profession

The analysis of figs. 10.10, 10.11 and 10.12 may, however, be indicative not only of variations in intelligence and home environment but also of variations in the quality of the facilitative environment created by L.E.A.S. To provide additional evidence for testing this supposition L.E.A.s are ranked

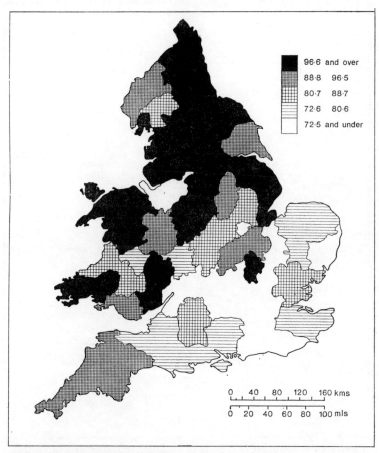

FIG. 10.12a Entrants to colleges of education expressed as a percentage ratio of university awards for 1966 and 1967. County L.E.A.s and Greater London only. Mean annual ratio for England and Wales, 80·7

on table 10.3 according to a twofold grading based on their ratios of (a) awards to university students and (b) entrants to training colleges. The centre of the table represents the national mean for both categories of student, and the four corners indicate different kinds of extreme departure from the mean. L.E.A.s could not justifiably be graded as to the quality of their overall educational performance solely by reference to their comparative positions on table 10.3, but there is clearly ample indication that some of them are far more successful than others where higher education is concerned. Moreover, there is little evidence that large authorities are better than small ones in this respect.[1]

Clearly, there is a fascinating field of study here awaiting further research. Without this our maps simply pose questions which will doubtless lead in turn

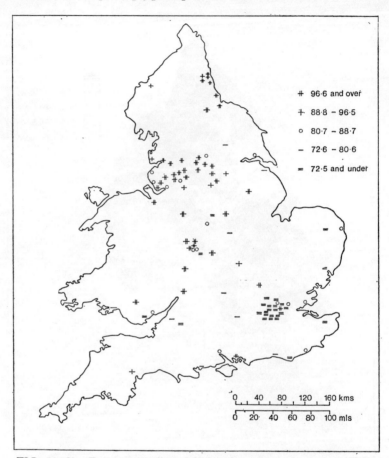

FIG. 10.12b   Entrants to colleges of education expressed as a percentage ratio of university awards for 1966 and 1967. County borough and outer London borough L.E.A.s only. Mean annual ratio for England and Wales, 80·7

to the need for more elaborate analysis. It is important, however, that research in greater depth should soon be undertaken, because its results would hold the key both to the best means of tapping the available reserves of ability and to the way ahead towards greater individual satisfaction and the realization and effective use of talents.

[1] *Royal Commission on Local Government in England 1966–1969*, Cmnd. 4040. Vol. I, Note of reservation by J. L. Longland, 152–160, especially paragraphs 5–8, and Vol. III, Appendix 11, Department of Education and Science: enquiry into the efficiency of local education authorities, 227–36

per 1,000 of the relevant age-group 1965, 1966 and 1967

Rows: Training College Entrants per 1,000 (rounded). Columns: University awards per 1,000 (rounded). Top axis "INDEX No." 80 → 120; side index 80 → 120.

Training College Entrants per 1,000	University awards: under 46/1,000	46/1,000	51/1,000	57/1,000	63/1,000	68/1,000	over 68/1,000
over 53/1,000	County Durham, Gloucester, Herefordshire, Preston, Worcester	Blackburn, Halifax, Lindsey, Rochdale, Wakefield	Denbighshire, Doncaster, Flint, Monmouthshire, North Riding, Northumberland	Blackpool, Bolton, Cornwall, Darlington, Glamorgan, Huddersfield, Lancashire, Merioneth, Montgomery, Pembroke	Anglesey, Chester, East Riding	Bath, Breconshire, Caernarvonshire, Cardiganshire, Carmarthenshire, Cheshire, Exeter, Oxford, Radnor, Solihull, Southport	
53/1,000	Burnley, Rotherham, South Shields, Staffordshire, Wigan	Oldham	Merthyr Tydfil, West Riding	Northampton, Swansea	Newport, Dorset	Herts, Kingston, Richmond, Wallasey	
49/1,000	Barnsley, Bradford, Dewsbury, Grimsby, Lincoln, Middlesbrough, Sunderland, Tynemouth, Wolverhampton	Bedfordshire, Carlisle, Derbyshire, Luton, Newcastle, Shropshire, W. Hartlepool	Essex, Stockport	Devonshire, Hampshire, Southend, Warwickshire, Worcestershire	Westmorland	Berkshire, Bournemouth, Bromley, Cardiff, Croydon, Eastbourne, Harrow, Redbridge	
45/1,000				National Mean for both			
40/1,000	Huntingdonshire and Peterborough, St Helens	Cumberland, Hastings, Manchester, Northamptonshire, Nottinghamshire, Wight, Wiltshire	Leeds, Somerset, Southampton, York	Bristol	Reading, Gloucestershire	East Sussex, Surrey, Sutton, West Sussex	
36/1,000	Coventry, Norfolk, Nottingham, Walsall	East Suffolk, Leicestershire, Portsmouth, Sheffield	Birkenhead, Kent, Rutland	Bexley	Ealing, Enfield	Barnet, Buckinghamshire, Cambridgeshire and Ely, Hillingdon	
under 36/1,000	Barking, Birmingham, Bootle, Burton, Derby, Dudley, Gateshead, Great Yarmouth, Holland, Hull, Kesteven, Liverpool, Newham, Salford, Stoke, Waltham Forest, Warley, Warrington, West Bromwich, West Suffolk	Brighton, Bury, Havering, Leicester, Norwich, Plymouth	Haringey, Inner London, Ipswich	Barrow, Canterbury, Hounslow, Oxfordshire	Greater London	Brent, Merton	

T

AWARDS TO STUDENTS

Local education authorities make two kinds of award to students: duty awards and discretionary awards. The granting of a place at a university or college of education to a student resident within the area of a particular L.E.A. entitles the student to an award as of right. Awards to students at other higher education establishments are discretionary if the course pursued is not designated by the Department of Education and Science as equivalent to training for a first degree. As the term 'discretionary' implies, authorities are not obliged to make such awards at all or in full, but some authorities assess discretionary awards as though they were duty awards.

The national mean per annum for the sum of both kinds of award was 169 per thousand of the appropriate age-group for the years 1965 to 1967. Fig. 10.13a and 10.13b show the broad variations above and below the mean for counties and county boroughs respectively.

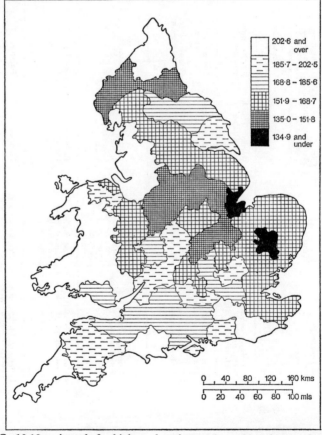

FIG. 10.13a   Awards for higher education, 1965, 1966 and 1967. County L.E.A.s and Greater London only. Mean annual number of awards per 1,000 of the appropriate age-group. Mean for England and Wales, 168·8 per 1,000

Many counties (fig. 10.12a) fall below the mean. Holland and West Suffolk, low on many other maps in this chapter, are the worst with 132 and 133 per thousand respectively. Durham and Cumberland are also low. But the semi-desert for awards that is clearly apparent in an arc of midland counties

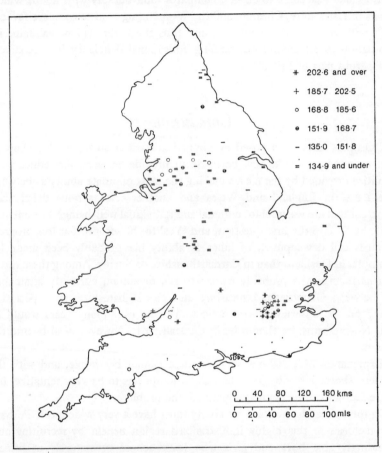

FIG. 10.13b Awards for higher education, 1965, 1966 and 1967. County borough and outer London borough L.E.A.s only. Mean annual number of awards per 1,000 of the appropriate age-group. Mean for England and Wales, 168·8 per 1,000

is by far the most disturbing feature shown on the map. Wales and the East Riding in contrast maintain their reputations, and Lancashire, Northumberland and much of the south-west, are graded high on the map.

Since some counties make more use than others of the discretionary principle and do not make full awards or even any award at all under this heading, it may be that *light shading* on fig. 10.13a does not imply local generosity. The map may also fail accurately to represent the numbers of students proceeding to higher education. That it should reveal such marked variations, however, is ample cause for concern.

Fig. 10.13b shows the proportion of awards made by borough education authorities. Southern authorities on the whole make many awards; the northeast, as one has come to expect, compares unfavourably with South Wales; towns in Lancashire, Cheshire and the West Riding tend to compare favourably with those in the Midlands, and thus the latter region maintains its reputation as an area of outstanding educational deficiency in a relatively prosperous part of Britain.

Conclusion

Questions have been posed or implied at various stages in this chapter, and an attempt should now be made to provide answers. Are educational facilities provided by the L.E.A.s making the most of innate ability as between one L.E.A. in England and Wales and another? Are serious deficiencies apparent that are wasteful for national and individual well-being? The answers must be 'No' to the first question, and 'Yes' to the second. Far less progress towards full development of inherent ability has probably been made for example, in Durham, than in Carmarthenshire or Surrey. Among these three, Carmarthenshire is probably closest to the maximum currently attainable. As between Glamorgan, Lancashire and Nottinghamshire, an expectation based on the criterion of economic well-being over many years would be that Nottinghamshire should be in the lead. It is, however, well behind others.

Explanation of variations such as these cannot be simple, and with the present shortage of objective data any attempt has to be very tentative, but some further comments may illuminate the problem.

In the Midlands the trawl for ability must have a very wide mesh. Perhaps the factories of this highly industrialized region benefit by recruiting outstandingly able boys and girls who leave school prematurely at fifteen. Perhaps, on the contrary, they suffer from a surfeit of talented but subconsciously frustrated workers on the shop floor. There is no way of telling. But we do know that there is a dire shortage in the Midlands of direct-grant schools that leaven the educational bread of Lancashire. Lancastrians may thus be deemed fairly interested in self-help in education while midlanders are not, for the latter have clearly done far less to supplement what the state and the L.E.A.s provide. In an environment of disinterest at home and among the electorate it is less likely that the local authorities themselves would show a very lively interest, however keen their officers might be.

In Wales there are two languages and many people are bilingual. The differences between the two and the problems of accurate translation may induce a higher level of academic interest among the populace in general than is achieved in England. This supposed factor is nurtured by national identity and pride coupled to a strong Welsh interest in music, poetry and the culture of the language. Wales suffered heavily in the 1930s. Education, especially for professional qualifications, meant security. There was and probably remains an aversion to following in father's grimy footsteps. White collar jobs were preferred, and to get them a sound education was needed.

No doubt there are other positive factors, but whatever has created in the home environment a keen interest in education, the resulting large demand has been well served by vigorous facilitative action on the part of local education authorities. Places in maintained grammar schools have been generously but not it would seem extravagantly provided, and following the example of Anglesey the comprehensive system is now spreading quickly. Innate ability is surely being effectively fostered in Wales.

In south-east England wealth and a high level of education among parents, many of whom have migrated from other parts of Britain, provide strong support for sixth forms and encouragement for university entrance. But the greater opportunities for better-paid jobs than in teaching, and the lower value placed upon higher education for girls tend to restrict numbers from entering colleges of education. Probably there is a brain-drain of newly trained northern primary teachers southwards to settle permanently, and progressively to swell the high I.Q. reservoir of the south-east with their own offspring.

Authorities in the south-east are probably for the most part quite effective in providing facilities for education, and they are aided by a strong private sector. It is, however, impossible to be as confident about their efficiency as it is about those in Wales. Inner London, it should be noted however, seems to compare favourably with the centres of other conurbations.

It would be inadvisable to develop these notions further without testing them by detailed local investigation of present and past conditions.[1] The need for such research and for the use in probing this topic of a regular grid by means of which to collect, analyse and correlate data should be clearly apparent. It is hoped too that the existence and value of a geography of education has been demonstrated.

By way of codetta to this chapter, reference to a recurrent minor theme may be salutary. Individual authorities have not been discussed here in detail because there is far more to educational efficiency than sixth forms and places at university and training college. Half our future is in the middle and primary school sectors, and authorities which look bad according to the

---

[1] In West Suffolk, for example, which reads low in the data presented here, local investigation reveals that the educational system is being virtually rebuilt from the primary level upwards. Such restructuring takes time to become effective statistically in the 16+ age group, but should result in rapid advance during the later 1970s

criteria used here may be excellent in other respects.[1] But there are a few authorities that could be picked out for special mention without fear either of prejudicing their future plans and misrepresenting their present achievements or of maligning their officers and committees.

The administrative county of the East Riding of Yorkshire is one of these. It is a largely rural, agricultural area with the more prosperous outer suburbs of Hull within its bounds. But Hull is not a very prosperous town attracting large numbers of able migrants from other parts of Britain. There is thus no good reason to believe that people in the East Riding are more intelligent or fundamentally more interested in education than people in small towns and rural areas anywhere in the northern three-quarters of England. Moreover direct-grant and independent schools are hardly plentiful in the county. Yet in proportion to its population in the appropriate age groups the East Riding achieves more sixth-form places, makes more university awards, has more entrants to colleges of education, and makes more awards for education beyond the age of eighteen than most other rural and many urbanized counties in England. There can surely be no other explanation for these achievements than the highly effective system of grammar and bilateral schools that the county has been running for several years. Bilateralism may not be either the best or the most politically acceptable system but, like the totally comprehensive scheme in Anglesey, it can be made to work very effectively indeed. This said, however, there is every likelihood that as the East Riding changes over to a comprehensive system its achievements will be enhanced still further.

[1] (i) *Half our Future* (Newsom Report), Ministry of Education, H.M.S.O., 1963
    (ii) *Children and their Primary Schools* (Plowden Report), Central Advisory Council for Education (England), H.M.S.O., 1967
    (iii) Clegg, A. and Megson, B., *Children in Distress*, 1968
    (iv) Taylor, George and Ayres, N., *Born and Bred Unequal*, 1969

11

Some Conclusions

This chapter has two major purposes, first, to draw together some of the findings of preceding chapters and, secondly, to discuss how deficiencies in portrayal, and thus understanding, of spatial variations in human geography may be remedied.

Many of the maps in this book confirm the existence of 'upward' trends towards London and south-east England. Often in the past the phrase 'drift to the south-east' has been used to summarize these tendencies, although their existence was inferred mainly from analyses made only of inter-censal changes in population. Clearly the south-east is a favoured area in many respects and its 'magnetic' field of influence upon people is stronger than that of other parts of the United Kingdom. But its favourability is neither simple nor comprehensive, and different kinds of people are attracted to it for different reasons.

Components of Favourability in the South East Region

More important than the high mean incomes found in a large part of the south-east is the great concentration there, both proportionately and absolutely, of exceptionally high incomes. Fig. 11.1 illustrates well the proportional disparities among the standard regions that were in use in 1959–60, and it is clear from the discussion in chapter 2, especially of figs. 2.6a to 2.6e, that the ladder of incomes slopes more steeply upwards in the area in and immediately around London than elsewhere, and that in the south-east there is far more 'room at the top'. For the man or woman with ability and drive who is granted the opportunity to use these attributes, the ladder of incomes in the south-east has fewer landings and obstacles hampering a quick ascent than in any other part of the United Kingdom. Furthermore, for people who lack those attributes there is less chance of poverty in much of both the Midlands and the south-east than elsewhere.

A concentration of high incomes in a particular region implies, first, a parallel concentration of those occupations that normally command high salaries and wages irrespective of location, and secondly, regional scarcity of

labour, thus placing it at a premium. Both factors tend to induce an increase in
the working population autochthonously and by migration from less favoured
areas.

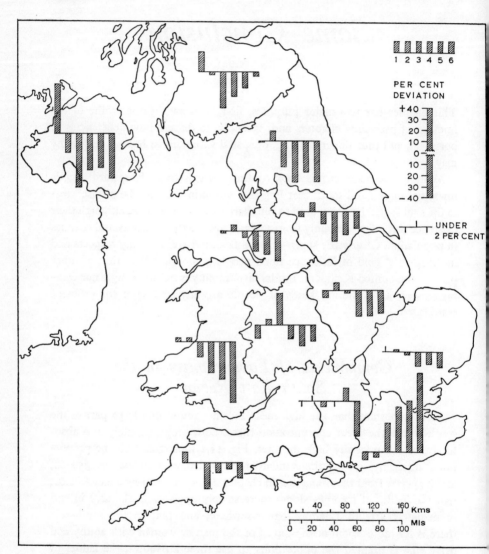

FIG. 11.1   Deviation in Income Brackets by Region, 1959–60: each column shows
the percentage deviation in each of six selected income brackets from the proportion
of the total number of incomes in the same income brackets for the U.K. as a whole.
The numerals below the columns in the key refer to the following income brackets:
(1) taxable incomes below £500, (2) £500–999, (3) £1,000–1,499, (4) £1,500–1,999,
(5) £2,000–4,999 and (6) incomes above £5,000. Thus, for example, the London
and South-Eastern region had proportionately fewer incomes below £500 and
between £500–999 and, conversely, a marked and increasing excess in the four
upper income brackets when compared with the average for the U.K. (Originally
published in *Westminster Bank Review*, February 1966, p. 37)

The studies presented in chapters 3, 4 and 5 illustrate the extent to which several different categories of employment responded spatially to these and other factors between 1951 and 1961. Male employment (fig. 5.1a) exceeded all other categories examined, in the strength of its south-easterly trend and was followed closely by employment in manufacturing (fig. 3.2b). Female employment showed a less marked trend (fig. 5.1b); services less still (fig. 3.2c), and the change in married women's employment (fig. 5.1c) had the least south-easterly trend of all. Male workers and employment in manufacturing were, therefore, setting the pace during the decade for the drift to the south-east. What facilitated the growth of this phenomenon most was probably the decision soon after the second world war to set up a ring of new towns around London. The rapid development of manufacturing industries in these and other places around London effectively counteracted policies for industrial dispersal to other parts of Britain. Paradoxically, however, London and the south-east was and remains short of manufacturing industry in relation to the total size of the regional work-force. Fundamentally, therefore, to set up new manufacturing towns in the south-east was a sensible measure to reduce regional imbalance. This, of course, was not its designed purpose. Had it been, then a counterbalancing policy aimed at redistributing service industries from the London area should surely have been adopted. But such a policy was not adopted, and remains largely neglected even today.

Government and commercial behaviour, geared often quite unwittingly to suit London and the south-east over many decades probably at least since 1891, has produced the favourable income and employment structures found within the region. This regional 'favouritism' had progressed so far by the end of the first world war, that incomes held up better in the London district than elsewhere during the ensuing slumps within the trade cycles of the inter-war period. It followed, therefore, that the sale of goods and services was also better sustained in and near London than elsewhere. Thus there was a genuine spatial advantage for the vigorous, small and expanding firm to be located near London. The theory that a strong home market is a prerequisite for growth and economic success is thus seen in practical operation regionally within a single fiscal system rather than internationally as is the more usual context for the application of this theory. Imitation by larger firms and a marked social preference among top management for the location in and near London, not only of their head offices but also of their entire enterprises, reinforced the effect of market orientation operating among the small, expanding firms.

Two widely accepted beliefs, both of them locationally spurious for the most part, gave an air of respectability and inevitability to what was happening. There was, it was believed, little to be done either to lessen the growth of London or to restore prosperity and social well-being to the provinces in decline, first, because the doctrine of *laissez-faire* implied that entrepreneurs tended to optimize their locations as part of the process of maximizing profits and, secondly, because geography taught that choice of location was subject to the doctrine of environmental determinism.

Laissez-faire indicated that above all the entrepreneur knew best, and that bankruptcy and voluntary liquidation of firms were the best devices for weeding and cultivating the land of the United Kingdom and thus maintaining a healthy output of goods and services. Little thought was given to the other processes of economic cultivation, namely, sowing and reaping. As a result, much of the land received few seeds. Many regions maintained a declining ratio of goods and services, and as the yields from their ancient crops diminished, so they became increasingly fallow.

A hazy awareness of the geographical doctrine of environmental determinism, which really meant physical and natural determinism, was recalled by decision-makers to justify the cultivation of the south-eastern and midland fields of the national farm and the neglect of the remainder. This doctrine was the only snippet of geographical theory likely then to have been acquired by most people during their time at school. Moreover, it was retained long afterwards, and lingers on even today among the many who still unquestioningly accept that the cotton industry grew up in Lancashire because, as someone once told them, the air is very suitably damp there. They tended, therefore, to believe without thinking very seriously about it that something natural or physical must explain not only the success of manufacturing and service enterprises arising in the fertile fields of the Midlands and the south-east but also the poor yields from enterprises elsewhere. This spurious theory justified an attitude of comfortable, but false, complacency among the decision-makers who themselves for the most part lived and worked in the south-east.

The real reasons for the prosperity and diverse structure of employment of south-east England have, however, been predominantly man-made since at least A.D. 1700. London is not only the capital, it is also the largest port, the largest town, the greatest single concentration of population, the social Mecca, and the commercial hub of the United Kingdom. Indeed many go 'up' to London and, apart from Oxford and Cambridge, down to everywhere else. Most major decisions are made in London, and it is largely the members of the so-called 'establishment' who make them. There is thus an environmental factor functioning, but its operation is neither natural and immutable nor, probably, desirable.

It is impossible precisely to map anything as ill-defined as the membership of the establishment, but the pages of *Who's Who* provide a fair indication of the distribution. Fig. 11.2 shows a regular sample of entries in *Who's Who*. The pattern is clearly centred upon London and differs markedly from the distribution of population as a whole. Power is vested in people who live in the south-east, and it follows that these powerful people will tend to give

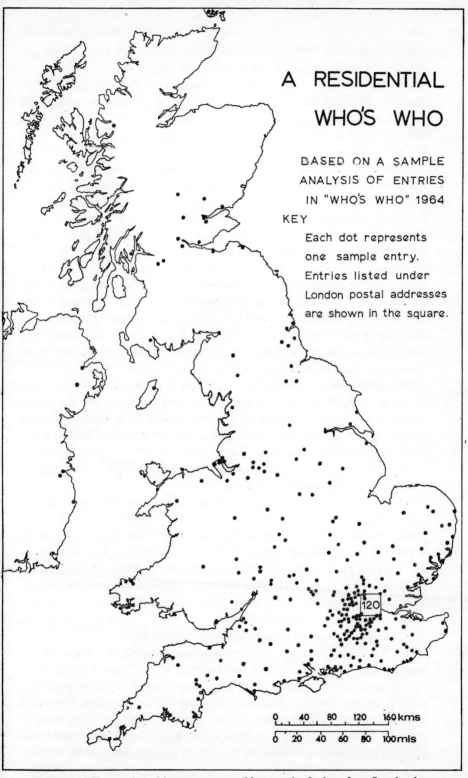

A RESIDENTIAL
WHO'S WHO

BASED ON A SAMPLE
ANALYSIS OF ENTRIES
IN "WHO'S WHO" 1964
KEY
Each dot represents
one sample entry.
Entries listed under
London postal addresses
are shown in the square.

120

| 0 | 40 | 80 | 120 | 160 kms |
| 0 | 20 | 40 | 60 | 80 | 100 mls |

FIG. 11.2 For entries with two or more addresses, the farthest from London has been taken

preference to their region by their decisions. What they create there will attract others ranging from the unemployed worker seeking a job to the immigrant dentist seeking a pleasant but adequately lucrative practice. Regional imbalance can never be solved, if such is the accepted wish, until the creators of the magnetism of the south-east redistribute themselves to find and create outlets for their energies and interests more evenly over the United Kingdom.

Diverse opportunities for employment and high incomes are not the only assets or positive characteristics of the south-east. People born overseas who have come to live in the United Kingdom have long tended to settle in parts of the region, and this tendency has become even stronger since 1951. Service and professional occupations especially have benefited from this influx, which must in addition have restrained somewhat the power of the region to function as the inflation-leader for the country as a whole. A more even distribution of immigrants would present fewer social problems, and a continued, steady immigration would probably be beneficial to the national economy, but neither could be achieved without steady, and spatially more evenly distributed, growth in the gross domestic product. There would need to be far greater inter-regional balance in both economic and social istributions than exists today.

Among the health services, the south-east is favoured in several ways. It has a larger proportional share of teaching hospitals and consultant specialists than other regions; a larger share of hospital beds; more dentists in relation to population and three-quarters or more of immigrant dentists (largely from Australia and New Zealand) and in much of the south-east the average list size of general practitioners is smaller than in most of the industrial counties of the Midlands and the North.

Infant mortality rates are favourable in much of the south-east, though they are slightly above the mean for England and Wales in Inner London, parts of which are doubtless as bad as some of the boroughs and counties of Wales and the North (fig. 9.2). Deaths from bronchitis and tuberculosis of the respiratory system are rather less marked also in the south-east. On the whole however, while this region is clearly favoured when compared with other populous parts of England and Wales, its health services and mortality rates are probably not as much in advance of those of other areas as are the opportunities it offers for employment and high incomes.

The south-east reasserts its pre-eminence, however, in several of the aspects of education that are examined in chapter 10. Places at independent schools are plentiful in many south-eastern counties. A larger proportion of children continues at school into the sixth form than in other densely peopled areas, though some less populous districts, notably many in Wales, equal or out-perform many districts in the south-east. It supplies the universities with a larger proportion of students than its share of the population would warrant.

Moreover, its urban areas are in general outstandingly better in this respect than towns elsewhere in England and Wales.

Favourable Characteristics of Other Areas

The south-east is not by any means favoured either in all things social and economic, or evenly among its parts. Nor is there a close relationship in most patterns between 'pecking order' and distance from London. Some of the maps in preceding chapters reveal apparently haphazard mosaics rather than fairly smooth trends outwards from the metropolis. Health services and education yield more mosaic maps than do the other topics.

Fig. 7.2 shows an oddly composed pattern of the availability of places in mental hospitals. Table 7.4 shows that there is an equally odd distribution of overseas-born doctors working in junior posts in British hospitals. The list-size of general practitioners (fig. 7.4) varies with a number of factors, but it is notable that Lanarkshire is better served than Warwickshire; Hertfordshire is as bad as Durham, and Glamorgan is as good as Surrey. The pattern of the school medical service (fig. 7.5) is a haphazard mosaic *par excellence*. Lancashire is equal to Surrey; adjacent counties are often in widely different grades, and the best areas of all in England and Wales are Merioneth, Montgomery and Cornwall. The school dental service (fig. 8.8) likewise presents a mosaic, but a very different one. Scotland clearly leads but Ayrshire, Renfrew and Lanarkshire contrast very unfavourably with most of the rest of that country. Derbyshire is far worse dentally than medically while Westmorland registers the converse. West Sussex, however, is bad in both services.

From the maps on education, the existence of mosaics is less easy to substantiate since for the most part county L.E.A.s are shown separately from those of the county boroughs. There can be little doubt however, as fig. 11.3 shows for the educationally sub-normal, that wide disparities occur over short distances and between adjacent L.E.A.s. Generally in education, however, the East Riding is an outstanding example of a bright piece set among duller ones in the mosaics, and the county boroughs of Lancashire and the West Riding are variegated pieces, some brighter some duller, but set in the grey hue of their surrounding county areas. Durham often contrasts markedly with adjacent Westmorland, and the grades in the mosaics of most of Wales compare favourably with those in most of England. Hertfordshire and Dorset (fig. 10.11a) contrast with much of southern England by having a high proportion of entrants to colleges of education.

These examples from both health services and education indicate the great and rather haphazard spatial variety that exists in at least two aspects of the social geography of Britain, seemingly quite unrelated to the marked south-easterly trends noted earlier. There are, however, some areas that have very few redeeming features so far as their social and economic geographies are concerned.

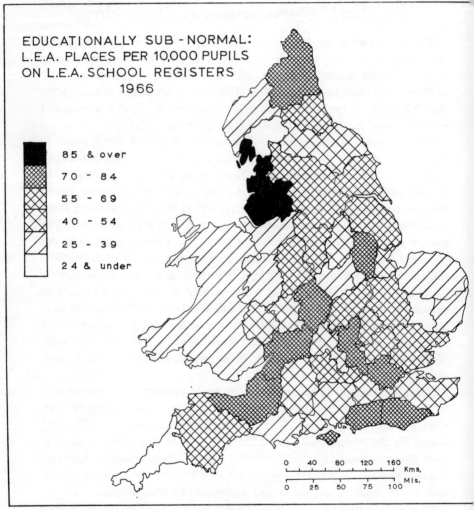

EDUCATIONALLY SUB - NORMAL:
L.E.A. PLACES PER 10,000 PUPILS
ON L.E.A. SCHOOL REGISTERS
1966

85 & over
70 - 84
55 - 69
40 - 54
25 - 39
24 & under

FIG. 11.3

Several counties in the Midlands, where incomes are reasonably high because opportunities for well-paid factory jobs are good, are socially unfavoured areas according to the limited range of criteria examined earlier. In the counties of Leicester, Nottingham, Stafford and Warwick the lists of general practitioners seem unduly large. In Derby, Nottingham, Stafford and Worcester dentists are scarce. Derby, Nottingham and Leicester are very short of school dental officers. Both direct-grant and independent schools are largely lacking in Derby, Leicester, Nottingham, Stafford and Worcester. The take-up of sixth-form places is generally mediocre in much of the Midlands, and the proportion of eighteen-year-olds who proceed to either universities or colleges of education is worse than mediocre in all midland county boroughs except Solihull and Northampton. A particularly unfavourable feature over much of the region is the low proportion of awards for further education (figs. 10.13a and b). Thus although one may speak with considerable justification of the existence of a ridge of high incomes and opportunity for jobs that stretches from Surrey and Essex into the Midlands, one must remember that the patterns of social facilities do not follow the same trend. Much of midland England falls in many respects far below the standards attained in the south-east.

But there are some areas even in England and Wales that return low readings for virtually all topics discussed in this book. Probably among these areas would be found Cumberland, Durham, Hereford, West Suffolk, the Holland Division of Lincolnshire and, indeed, much of eastern England between the Humber and the Suffolk Stour.

There is little point, however, in attempting to grade areas according to a wide range of criteria when the latter are observed to vary largely independently of each other. Income and employment combine into a powerful force to endow much of the south-east with a better social and economic environment on the whole than other parts of Britain. But there are local forces working everywhere in the country, in some areas beneficially in others not, that distort what would otherwise be a relatively smooth trend outwards from London. The important finding to note is that many spatial variations, including the trend of the combined factor, are to be observed that would surely be unacceptable severally or separately to an *informed*, democratic society claiming equality of opportunity as one of its goals.

A Well-informed Society

Unfortunately society is not well informed and, where ignorance is bliss, spatial variations that are unjust, harmful and inefficient are accepted not only by those who govern both nationally and locally but also by those who, did they but know it, suffer badly because they happen to live and work in particular areas. The decision-makers and the local inhabitants alike lack the foundation for sound judgment as to available possibilities and desirable actions.[1] Migration of people and regional policies are responses to a largely subjective awareness that harmful spatial differences exist. They are not separate responses to sound, objective measurement of these variations.

[1] Shackle, G. L. S., *Decision, Order and Time*, 1961. This book lacks a section on space, otherwise it would be better known to economic geographers. Bray, J., *Decision in Government*, 1970, see especially ch. 6–11

Presently available means of measurement are defective, including those used in this book. The defects arise, first, because data are uneven in quality to the extent of being virtually absent in some legitimate fields for geographical inquiry on the human side of the subject. There are, for example, few worthwhile data dealing either with expenditure, so this aspect of geography is neglected, or with the variations of commercial profit and output from place to place. The study of production in economic geography tends, therefore, to examine variations in employment. A factor of production, labour, for which data are fairly good, stands in for production itself in most analyses.

Secondly, unlike geology, geomorphology, climatology or meteorology which examine continuities[1] varying over the earth's surface only in the trends they exhibit to the surveyor (a particular trend may be found to change little, gradually and smoothly, or abruptly according to the topic and area of investigation), human geography studies phenomena that are discontinuous and discretely distributed. There can thus be no direct equivalent of the augur, the level, the aneroid barometer, the Stevenson Screen and the radiosonde to help the human geographer sample the trends he seeks to find and understand. Spatial sampling in human geography may ultimately be proved feasible but it lacks at present the foundation for confidence that spatial continuity gives to the physical branches of geographical research.

Thirdly, such data as are collected suffer in their amenability to spatial analysis from the frameworks according to which they are assembled and published. Few frameworks coincide spatially, for it is a common practice to lay out a different spatial framework for each class of data (i.e. the boundaries to the areas used in the processes of collection and publication seldom coincide as between one set of data and another). Collecting agencies do not co-ordinate their efforts spatially. Even if they did, however, the resulting benefit would be small unless the standard framework were sensibly designed. For most of the maps in this book a standard county framework has been used, and certain advantages and benefits of consistency result. But the differences in the size and shape of the counties and the distortions inherent in the placing of the county boundaries greatly diminish confidence in the value of the findings. The maps lack spatial precision by virtue of the defective framework, notwithstanding that the data have been plotted as faithfully as possible.

An attempt has been made to show in this book that variations from place to place in selected aspects of human geography are a cause for concern and are worth measuring. If the problems of discreteness and framework can be solved the lack of good data should quickly be appreciated and rectified. Establishing a sound framework is thus the key problem, but the discontinuity

[1] All places have a climate, weather, 'landforms' and geology

of phenomena in social and economic geography should be discussed first by way of justification for tackling the initially larger framework problem.

If the distribution of phenomena in human geography and in human spatial behaviour are to be properly understood and amenable to scientific analysis, each distribution of spatially discrete quantities must be converted into a notionally continuous form. Each distribution must be mapped, therefore, as though it were a continuity. The contour or isopleth is the most feasible device for this purpose.

The human geographer, like the geologist and geomorphologist wishes to reconstruct the past so that he may better understand the present.[1] He is, however, rather more interested in predicting the spatial future than they are. His attitude compares better to that of the meteorologist. One of the great virtues of isopleth maps portraying the economic and social geography of any area is that, like weather charts, they would reveal the spatial changes taking place through time if they were produced speedily and at suitably frequent intervals. Not only could refined versions of figs. 2.3a and b be prepared perhaps annually as a guide to policy on incomes and taxation but they could be analysed in relation to similar maps for employment, commercial profit, and so on. The possibilities of multivariate cartographic investigation would be limitless. *Inter situs* as well as *in situ* analyses could and should, however, be undertaken, for when causes are sought with a view to remedial action in one area they may be found far away in another. The *inter situs* problem will not be understood until economic and social isopleth maps have been produced and studied over a considerable period. Both long and short range weather forecasts are somewhat similarly dependent upon the study of past measurements and the solution of the *inter situs* problem.

Without a suitable framework, prediction of spatial trends in the economy and sociology of an area cannot make much progress. The ideal framework might be a hexagonal mesh, but the acceptable one is likely to be based on the square. The one-inch (1 : 63360) Ordnance Survey map has a grid superposed upon it, each cell in the grid being a square representing one square kilometre. For the Census of Population in 1971 a regular hectare (100 × 100 metres) mesh based upon the Ordnance Survey grid overlay is adopted for enumeration.[2] The cartographic potential of this very close mesh is close to the optimum for conversion of discrete distributions into continuities. It is desirable too that the collection of data other than by the Registrars-General should be undertaken according to the same framework.

Since each hectare has a unique map reference expressed in numbers as a spatial co-ordinate, the processing of the data collected can be carried out by computers, which can be equipped to draw the isopleth map of any

[1] See chapter 1, p. 2
[2] See also chapter 2, p. 10, and *1971 Census, Information Paper 1*, Census Division, General Register Office, 1970

U

phenomenon surveyed. They could also in due course produce the maps resulting from the multivariate spatial analyses which they themselves would be programmed to undertake.

Maps based on computer-plotting from a uniform framework have already been produced.[1] The results are specific and experimental, but they are expressed by demographic contours, and sections portraying unidirectional trends in demographic relief are drawn. A customary exercise in mapwork for boys and girls in school as well as for students at university is the drawing of sections, profiles and summit levels from the relief map. The possibility now arises of undertaking similar exercises that will reveal the scarps, dips, and even drumlins, of economic and social geography. The *human* face of the earth may not, after all, be beyond effective portrayal.

Technical Problems

If the computer were to plot the data straight from the hectare grid without any modification, the resultant map of a highly varied area such as the United Kingdom would be very confused indeed. Aggregation is clearly desirable therefore, but to what extent should it be undertaken? Only experiment can answer this question satisfactorily, for it is not certain whether a large, medium, or small-scale framework for aggregative analysis and scanning of the data is to be preferred.[2] The best recommendation must be to carry out data scanning at many levels of aggregation from, say, 2^2 km. upwards to 100^2 km. The contour pattern would, of course, differ from one level of aggregation to another but, since spatially causal factors operate over varying distances and over differing fields of influence, the effect of one factor might be indicated at a smaller scale of aggregation and that of another factor at a larger scale. Experiment and geographically disciplined judgment will progressively reveal the explanatory relevance of different scales.

A second technical problem is to decide what shape or shapes of aggregation should be used. Any shape from a regular figure such as a square or an approximation to a circle (the latter was used by Hägerstrand, 1967) to an irregular but standard shape is possible. Perhaps for some topics it might be found useful to vary both the size and shape of the aggregation according to the area being studied, since the operational range of a factor may be found to vary not only from area to area but also in direction outwards from the

[1] (i) Hägerstrand, T., Moden, S., and Rystedt, B., *Urbaniserings processen*, 1967, 1 and 5

    (ii) Hägerstrand, T., 'The computer and the geographer', *Trans. Inst. Brit. Geog.*, **42**, 1967, 1–19

    (iii) Mason, J. B., 'Forecasting weather by computer', *Electronics and Power*, January 1968, 4–7

[2] See chapter 2, p. 41 and chapter 3, p. 47

focal point of operation, if such is found to exist. But these are merely conjectures. To begin with, a square or circular aggregative scanner would be
adequate, and would be most closely analogous to the field measurements of
the land-surveyor. The module of the single hectare cell may be deemed
comparable to the land-surveyor's base-line, while the scales of aggregation
compare with his triangulations.

There is, however, a seemingly desirable refinement of aggregative method.
By moving the scanner forward only one or a small number of hectares at a
time, a running spatial mean is contrived.[1] Every time the scanning frame
halts as it moves over the data an entry, probably the mean, is registered on
the map at the centre of the frame. Thus if the scanner halts at either every
hectare or every kilometre square, for example, each of these over the whole
of the map will be allocated a reading commensurate with the mean for the
area encompassed by the scanning frame when centred in turn over each
module.

In this way society and those who represent it in local and national government may be better equipped to assess possibilities and to take sound decisions. They will understand far more about the problems of their own and
other areas than they do today, and social and economic management will
acquire the spatial perspectives it so badly lacks. Trend surfaces will be
readily apparent and 'region' will no longer be an equivocal term. There will
be ample scope for application, testing and refinement of spatial quantitative
techniques.

But to achieve an effective 'meteorology' of the economic and social geography of Britain a central institution must be established. The General
Register Offices are likely to serve, in this respect, as prototypes from 1971,
but this arrangement should not be allowed to last, for the data to be handled
must in due course be extended beyond the purely demographic. A specialized
central institution designed for the purpose will ultimately be necessary. It
should be charged at least with the collection, processing, analysis and
mapping of the data and should be called the 'Geographical Survey', since
among all disciplines the spatial approach which geography alone centres
its attention on will be the key to the success of the Survey.

Hurricanes can be tracked and warnings of their approach given. They can
be bombarded experimentally with silver iodide in the hope of lessening their
impact, but they cannot yet be controlled. Economic and social storms are not
even tracked, for there are as yet no truly refined and objective charts on which
to trace their movement. But once these are available, such undesirable,
man-made features as they portray will be more readily controllable than the
natural storms of the atmosphere are today.

[1] Hägerstrand, T., 1967, p. 14. 'The curves [isopleths] then indicate how the number of inhabitants varies over the country with reference to a "floating circle" with a
radius of 30 km.'

We have tried in these pages to be as objective as possible but, of necessity, only in a rudimentary fashion. We know that the topics we have reconnoitred should be studied in far greater depth than time has allowed and with more and superior resources than we possess. We are convinced that it is most important to society that these and related topics should soon be studied with at least as much vigour as are the problems of meteorology. The tasks involved are immense and will be costly to undertake, but they are now technically feasible and their accomplishment should surely be enormously beneficial. A budget rising quickly to equal that of the Meteorological Office would ensure an effective start.

Index